Boy
Number
26

Boy Number 26

Tommy Rhattigan

Mirror Books

This book first published by Mirror Books in 2019

Mirror Books is part of Reach plc
One Canada Square
London E14 5AP
England

www.mirrorbooks.co.uk

ISBN 978-1-912624-17-1

For my beautiful wife and family – for the love,
care and understanding.
Thank you. x

Contents

Oh Happy Day

The playground of St Vincent's Approved School in Formby near Liverpool is lit by a bright, early-morning sun. It's 1966 and I am 10 years old. I'm not alone, though I wish I was. I am in the company of 47 other young boys aged between eight and 14, many of whom are in floods of tears. I, on the other hand, feel very happy. The unexpected news we've just heard from Sister Ignatius came as a pleasant surprise to me and the dozen or so boys who are not crying. And I am truly baffled as to how the events unfolding on this autumn morning could possibly have anything to do with the outpourings of grief I am witnessing from this bunch of wailing idiots.

Any stranger happening by could be forgiven for assuming we are mourning the passing of a dearly departed friend, or that an outbreak of mass hysteria has suddenly swept over the whole show. But – though it's true I only have a handful of friends (none of whom are dear to me) – I don't think I've missed anyone suddenly departing from St Vincent's Approved School, unless you count Sean Murphy, who did a bunk a few days back and hasn't returned – yet.

1

The cause of the mass hysteria was a surprise announcement made moments earlier by Sister Ignatius, Mother Superior of the Order of the Sisters of Mercy, and batterer of little children's arses.

She was standing on the portable wooden rostrum, used for outdoor prayers, looking down upon us like a saggy, red-necked vulture on the hunt for dead meat. And as the rostrum groaned under the weight of the hippo-sized nun, I muttered a silent prayer to Jesus, asking him to make the whole thing collapse. But, as usual, Jesus wasn't listening to me, and the rostrum – creaking under its burden – held fast. "Quiet, children!" barked Sister Ignatius in her thick Irish accent. We had no idea what she was going to say next, but we knew it was big news.

For the past few days, a rumour had been going round the school that an important announcement was on the cards. And along with the rumour came the usual gossip: Mr Guinness, the school's 69-year-old storeman, was having an affair with 75-year-old cleaner Mrs Cuthbert, and both were going to be sacked; Sister Jennifer was up the duff and had been excommunicated from the church; Mr Sands, the school's 80-year-old shoe repairer, had really died this time. There'd been many false alarms about Mr Sands' abrupt end, which were understandable given how he would suddenly drop off to sleep at any given moment – midway through hammering a nail into the heel of a shoe, for example, or just as he'd taken Holy Communion at Mass. The fact we hadn't seen him around for a few days added credence to the story, making it the likeliest of all the rumours.

But, as usual, we'd all been wrong. The bombshell delivered by Sister Ignatius had been much better than that.

"It saddens me ta have ta pass on this news ta yah all," she began. "With the exception of the domestic staff, who'll be retained at the school, The Sisters of Mercy will be leaving St Vincent's, with immediate effect."

With immediate effect! That meant now! Today! Yippee! I'd been unable to contain my emotions and was clapping like a sea lion in a circus, making my hands sting. But the pain was worth it, knowing she and her coven of witches were leaving St Vincent's. Today! For good! Forever! They'd already packed their bags and broomsticks and were on their way.

"Hip-hip-hurray!" I shouted as I clapped and danced a jig. And some of the boys followed my lead, cheering on the good news, whilst most of the others wailed like hysterical children abandoned by their mothers.

"Yah can stop all that," snapped Sister Monica, giving me a clip around the ear. "Don't be so disrespectful to the Holy Mother."

"But I'm not being disrespectful to the Holy Mother, Sister Monica. It's great news, isn't it?"

She responded by giving me another stinging clout around the same ear. But I didn't care, I was overjoyed. This was the most welcome news I could ever have dared to dream of. For nearly one whole year, I'd had to put up with these distant, frocked shadows, floating like ghosts in and out of our everyday lives. And I couldn't wait to see the back of them.

As for the Mother Superior, I could have sworn she was a man. In fact, all the boys had been taking bets on who would be the first to expose her dark secret. We'd stand at the bottom of the concrete steps leading up to the dormitories, peering upwards as she walked up or down them. Or we'd "accidentally" trip over ourselves in front of her or pretend to faint, just to get a quick peek up her flowing black habit. But besides seeing her long, hairy legs, whatever secrets she'd had hidden further up remained a secret between herself and the Devil.

"This," continued Sister Ignatius, "is Mr Lilly. Your new headmaster." As she casually dropped her second bombshell, the Mother Superior gestured towards a short, plump man, one of a group of unfamiliar faces we'd seen earlier on. He was dressed in a three-piece tweed suit and had a chequered trilby with a few small, coloured feathers poking up from the ribbon trim sitting snugly on his large head. Standing with his hands clasped tightly behind his back and his chest puffed out, military style, the new headmaster peered at us dispassionately through the small, gold-rimmed spectacles resting on the end of his nose. Above his smug, thick lips sprouted a Hitler-style stubble of hair.

"Mr Lilly originates from Austria and speaks fluent German," said Sister Ignatius. "He is also a member of the Round Table and the Magic Circle." No mention of the Nazi Party. "So, come now children! Let us show our appreciation for your new headmaster!" She clapped her huge hands together, as did the few of us who were not crying. The other nuns clapped extra loudly, attempting to make a good show above the hysterical sobbing. I didn't understand the tears. As far as I was concerned, any change at St Vincent's was a change for the better.

With 48 delinquents from all walks of life and every corner of Great Britain forced to live together under the same roof, it

4

was inevitable that rivalry, antagonism, hatred, sodomy and, on the odd occasion, outright war would play an integral part in our daily lives at St Vincent's Approved School. We were, at worst, appallingly heartless and cruel to one another, and at best, just able to tolerate one another.

By the time the nuns announced their departure, I had endured 11 months there. Every day was a trial as we battled for the higher ground, constantly jockeying for a better position in the pecking order of acceptability amongst our own peers. By "higher ground" I don't mean the moral high ground – we didn't have any morals.

Beyond the eyes and the ears of the grown-ups, another world existed in St Vincent's. It was a world beyond the imagination of normal, right-minded, thinking people. It was a place where we competed amongst each other for almost anything, from the mundane to the ridiculous, from the highly dangerous to the insane. Who's the best footballer, the best athlete, singer, altar boy, the biggest snitch? Who can smoke a roll-up made of toilet paper and dried leaves from the sycamore tree with the lowest number of coughs? Who can masturbate the most times in succession without going blind? Who can stand the longest up against the wall without moving, while a football is kicked at it? And the most insane game of all: who can stay unconscious the longest?

To play this game, the challenger did 25 squats in quick succession. On the last squat, he exhaled all his breath as another boy came up behind him and gave him a bear hug – literally squeezing the remaining air and the living daylights out of him. Rendering the challenger unconscious.

Jimmy McDermott, a small, skinny lad from Liverpool, broke the record and then spent a couple of days lying in a coma in Liverpool's Royal Infirmary. After he was discharged, he was paraded in front of us at morning assembly, where he'd stood smiling proudly as we were made to say a prayer of thanksgiving for him having survived his ordeal whilst only suffering minor brain damage. Though to be honest, I didn't see any change in his usual demeanour. The upshot of it all was a total ban on all illegal competitions between us, with Sister Ignatius threatening to punish any wrongdoer with the cane, plus a week's loss of all privileges.

As an incorrigibly inquisitive child, I was always begging the question, seeking out clarification just so I knew where I stood, which was often mistaken by my superiors as blatant insolence. After being told countless times by the nuns how grateful I should be for the privilege of being at St Vincent's, I couldn't help but ask whether the one-week's loss of all privileges included not having to attend daily Mass.

"Mass is a duty, not a privilege!' Sister Ignatius had barked at me, before caning me on the bare backside for my insolence and giving me a one-week loss of all privileges – excluding Mass.

Perhaps the hardest part of being at St Vincent's was that I was alone, without my family for the first time in my life. I couldn't care less where my drunken, feckless parents were, but the loss of my brothers and sisters, especially Martin, was an ache in my heart. There wasn't a day went by when I didn't think about them and wonder if I would ever see them again.

The last time I had seen my siblings was two and a half years earlier, outside Nazareth House Children's Home in north Manchester. With our Daddy in prison and Mammy constantly disappearing, it had only been a matter of time before Social Services caught up with the nine of us still living at home. They decided that we could no longer stay at the family home alone but needed to go into care. And so, in January 1964, we were driven in a van to Nazareth House, our new home for the foreseeable future. It was the last time I was to see my brothers and sisters all together. As much as I loved them, I couldn't stay with them: incarceration in a children's home was not for me. Martin and I didn't even set foot inside Nazareth House. As soon as the police van pulled up outside, we'd legged it, running as fast as our legs would carry us, leaving our siblings to the mercies of the care system, determined we weren't going to be taken into care. Or so we thought... Martin and I had a much better plan: we were going home, back to 24 Stamford Street, Hulme.

Looking back, I think Martin and I must have walked hundreds of miles around Manchester during the three years we had lived in Stamford Street. We roamed the streets, criss-crossing Hulme, Longsight and Gorton, with no planned destination and just the one purpose in mind, which was to take advantage of any opportunity that should come our way. Those three years – surrounded by my family, feeling that I had the freedom of the streets – were the happiest days of my childhood.

Hulme! What a place! With many parts of it still frozen in its Victorian time warp. Even now, when I picture it, I see gas-lit cobbled streets and row upon row of back-to-back bathless houses with smoke-spewing chimneys. I think of an endless maze of back alleys, which you could walk along for mile after mile, hardly having to show your face to a living soul. I see clotheslines stretched from one side of the street to the other, straining under the weight of bed sheets caught by the wind, like the sails of a tall ship going nowhere; the front door steps scrubbed clean and donkey-stoned in yellow; the rag 'n' bone man with his horse and cart, in no hurry to end the day as he strolled up and down the cobbles with his familiar song. I hear the voices of children, out on the streets playing football, hopscotch, marbles, swinging off the lampposts, skipping over long pieces of rope, chorusing "The big ship sails on the ally ally oh! The ally ally oh!"

And let's not forget the pigeons, hundreds of them, which our older brother Shamie told us were flying rats with wings. It seems like only yesterday that Martin and I walked into Dale Street, where we came across a flock of pigeons pecking at full slices of mouldy bread. Always hungry, we snatched up a stale piece each and headed off down the street towards the Stretford Road, picking off the worst of the green mould as we went, before eating it. Mammy and Daddy never threw away any mouldy bread. Instead, Daddy would toast it over the flames of the coal fire for us.

"All dat green stuff is good for yer health," he'd tell us. "That little fella whatshisname, with the long, scruffy white hair all over the show and the long moustache drooping from under that big hooter of his? Einstein! That's the fella. It was him who'd invented penicillin from this shite. And now they inject it inta yer veins every time yah go inta hospital for an operation. That's why we're all healthy as can be expected."

But if Hulme seemed frozen in a bygone era, it was also a

place of new possibilities. Its colourful and diverse mix of cultures – Irish immigrants, Pakistani, Indian, Chinese – were living in a lost time, but they were also part of a landscape that was changing daily. As the slums tumbled, vast areas of wasteland, which we called crofts, appeared. Waiting for a new beginning.

Even our familiar home at 24 Stamford Street seemed changed when Martin and I returned to it after making our escape from Nazareth House Children's Home on that cold January day in 1964. We'd only been gone a few hours as we had tried – and failed – to evade the Social Services, but already we had felt the difference without our parents or our siblings for company and warmth. How deathly quiet and empty it seemed.

I don't know what we were hoping to find when we fled there, if anything at all. We just went home, because where else would we have gone? On our many journeys around Manchester I had always loved being in derelict buildings, because I'd felt such a deep peace inside those silent sanctuaries. But not this time. As Martin and I hid out in Stamford Street, our former home – once filled with cries of laughter and tears – felt abandoned, cold, and devoid of any feeling. We probably knew, deep down, that it was useless to hope Mammy, or anyone, would come back for us or that we could carry on as before. This would never be our family home again and our lives were set on a different course forever. After three cold, hungry days, we took one last look around the house before setting light to mammy's bedspread and walking out into the street, shutting the front door behind us.

Rovers' Return

Crossing over the Stretford Road, we made our way up along Welcome Street. It was here that we could see how the turmoil of the clearances had spread, like a disease. The long row of terraced houses that had stood to our right only weeks earlier were now gone forever, except in the memory of those who had once lived in them. Nearby, there were some houses only half demolished, with smouldering remnants of small fires scattered among them.

Further along the street, we noticed a group of young children smashing the windows of yet more empty houses. And it was strange, almost surreal, for us not to run over and join them as we would usually have done, playing our own part in the demolition process.

"Martin! Tommy!" Our cousin, Paddy Ward, had spotted us and hurried over, wanting to know where we were off to.

"Nowhere interestin' to be goin' in the first place," said Martin.

"Can I –"

"No, yah can't come with us," Martin cut in.

"Have yah seen any big puddles lately Paddy?" I asked, a wide grin spreading across my face as I thought back to the time he and Martin had the puddle competition to see who could make the biggest splash. Paddy, insisting he went first as he was slightly older than my brother, had disappeared under the pungent, sludgy surface of a pond that had once stood in the back garden of a house no longer there.

Looking back at me with a blank expression, Paddy was about to say something and then suddenly ignored me out of hand, either not wanting to remember or because he'd completely forgotten about the incident. This wouldn't have been all that surprising to us, considering his dad, our Uncle Bernard, had told us his son Paddy was half a Guinness short of a pint.

"Is it a secret? Where yah goin' I mean?"

"We're off ta the police station ta give ourselves up, that's all Paddy." I told him the truth, hoping he'd accept it and be off on his way.

"Give yourselves up! Jaysus what have yah done? Is it serious?"

"We can't be tellin' yah that Paddy," said Martin. "Otherwise ye'll be telling the whole of Hulme, if not Manchester."

"I wouldn't even tell the divil himself, Martin, sure I wouldn't an' yah know that don't yah? I mean, we're family an' all."

"But there's nothin' to tell, Paddy."

"Ah, ye'd say that so yah would Tommy. I can see the lies written inta them shifty eyes of yers."

"Paddy's too clever for us, Tommy," said Martin. "So, we might as well tell him."

"Tell him what?"

"Shallup Tommy!" Paddy glared at me. "Go on Martin. I won't say a word ta anyone, not even to me auld Granny, God rest her soul."

"Tommy's tellin' the truth. We are givin' ourselves up ta the coppers so we can be with the rest of our brothers and sisters, but we don't know if we want to tell dem about the money."

"What money?" both Paddy and I asked in unison.

"The money we stole from the church an' buried over there." Martin gave me the look, before pointing across to the croft next to the recently demolished houses and I noticed that Paddy's eyes had suddenly lit up.

"Oh! that money!" I suddenly remembered, falling in with my brother's concocted tale about us robbing the collection money from St Mary's Church in Upper Moss Street the previous evening.

"That can't be right, stealing from the church – can it?" said Paddy.

"Only if it's not a Catholic church," said Martin. "Well, we have ta go now Paddy. We'll see yah when we see yah."

"Yer coddin' me aren't yah? I mean, yer not really giv'n yourselves up ta the coppers? Are yah?"

"Aye, we are that, Paddy," said Martin.

"Yah won't be touchin' that money now Paddy will yah?" I added.

"What do ya take me for Tommy!" Paddy looked hurt. "I wouldn't do such a ting ta me own kind, so I wouldn't." He stood on the same spot eyeing us suspiciously as we walked off up the street.

"He'll murder us for sure if he ever finds out we made it all up."

"Well he won't find out unless he's stupid enough ta dig up the whole croft," laughed Martin.

Continuing our journey along those last few streets, which had played such an important part of our childhood, I felt afraid to look back over my shoulder in case we'd spot someone, or they'd spot us, which could so easily have influenced us to leave the path we were set on.

I didn't want to give myself up. I didn't want to leave those damp, dark streets that were just as much a part of me as I was a part of them – and certainly the place where I had felt safest. But I missed my brothers and sisters. And as tough as times were for us all, it was always comforting to be in their company, sharing everything we had, including the warmth of our bodies when we had snuggled up together in bed under all the old overcoats and whatever other rags we could find to keep ourselves warm.

I so missed my sister Bernie's infectious laughter and the brilliant ideas she would often come up with, for someone so young. Ideas that had got us into big trouble. Like the time she'd taken us on that ride in Mr McCarthy's horse and cart through the streets of Manchester and up along Piccadilly Plaza in the city centre.

I missed our big sister Maggie's sour puss when Mammy and Daddy were not around. And though she pretended nothing ever bothered her, we knew she'd be worrying so much about us over any little thing, especially our habit of stopping out much later than we ought to have done. I missed the affection Elizabeth had for us all, her reassurance and encouraging words that kept us all going, at times, helping us to forget our hunger. Martin and I needed her. We needed all of them. And for that, we were both willing to give up our own freedom.

"Look!" I'd been the first to spot the tall aluminium television aerial still attached to the chimney of the house with its roof now collapsed in on itself. And in that moment, it seemed that I had suddenly forgotten that we had a purpose for that day. Until Martin reminded me.

"Leave it Tommy! It's no use ta us any more."

"It's got to be worth at least tuppence."

"But not ta us – not any more." He held out his hand to help me back across the uneven surface of the ground. And that's when it had all suddenly dawned on me and I came to accept that this chapter in our lives was close to its end. Hulme had nothing left to give us but our memories, and for those we were grateful. We were still holding hands when we turned into Park Street and walked into the police station.

I can still see the look on the fat Sergeant's face as we ambled inside the station and stood peering up at him in silence. His jaw nearly dropped onto the large oak counter. You could almost hear a pin drop as he stared back down on us, before squeezing his eyelids tightly together, as if checking whether we were just a figment of his imagination. Then he went away, leaving us standing there for a few seconds before he reappeared with a posse of faces, which stared over the counter at us, their murmured whispers finally breaking the silence.

"You've seen some sense at last, have you?" The Sergeant's hardened face had softened into a smile. But if he'd been waiting for an answer or a smile back from us, he would have been waiting for an eternity. Our lack of schooling had left us with a somewhat stunted vocabulary, so our conversations were very short and sweet, influenced more by the foul language we'd picked up from our elders. For Martin and me, that day was not a victory or a disaster. There were no sentimental emotions running through my head. In fact, there were no thoughts at all – they would come later. For now, I remained silent, staring up with expressionless eyes into the Sergeant's face.

"Come on," he sighed, breaking the spell. Lifting the heavy counter flap up for us to come behind, he handed us over to the jailer, telling him to look after us.

We were put into a large cell with an iron-barred frontage, which I can only assume was used as an eating area for the policemen working at the station. It was furnished with a long, heavy table and an assortment of six or seven chairs, with drab-green painted cupboards fixed to the walls and a large floor-standing three-bar electric fire in one corner. The jailer said he was going off to fetch us something to eat and as he went, he closed the gate behind him and was about to lock it. But then he paused, seemingly having second thoughts, before swinging the large iron gate back open, leaving it ajar as he left us alone.

He arrived back with a portion each of sausage and chips covered in a thick layer of mushy peas and all wrapped in newspaper, which we'd gratefully swallowed down with the help of a large tin mug of strong, sweet tea. Afterwards, we were interviewed by two social workers, Miss Barton and Miss Young, who arrived in the late afternoon.

Miss Barton, the older-looking of the two women, was small and plump with short, silvery-grey hair. The other was much taller and wider with black hair in a bob and a face like a constipated gorilla. I didn't like the pair of patronising old biddies, who started off with their false, sweet smiles, calling us Martin and Tommy as if they'd known us for ages. They were desperate to get information out of us.

"Where's your mother?"

"Don't know, don't care."

"Did your father come home from prison?"

"Don't know, don't care."

"Who has been looking after you both?"

"We don't need anyone looking after us, missus."

"So, there was no one looking after you?"

"We'd not said that, so don't be puttin' words inta our mouths," snapped Martin.

"Then who has been looking after you?"

"Don't know, don't care."

"And how did you eat?"

"With our mouths." I sniggered at the stupid question.

"We are obviously not getting anywhere with this." The snooty, silver-haired woman, having grown tired of our unhelpfulness and seeming to be getting humpier by the minute, spoke through gritted teeth. It had taken her a moment to gather her composure, before telling us we were being taking to Lynwood Children's Home for a few days, until they could find us a more permanent place. Nazareth House was mentioned as a permanent possibility and that news had lifted our spirits, giving us hope that we could soon be reunited with most of our family.

"So," said the darker-haired woman, "if you've any questions you would like to ask us before we set off, now is your chance." She stared hard from Martin to me.

"Have yah been ta a zoo?" asked Martin.

"That's an odd question, under the circumstances. But since you ask, yes, Polly and I visited Chester Zoo only last week." She threw a big smile at her silver-haired companion.

"How did yah escape?"

On the way out of the police station, the smiling desk Sergeant, probably smiling at the thought of never having to see us again, stood holding the front door wide open for us. We gave him our best scowls and I just had the word "fatty" on my lips when he suddenly handed us each a pack of fruit Spangles, telling us to take care of ourselves. And for the first time ever, I had seen a softer side to this big fella who, on many occasions, we had harassed and threatened with all sorts of dire consequences if he so much as looked at us.

A New Home

With the pair of us sitting in the back of the two-door Morris Minor, we were taken on the short journey of around three miles to our destination. The silence was interrupted only the once, when a football bounced off the pavement into the path of the car. The Gorilla, who was driving, deliberately aimed the car straight at the ball and popped it, to the amusement of her colleague, while three small boys stood on the pavement with their two fingers in the air, screaming abuse at the car.

"What chance has the world got with this lot?" sneered the Gorilla, peering into the rear-view mirror (probably admiring her handiwork), where she caught my gaze and held it. But determined as I'd always been, I glared back at her with a grin spread right across my grubby face – knowing she would have to back down first or crash the car. "And that's just the children," she declared, as I won the battle of wits.

It was already dark when we arrived at Lynwood House Children's Home. Both social workers escorted us into the hallway and had the briefest of discussions with a middle-aged fella they'd addressed as Mr Howard who to all intents and purposes looked as if he'd just woken up and climbed out of his coffin. He kept blowing his reddened hooter, excusing himself for his bad bout of flu. Pale-faced and as bald as a coot, he looked to us like he was at death's door. It wouldn't have surprised me one bit if his clothes, which hung off his bony body like sacks, had fallen off him when he sneezed twice in succession.

"I'm Uncle John," he said hoarsely.

"What's the queer fella sayin?" asked Martin under his breath.

"I tink he said he's our Uncle."

"He looks like Granddaddy standin' in his coffin, I'll give him dat!"

"So, he is our Uncle?"

"Shallup Tommy."

"The children here call me Uncle John," he explained.

"Well, we're callin' yah nothin' of the sort, mister. An' don't yah be pretendin' yer related ta us when we've never set eyes on yah till now." Martin put him in his place.

"This is Aunty Pauline," said the dead-looking fella, ignoring Martin and introducing us to the fat, slobby-looking girl who had suddenly squeezed herself out into the hallway through a side doorway.

"Jaysus, will yah get a look at dat. No wonder the queer fella's dying of starvation, with the size of her." Martin muttered the words out of the side of his mouth, causing me to almost choke on my laughter.

"Aunty Pauline will look after you and I'll speak with you tomorrow morning," said the ill fella, suddenly walking off and leaving us with the blonde fat girl, who couldn't have been much older than our sister Mary – though probably three times as wide. I'd taken an instant dislike to her, with her gawking eyes sizing up the pair of us and her nose in the air, as if she thought she was above us. I'd been on the point of firing off the first barrage of abuse at her when, right on cue, she suddenly turned her back on us and walked away.

"Follow me – if you're hungry."

Aunty Pauline rustled us up some cheese sandwiches and a home-made Victoria sponge, along with a glass of watery, diluted orange juice to swill it down. We sat at the large kitchen table, forced to listen to her going on about her life, which hadn't amounted to all that much. She lived in Moss Side, hardly ever went to school, was put into care aged 12 after her mother had got rid of her baby – the one her granddaddy had given her. Now aged 16, she bemoaned the fact she had been removed from every foster care placing, having been accused of being a nympho-something-or-other.

"I suppose I'm one of the lucky ones living here and them giving me a job as well," said Aunty Pauline, who perhaps wasn't so bad after all.

She seemed happy with her lot. So, when she helped herself to a large lump of the Victoria Sponge, Martin and I quickly grabbed our lot, leaving her to pick off the crumbs left on the plate.

I wondered why her mother had given away the baby her granddaddy had given to her and where he'd got it from in the first place. Daddy said he'd found us under a bush by the Manchester shipping canal. I wanted to ask her if that's where her granddaddy had found her baby. But I changed my mind at the last minute, not wanting to upset her, especially as we all seemed to have been getting on well. It did have me thinking about why our own mother had left us the way she did, which brought to my mind the song our sister Mary used to sing us to sleep with.

I once had a dear old mother
who meant the world to me
and when I needed her
she'd always cuddle me.
One night as I lay dreaming
upon my little bed
an angel came from Heaven
to tell me mother was dead.
I woke up in the morning
to see if it was true
And she'd gone to Heaven
above the sky so blue.
So listen all you children
and do what you are told
for if you lose your mother
you'll lose a heart of gold.

I liked the song very much and was able to understand its meaning, though it meant nothing to me, in the sense of losing something as precious as a mother. I'd lost my mother and I had no emotional attachment to that fact. But I had been left with the question, if a good mother has a heart of gold, what was my mother's heart made of?

We followed Aunty Pauline upstairs to the bathroom where she ran a bath, telling us to strip off and get in. We were only too happy to oblige, before being interrupted by a breathless, grey-haired old woman who came barging in on us.

"I'll deal with the boys," said the bespectacled old woman, scowling at Aunty Pauline and telling her, between deep breaths, to leave the bathroom. Then she turned on us and snapped, "Come on! Off with those dirty rags and into the bath." But we were not so obliging for her, and we stood our ground, scowling back at her.

"Come on. We haven't all day."

"We're goin' nowhere missus, are we, Tommy?"

"Not today we're not." I grinned at the woman. "Anyways, yer not gettin' a peek at our flutes."

"Flutes? What are you talking about!"

"Our mickeys."

"Mickeys indeed. Get yourself in the bath and I'll be back with some clean clothes for you. Flutes!" She walked out of the bathroom closing the door behind her, as we hurriedly stripped naked.

I still don't know why we did what we did next, but the intentions of getting a bath changed instantly when Martin, with a mischievous grin, stepped into the bath and opened the sash window above it. I watched as he climbed out of it and down the soil pipe to the ground and then I followed him.

"Are we runnin away, Martin?" I scanned the small passage-way we'd found ourselves in, looking for an escape route.

"Let's pretend ta be dead." He got down on the ground and laid on his back, and I followed suit, lying on my back on the cold concrete surface, as naked as the day I was born. With my head resting on Martin's stomach, I squinted through half-closed eyes at the open window of the bathroom above us.

Not long afterwards we heard this almighty, blood-curdling scream, and saw the old woman's grey head looking out of the window, peering down into the dark at us.

"Oh Lord! They've fallen out of the window! They've fallen out of the window! The poor buggers!" The woman was beside herself as we listened to her voice fade away.

"Quick!" said Martin, pushing me up off him.

Climbing back up the soil pipe, with me following close behind him, we clambered back into the bathroom and pulled the window shut, before sitting in the bath and washing ourselves.

"But I know what I saw! They were both lying there! I didn't imagine it!"

We scowled at the group who had suddenly rushed into the bathroom, led by Mr Howard, still blowing his hooter. The distraught old woman standing alongside him stared at us with disbelieving eyes and, shaking her head from side to side, insisted she'd seen what she'd seen. And no one could tell her otherwise.

I caught Aunty Pauline's gaze and was sure she knew what we'd been up to, as her concerned look suddenly bloomed into a wide grin.

"I think you should take the rest of the week off, Mrs O'Neil," advised Mr Howard, as we continued to scowl, while shaking our heads at the distraught woman. "You have been overdoing it again."

"But I swear, they were lying outside. I saw them both. I did!"

End of an Era

Our expectations that we would be moved on quickly to Nazareth House to join our siblings, as originally mentioned by Social Services, never materialised. Longing to be reunited with our brothers and sisters, we'd cried in private until we'd no more tears left to shed. We had lived on the promise of being reunited with them and were told time after time, "Soon", "Not long now", "Just be patient." Eventually, time was to blunt the sharpness of our separation from them.

A few days after Mrs O'Neil (Aunty Julie) came back off sick leave and we'd got to know her better, we owned up to what we had done on the first evening at the home. She told us she was very cross, more so because we'd nearly given her a heart attack when she'd seen us lying below the bathroom window and had thought the worst. But she was very forgiving and smiled it off, grateful that everyone now knew she'd been telling the truth after all.

Uncle John, looking more alive than when we had first met, had given us a half-hearted lecture on the consequences of our behaviour. Not only because of the upset caused to Aunty Julie, but the fact that she could have lost her job. After we had apologised, promising never to do anything like it ever again, we were instantly forgiven – without having to do any penance.

At Lynwood House we were being cared for much better than we could have expected. Not that we'd had any previous experience to give us higher expectations above and beyond our past lives. And so there was an acceptance of everything thrown at us. Given the opportunity, I would have liked to have stayed at Lynwood for as long as possible, but the chance of being able to do so was never on the cards – and that was purely because of us.

What we received in care, compassion and understanding was, regrettably, never returned by Martin and me. We bunked off school daily, preferring instead to spend our days wandering the streets, or up along the canals. We had no sense of purpose: everywhere we went, everything we did, every choice we made was a compulsive one, based on what we'd been used to and what we loved best. It wasn't enough that we had become cared-for children for the first time in our lives. It meant nothing to us at all. Whilst most of our needs were being taken care of, there was always something missing from our lives. And no amount of caring or loving was ever going to be a substitute for our inborn desire to be free.

At the end of each day, if the police were not bringing us back to the home, we would get rid of any bicycles we'd stolen, either giving them away freely to other kids we'd met on the streets or leaning them up against a wall for someone to help themselves to. Anything else we'd collected during our many journeys would be hidden in our den beneath the demolition site, just across the street from Lynwood House.

We'd discovered the small entrance hole beneath a large slab of concrete just a few days after our arrival. It was just wide enough for us to be able to crawl through and down into the cellar of a demolished building. Over the first few weeks we turned it into an Aladdin's cave, filling it with all sorts of things we'd stolen or found in empty houses, or up along the alleys. Our haul included unwanted toys, board games, books, scrap metal, pots and pans, old bed covers, road lamps – anything and everything we had no real need for, except to be able to call it our own.

One morning, I woke from a dream that I was playing on the lamppost outside our house in Stamford Street and this put the idea into my head that I wanted to visit the place again. I told Martin about my dream and my thoughts of going back to Hulme, just to see it once more. He agreed it was a great idea.

We made our way to school as usual and hung around the bike sheds until the school assembly bell rang out and the coast was clear. Finding a couple of unchained bikes, we discarded our red school blazers and were on our way, pedalling out of the main gates.

We had no idea what to expect when we got there. When Martin and I had walked out of our old home for what we thought was the last time, I had thrown a burning cigarette lighter onto Mammy and Daddy's bed as a farewell gesture. I wasn't sure why I had done it. So, as we pedalled along the pavements, filled with excitement and trepidation, I had many questions running through my head. Had the house caught fire? Were Mammy and Daddy back home? Had any of the others come home? If so, what sort of reception would we get?

The journey had taken us into the latter part of the morning, not that we were in any hurry to reach our destination. We'd stopped off at a small chapel en route, saying prayers and lighting lots of candles for our Granddaddy and all those members of the family who (Daddy had said) were either up in Heaven or being roasted on a spit in Hell. I think we'd lit almost all the candles in the church before we were chased out by a pair of old female codgers coming out of a side room with vases of flowers.

We rode up along the Stretford Road, which took us directly into Hulme. The high street didn't look any different since that fateful night a few months earlier when we'd stood outside the Chinese restaurant, looking in on people eating, before we had been taken away in police vans. Despite the shining sun, the place maintained the drab, grey dreariness we remembered so well. It was almost as if it had been waiting for our return.

We noticed the changes as we cycled along Vine Street, with some of the familiar buildings now gone and others in various states of demolition. Crossing over Dale Street, we continued up the hill, having to get off the bikes halfway up and walk them the rest of the way.

When we reached the top of the hill, my heart sank. We were frozen in our tracks as we were hit by a sea of emptiness. I could feel the overpowering sense of bewilderment and panic rushing through my whole body, almost causing my legs to buckle, as my gaze had searched in vain for Collins Street, Durham Street, Bonsall Street, Philips Street, Stamford Street. But they were no longer there. All those streets that had played such a big part in our daily lives – the houses, the people, the children, the lampposts, the back entries, the noise, the smoke, the flying rats – all gone.

Leaving the bikes where we'd let them fall, we walked through the deafening silence over the rough landscape that was now so alien to us. It took us a while to work out where Stamford Street had once stood, only finding it after Martin had spotted the edge of the twisted tin street sign poking out from the debris.

Martin straightened out the sign as best he could, beating it with a lump of masonry before he stuck it upright into the dusty ground, steadying it around its base with lumps of debris. And there, in the eerie silence, we stood with our heads slightly bowed as we came to accept our lives were now set on a different path and could never be the same.

Heading back across the rubble in the direction of our bikes, we said not a word to each other. I didn't know what Martin was thinking, nor did I feel the need to ask him. And though we hadn't had any real expectations of finding anyone at home, it had still been a shock to see our past had gone. Not that the feelings of loss or grief were touching my heart. I am not sure that I understood what mourning meant at that time. For me, standing in solemn silence for a house we had lost was no different from the times we had walked up to a graveside and had stood alongside the mourners (strangers to us), joining in the prayers and throwing the traditional handful of soil down on to the coffin below.

As we approached our bikes, we noticed the three lads, about a year or two older than us, standing over them. The tallest lad had picked up one of the bikes and thrown his leg over it, but before he'd had time to ride off, Martin rushed across and pushed over both boy and bike.

"Dem's our bikes, so feck off!" warned Martin, picking up the bike as I grabbed the other one.

"We found them first," said the blond boy, who was probably a foot taller than me.

"They weren't lost ta be found in the first place," said Martin, reclaiming his bike and kicking the lanky boy as he started to pick himself up off the uneven, dusty ground.

"Finders keepers," said one of the other lads, suddenly grabbing hold of my bike.

"Put yer dukes up an' we'll fight for it." The lad agreed to my offer, taking his hands off the bike as he brought his fists up to protect his face. This gave me enough time to grab the tyre pump off the frame and whack the thieving fecker to the side of the head, causing him to howl, before he ran off with threats of fetching his daddy. The other two lads just stood scowling at us, not saying a word, as we climbed on our bikes and rode past them in the opposite direction.

Trapped

The following morning the sky was a dark grey and it was pouring down, so we decided to take refuge in our den. We could see the demolition men working inside some empty houses further across the site from us, so we sneaked into their work hut and helped ourselves to a lunch box, along with a heavy tea flask. As I followed Martin back out of the hut, I snatched up the large radio on the table and hurried after him.

Martin was the first into the den, with me pushing the lunch box, flask and radio in after him, before crawling down into the hole myself. Martin turned on the two yellow, battery-operated roadwork lamps we'd pinched some while back.

"Why did yah want ta bring that thing for? It's not like we can play it down here with everyone up there listenin'," complained Martin.

"I liked it."

"Jaysus Tommy. If yah brought everythin' yah liked down here, we wouldn't be able ta get in anymore."

"Do yah want a game of tiddlywinks?"

"Aye ok. I'm seven four up on the day."

"Dat's not fair, Martin!"

"Why isn't it fair? I beat yah a few days ago."

"Yeh! But you should only win on that day," I argued, "not carry it over for another day, otherwise yer always in front."

"Ah it doesn't matter anyhow, I'll still beat yah."

I surrendered on eight-three down, suggesting we play snap instead, because I could easily cheat at that. I was two-nil up when our card game was interrupted by a loud noise above. We could hear the loud engine of a digger drawing closer and men's voices, though we couldn't hear what they were saying. Then the ceiling and walls of the cellar began to vibrate as the ground all around shook and, in that instant, we knew the heavy machine was on top of us.

"We'd better be goin'," said Martin, quickly moving to the coal-hole exit, standing aside to give me a leg-up first.

But in the split second it took to put my right foot into Martin's hand, a stream of dust and small pieces of rubble had suddenly fallen into the cellar. I could see that our way out was blocked as the large lump of concrete standing over the entrance fell and the small view of the outside world had disappeared.

"The hole's blocked!" I only just said the words before feeling a bang on the head that knocked me senseless.

"Tommy! Tommy! Are yah alright? Jaysus Tommy, say something."

"Are we dead Martin? Are we in Limbo?"

"No, we're not dead Tommy. An' we're not in Limbo either. We're still alive."

"So, I'm blind then? Jaysus! I'll never be able to see meself agin."

"Yer not blind Tommy. The lamps are broken is all."

"But it's dark! An' me head feels bigger than before."

"A brick bonked yah on the nut. I'm going ta see if I can find a lamp."

"Don't leave me Martin!"

"I'm not leavin' yah. Just stay still."

I listened to my brother moving around in the dark, sifting through the rubble in search of a road-side lamp, and as I waited, listening to his every movement, I felt the initial sense of panic leave me. I was frightened, but not of the dark. I'd stopped being frightened of that after Daddy had told me, "It's not the dark dat harms people, but the people in the dark dat harms people." My sister Mary had already dispelled my night-time fears of ghosts by telling me, "Yah'll never find ghosts coming out in the dark Tommy, as they'd only be falling over themselves," which had made a lot of sense to me at the time.

I suppose it was the not knowing what was going to happen next that was my biggest fear. But at least I felt comforted by Martin being there with me, which was all that mattered. And I was sure that if anyone could find a way to get out of there, it was him.

Touching the top of my sore head, I could feel the throbbing lump and the stickiness of blood on my matted hair, glad of the darkness so I was unable to see the damage.

"Found one!"

I could hear Martin fiddling around with the lamp, before the dim yellow light suddenly flashed on to reveal his dust-covered, shadowy face. I was shocked to see the debris

32

filling half of the cellar after the ceiling had collapsed in on itself, followed by the huge pile of rubble above the ground.

"Jaysus Martin. We've the whole show on top of us. What are we goin' ta do?" I looked at my hand to see it was covered in a thick layer of blood and dust. "I'm bleedin' ta death!"

"Yer not bleedin' ta death. Let me get a look at yah." He moved the lamp close to me. "It looks like a little cut is all. Anyway, the dust has dried most of it up."

"How little is little?"

"I don't know. An inch maybe."

"How little is an inch?"

"Well it's smaller than two inches, I know dat."

"But I don't know how little two inches is."

"Jaysus, Tommy, it's dat size!" Martin indicated with his finger and thumb. "The size of a fly."

"A little fly?"

"Ah, for feck's sake. Whished! I heard somethin'." My brother got to his feet and moved closer to the coal-hole entrance. "I think I can hear more people up there talkin'."

"I can't hear anythin'."

"Will yah whished up for a second."

We listened in the silence but all I could hear was the odd movement of my brother's feet as he moved around on the debris.

"They've gone."

"Can't yah shout for help?" I asked, before suddenly screaming, "Help! Help! We're down here!" I'd shouted myself hoarse, but no one came to our rescue.

Martin found the lunch box and flask, and we tucked into the spam and pickled sandwiches. I loved spam. It was always the first thing I'd go for when we used to steal the food from the shops. Opening the tin with the metal key would sometimes be trying, especially when the metal rim snapped off before I could get all the way around the tin. Having to force it open the rest of the way, I always ended up with a few fine cuts to my fingers, which would sting for a few days. The tea in the flask was unsweetened and stewed, but it was hot and we shared a cupful between us.

After a short while, I decided to try and move the debris to see if we could find a way up through the cellar ceiling, but as I moved it, twice as much would fall back through from above.

"Leave it Tommy, or we'll be buried alive," warned Martin.

We had no idea how long we'd been trapped inside the cellar, and as time had never been all that important to us, it had been hard for us to judge, especially as we couldn't see any natural light from outside. We played a game of I Spy, which kept our minds occupied for a while. Martin as usual, was on top of his game, especially as he was a better speller than me. I kept giving in to him, but to be honest he could have been spelling anything wrong and I wouldn't have known any different. When it came to the few turns I had, I would have to half pronounce the sound of the object I had spied, so "Bri" was brick, making it much easier for him to guess.

I had managed to get him on one, which had peeved him off no end.

"I spy with me little eye somethin' beginnin' with U." I drew the letter U in the air with my finger.

"Undies?"

"Can't see them!"

"Up?"

"Dat's not somethin'."

"Ugly."

"I wouldn't call yah that."

"Upducky."

"What's upducky?"

"Nothin' darlin'."

"Dat's not fair."

"Well, I can only tink of umbrella an' there isn't one of them here."

"Nope."

"There's nothin' else, unless yer makin' it up, or spelling it wrong, which doesn't count."

"So, yah give in then?"

"I give in – go on," sighed Martin.

"You!" I point to him.

"Me? You said it began with the letter U."

"That's how I spell it an' that's what counts. Anyways, I couldn't say it any other way without saying 'you' could I?"

We finished off the remainder of the stewed flask tea and I asked Martin if he thought we would see the others again. I hadn't meant it in the sense of not getting out of the cellar alive. I hadn't thought of such a thing happening under any circumstances, only ever thinking of death as something that happened to older people – like our Granddaddy.

"I don't know," said Martin and went on to talk about other things. But I don't recall what he said because his soft voice had sent me drifting off into a deep sleep.

Lost and Found

When I woke, Martin was fast asleep at my side. He looked like a little mouse, the way he'd been curled up into a ball. I noticed that the light of the lamp had dimmed to almost nothing. But it was the smaller, brighter light beyond the lamp that had caught my attention, getting me all excited.

"Martin, Martin, wake up! There's a light!"

"What?"

"Wake up. Look, there's a light." I pointed to the hole where I could see the tiniest of bright lights glowing.

"Oh, thank yea sweet Jaysus. Thank yea Holy Mother of God." Martin had gone on like Mammy, thanking every saint he could think of. "We're saved Tommy! We're saved!"

We made a high step from the bigger pieces of bricks directly underneath the coal hole, until we could stand on it and touch the piece of concrete blocking our way to freedom. I handed my brother a long stick, which he pushed towards the tiny hole in the hope that he would dislodge any debris on the outside. But the hole remained the same size. Then Martin came up with the idea of switching on the radio in the hope that someone passing by would hear it.

We took it in turns to hold the blaring radio up to the tiny hole. I don't recall how many times we swapped places, but it seemed many. We'd been on the point of giving up when Cilla Black came on, singing, "You're my world, you're every breath I take," and miraculously we heard a man's voice calling down through the tiny hole.

"Is there anyone under there?"

"Help, we're trapped! Please help us!" Martin dropped the radio and I peed my trousers with the excitement of having been found.

"Hang on, hang on, I'll get you out. Fetch that long bar, son. Okay, I'm going to move this lump of concrete out of the way."

The outside world slowly began to reveal itself to us as the large slab of concrete was slowly edged away from the hole and the fresh air rolled in. It was dark outside, except for the dim yellow glow from the few streets lights. Then I noticed the moon off to one side of us and I wondered if that had been the light I'd spotted inside the cellar.

"Out you come."

The black arm came down and I gripped the man's hand tightly with both of mine as in one swift movement he hauled me up and out into the open. I was standing next to a young black boy, who couldn't have been much older than me. The boy said nothing, opting to look wide-eyed at me, as if he'd never seen the likes of me before. The man then got down on to his knees and seconds later Martin popped out, just as Cilla hit the words, "A power so divine".

"Man, how on earth did you both get yourselves trapped down there?" asked our rescuer.

"Some boys made us do it and then trapped us inside," lied Martin.

"Oh Lord! You could have been buried alive."

"We'd better be off home, before Mammy gives out to us," I said to Martin.

"Wait, wait. Your head looks bad, fella." The man was about to inspect my injured head, but I turned my back on him and had already started to walk off.

"It's only a scratch, thanks." I looked back at him and the wide-eyed boy as Martin walked to my side. "And thanks for saving our lives."

We legged it up the street and out of sight, making our way to Lynwood House and ringing the front doorbell. When no one answered, Martin pressed the button again, keeping his finger on it until the door was opened by the grumpy old night watchman, Mr Todd, who we'd only seen on one other occasion. Usually we would have been in bed and fast asleep by the time he and his wife came on duty, so we knew it must have been late in the night. He stood in the half-open doorway, blocking our way and eyeing the pair of us up and down suspiciously without saying a word. Until Martin broke the silence.

"It's us. Tommy an' Martin."

"And?"

"We live here."

"The two missing boys?"

"We're not missin'," I snapped.

"Heather!"

"Who is it Gerald?" asked his wife as she came rushing into the hallway. "Oh my word, look at the state of you both. Let them in for God's sake." She almost pushed her husband out of the way as she ushered us in and made a big fuss over us. "Get Mr Howard on the phone," she ordered her grumpy husband, before taking us down to the kitchen, where she cleaned up my injured head over the sink. It was only a small cut, just as Martin had said, and didn't need any stitching.

"Whatever happened to you both?" asked Mrs Todd, seeming concerned and almost tearful. But I said nothing, looking to Martin to come up with an answer.

"We were chased by a gang of older school boys throwing duckers at us. One big ducker hit Tommy on the head and nearly kilt him, didn't it Tommy?"

"It did Martin. I thought I was dead until you woke me up in that dark hole and told me I wasn't."

"Dark hole?"

"We had to hide down a coal cellar of a bombed house 'til it got dark enough for us to show our faces, is what Tommy means. We were so scared to come home 'til we were sure they were gone." Martin suddenly burst out crying, which was fascinating for me to watch, as he cried real crocodile tears. I couldn't, for the life of me, put on such a false cry, especially with all those facial expressions having to go with it. And though I had managed to pull a face with quivering lips, I'd not been able to get a single teardrop to spill from my eyes.

We were sent upstairs to get a warm bath, which Mrs Todd had run for us. And once we got into our pyjamas, we headed back downstairs to the kitchen, where we had a couple of buttered fruit buns, along with a cup of warm, milky cocoa.

Not long afterwards, Mr Howard came to see us. He seemed genuinely upset by Martin's account of our ordeal and my brother stuck to the same story about the gang chasing us. A short while later the coppers arrived, which is when we realised they were taking it very seriously. The coppers did a crafty one on us though, by separating us before they questioned us. But since I already knew the lies my brother had told Mrs Todd, I just repeated word for word what he'd told her.

They asked me how many boys had done the chasing. I gave this question a lot of thought, wondering what Martin might have said, but as I hadn't a clue, and not wanting to get caught out, I tried a different tack and decided to act the idiot.

"I don't know, I can't count ta save me dead granny's life."

"Were there two of them?"

"One, two," I counted on my fingers. "'More than that."

"Three?"

"How many is that more than two?"

"Is this lad for real?" said the agitated copper, turning to Mr Howard for help.

"Both of the boys are unable to read nor write," he explained.

"But surely they can count to ten?"

"It's not my fault if I can't count." I crossed my arms and sulked, refusing to look at the copper or answer any more of his questions on the matter.

Lucky for us, Martin had point-blank refused to answer any of the questions the other copper had put to him. And although they seemed to know something was amiss, they must have also realised they were not going to get any more out of us than we wanted to give them. So they left us in peace and we were able to go straight off to bed.

Moving On

We were kept off school for the next few days, before being informed by Mr Howard that we would have to appear before the Magistrates' Court. But the worse news was being told of the likelihood that we might not be returning to Lynwood House. The impact of such news left the pair of us distraught and speechless, and no amount of consoling from Aunty Pauline, or anyone else, could lift our spirits.

As expected, after standing for five minutes in the dock of the Magistrates' Court, we were informed by the miserable-looking, toffee-nosed old hen, sitting in between two more miserable-looking old hens, that we were to be remanded to Rose Hill Remand Centre, still in North Manchester, until a more suitable place had been found for us. Apparently, we were reckless and a danger to ourselves, besides being too out of control to be allowed back to Lynwood House.

"Yah humpy auld lesheens yah!" The old female magistrates looked on in shocked disbelief as Martin cussed and cursed them. "May the cat eat yah an' the divil eat the cat, yah dirty auld witches!" yelled Martin, throwing one of Mammy's curses their way.

They were saved from further hexes when one of the jailors put his hand over Martin's mouth before picking him up off the ground, carrying him across the dock and down the stairs to the cells. Meanwhile, one of the distraught magistrates ranted on (to no one in particular) about how she'd never heard or witnessed such behaviour from young children in all her years on this earth.

As she caught my eye, I gave her a double-handed, two-fingered salute before following the second jailor down the stairs to join my brother sitting on the concrete bed area in the small cell. And this time they locked us in.

"I'm afraid, Martin."

"Der's nothin' ta be afraid of Tommy."

"I want us ta go back ta the home, that's all."

"Dat's the thing. The home doesn't want us."

"Do yah tink Mammy an' Daddy might come an' fetch us?"

"We've more chance of seein' pigs flyin'."

"I've never seen flyin' pigs before."

"Dat's the whole point Tommy, we never will."

"I feckin' hate them."

"Pigs are fine if yah leave dem alone."

"Mammy an' Daddy, I hate them. We wouldn't be here if it wasn't for them. I feckin' hate them. An' I hope they drop down dead an' die." I cried, with so much anger and frustration burning inside me. I was unable to come to terms with the fact they'd abandoned us, and for the first time, the truth, that they didn't care for us, suddenly hit me. I'd seen Daddy pat a stranger's dog and Mammy stroke Churchill, our cowardly cat who wouldn't attack a fly, let alone a mouse. And yet the only time I'd ever felt their touches was when he was either throwing a punch at me or beating me with his leather belt. Or when she was scrubbing the dirt off me.

I could find some forgiveness for her. Being uneducated and unable to read and write was something beyond her control, since she was brought up in Ireland's travelling community. But to watch, without showing the slightest bit of emotion, as our daddy had beaten us black and blue for no good reason, drunk or otherwise, was always going to be unforgivable.

I'd once overheard Mammy say to my sister Mary, "Jaysus, I can't stop him drinkin' an' carryin' on all the while. What d'yah expect me ta do?"

"Leave the auld bastard an' take the lot of us with yah," replied Mary, who ran away from home with our sister Rosie not long afterwards. "I don't know how yea can put up with him beatin' yea an' us. An' doin' the tings he's doin' to us an' you lettin' him get away with it all the while. He's no feckin' good for yah mammy! He's no good for any of us."

But Mammy was having none of it. Instead, she blamed it on us, her family of "humpy bastards" who'd destroyed her life and made them both turn to the drink just to cope with it all.

"I don't have two pennies ta rub together an' I have ta feed and clothe yah all! An' if it wasn't for him ye'd have nothin'," was Mammy's answer.

She did often have her emotional outbursts, along with the same crocodile tears that Martin could bring on so easily. But she only ever cried when she was drunk and feeling sorry for herself, always moaning how life could have been so wonderful for her and Jim (Daddy) if it had not been for all "yous poxy bastards gettin' under our skin".

As for Daddy? I hated the fact that I was afraid of him. I hated the fact he was my daddy. I just hated him.

"Don't cry Tommy, at least not for them bastards." Martin threw an arm around my shoulder and began to sing me the song we always used to sing together.

I used to play my yellow banjo and rest it on my knee.
But now the strings have broken down it's no more use to me.
I took it to a mender's shop, to see what he could do.
He said the strings are broken down. It's no more use to you.
I took it to the minstrel man he said, I've one like you.
He changed the strings on my yellow banjo and now it's good as new.

I didn't know how long we'd been asleep in the cell, but it seemed an age until we were woken and taken out, handcuffed to each other, before being put into the police van, along with three other boys roughly the same age as us.

One of the boys, a short lad called George, was crying for his mammy, while the other two were teasingly smirking at him, calling him a little girl. When the lad with the long neck and goofy teeth kicked George on the shin, telling him, "Shut your fuckin' mouth up mate," Martin had to get involved.

"Leave the kid alone," snapped my brother.

Goofy didn't take too kindly to this and took a kick at my brother, which was the worst thing he could have done. Martin and I launched a sudden attack on him with our feet, kicking out at Goofy time and again, while his friend, who had been handcuffed to him, kept his legs out of the way so we didn't catch him.

"What the fuck is all that commotion?" The police van had suddenly screeched to a halt.

When the back door was thrown open, we saw the taller of the two coppers standing outside, glaring into the van with his truncheon raised at the ready. But none of us dared say a word. I remember looking from the truncheon to the copper's eyes and I was wondering if he'd ever hit anyone with it, when he suddenly brought it down hard on the floor of the van, making me jump in fright. "Keep it that way," he snarled through gritted teeth, before slamming the van door shut and locking it again.

"Touch him agin, longneck, an' I'll straighten them goofy rat's teeth for yah," threatened Martin, which was all that was needed to put the bully in his place. And we heard no more out of him for the rest of the journey to the Remand Centre.

It had started to rain by the time the police van drove down Longley Lane, before suddenly turning off the road and in through the double gateway. Driving past the dreary, grey-stoned gate lodge and along the long driveway, the van came to a halt outside the main entrance to the remand centre.

I was taken aback by the huge lump of rock standing just on the edge of the driveway, a foot or so off the ground and balanced on top of a large metal plinth. As we stood staring in awe at the size of the stone, which must have been almost as large as the police van, the shorter copper of the two told us it had fallen from Outer Space, landing right on the spot where it now stood.

"Was that metal bit already fixed ta it when it dropped out of the sky?" I was asking a serious question as I pointed to the metal plinth the rock was balanced on. "Or did the stone land on the top of it, like that?"

"Don't try to be smart lad, it'll get you nowhere," said the copper, glaring at me.

Once inside the building the two coppers set about taking the handcuffs off the other three lads, before turning to Martin and me. But we handed ours over to them, having already slipped our skinny wrists out of them.

"Next time they'll go on tighter," said the copper.

"There won't be a next time," said Martin.

"That's what they all say son. We hear it every day from the likes of you. And then back you come. Kids like you should be locked up and the keys thrown away."

On Remand

We'd been on remand for some months without any word of what had been planned for our futures. We questioned the staff about this from time to time, but they would just shrug their shoulders at us. Our daily routine was boring, with nothing much to do other than to remain in the playroom all day playing board games, watching television, or just sitting around calling each other names. Sometimes a small group of us, about 20 in all, would be taken by Mr Samson down to the gate lodge to listen to his records, or he would sit at the piano and teach us a hymn or two.

Mr Samson, like me and Martin, was from the Republic of Ireland, and he loved playing his Irish rebel songs on his battered old record player, which Martin and I enjoyed. We knew the lyrics to many of the Irish songs from listening to Mammy and Daddy and all our aunties, uncles and cousins. They would give their renditions of "Take Me Home to Mayo", "A Nation Once Again", "Dying Rebel", "Kevin Barry" – all beautiful rebel songs, written to stir the emotions, lift the heart and make half the true-blooded Irishmen want to give their all to Ireland's cause. The other half, not up to the fighting, filled the pubs of England to sing songs about all those brave men who'd stayed behind in Ireland to fight for the cause.

Sometimes a group of boys would be taken out to the local picture house as a treat, to see the afternoon matinee. Mr Butterworth, a regular staff member, would usually have a boy sitting on his lap and it had been well rumoured amongst us all that he often tickled the boy's goolies. He seemed different from the other staff, more aloof, in a proud sort of way. He was always turned out spotlessly, in cream trousers and navy-blue blazer with gold buttons, a cravat tucked inside his open-necked shirt and matching hanky poking out from the breast pocket of his blazer. He was more open and approachable than any of the other staff, and the children seemed to really like him.

Once, he called me in to his side office and asked me my name.

"And would Tommy like some sweeties?"

"Yes."

"Yes what?"

"Yes please."

"That was easy wasn't it? Which pocket? Choose the one you think the sweeties are in." He tapped his trouser pockets and I pointed to the left one. "Go on then, have a feel inside."

I rummaged around inside his pocket and was disappointed to find no sweets inside. But he pushed my hand deeper, making me feel his mickey, before he brought his hand across the back of my head and pulled me into him, squeezing my hand in his pocket so that it had pressed harder against him.

"Here." He pulled a small white paper bag of mixed sweets from his blazer pocket. "That's for being a good boy – and you don't mention to anyone where the sweets came from." He smiled. "It's our little secret, alright?"

Sharing out the sweets with my brother Martin and little George, the boy who'd been in the police van with us on our arrival at Rose Hill, I told them what Mr Butterworth had done. "It was only a little feel."

"That's not fair! I kissed him and only got two toffees off him," moaned George.

"Yah kissed his mickey!"

"Nah! He asked me for a kiss on the lips and I gave him a peck."

Mr Parker, the headmaster at the remand centre, was a strange, miserable, thin man with a bony face. He walked with a limp and had a silver-handled walking stick, which he would often hit the boys with. He was very much hated by the children, who seemed frightened to death of the fella. And I could sense the dislike he had for us because of the uncaring attitude he had in our company. I still recall the exact moment he'd taken his heartless feelings out on Martin and the terrible consequences – for him.

We were lined up along the corridor, waiting to go into the dining room, when he walked past us. It was the first time I'd seen him up close and he looked scary, hobbling along the corridor and paying us no heed, as if we weren't even there. Ahead of us, my brother, standing out of line, was talking with a couple of boys when, for no reason at all, this evil old bastard suddenly belted him with his walking stick from behind, catching Martin across the side of his face. All this because my brother happened to be in his way. I remember seeing the red mist as my anger surged. I'm not sure what came over me, but I could not stop myself from rushing the few yards up to the old cripple and giving him a solid shove in the back. I watched in horror as the bag of bones keeled over and hit the floor, face down.

"He's murdered him," said Goofy.

"One word an' I'll murder yea," warned Martin.

"I'm saying nowt," grinned Goofy, before suddenly taking a swift kick at the old man, catching him right up the backside as he'd started to get up on his hands and knees, causing him to fall back down again. Another lad, Richard Golab, picked up the walking stick and whacked it down on the headmaster's head, before throwing the stick up along the corridor. This seemed to have been the signal for others to mock the headmaster, as he struggled to pick himself up off the floor, with none of us willing to lend him a hand.

"Mr Samson's coming!" We heard the warning and quickly got back in line, leaving the dead-looking headmaster struggling to get to his feet, as we stood silently watching.

"Mr Parker! Are you alright, sir? What's happened?" Mr Samson glared up and down the line as he raced to the headmaster's aid.

"He slipped, sir."

"He fell over his stick, sir."

"His stick fell out of his hand and he tripped."

"He tried to do a jig, sir."

"I'll deal with you later, Murphy."

We were informed by Mr Samson later that day that Mr Parker had said he'd had a dizzy spell. Obviously, he'd been too embarrassed to admit he'd been attacked by a group of young children. And who knows what might have happened if he'd been left on his own with us for any length of time. Yes, when all was said and done, the cripple was an easy target. But then, so were we children…

During the early summer we played cricket, which I loved. I couldn't bowl, but I could bat and would hit the ball all over the show. Mr Johnstone said he could see I had a keen eye for the ball and that one day I'd make a good cricketer – even though I couldn't bowl in a straight line and hated fielding.

Martin, on the other hand, was a great all-rounder. He had a competitive streak about him and was able to find that extra push in himself, always on target when bowling or throwing the ball from the outfield to the wicket keeper. It was a talent I'd spotted in our many ducker-throwing gang battles on the crofts of Hulme and Moss Side.

Unusually, Martin held the cricket bat high above his shoulder, like an American baseball player. He'd swing blindly at every ball coming down at him, scoring some spectacular runs, but he never stayed in for long.

Once, when he had bowled a ball that was hit high into the air, he screamed "My ball!" and then stood underneath it, as it dropped back to earth, missing his hands, hitting him straight on his hooter and breaking it.

As the summer got underway, we would play football against each other on most Saturdays. The teams were always Man United v Man United Reserves, because no one would play under any other name. I did like playing football, especially when it had been raining, or was still raining and the pitch was wet and muddy. It was brilliant to slide on, even when I wasn't making a save.

I was always picked as the goalkeeper, even though I wasn't that good – but as I was even worse in any of the other positions, I couldn't really complain. For me, it was great fun just to be out in the open air, slipping and sliding in the mud. That said, I hated playing in the winter, having to stand for an hour or so shivering to death, with my cold hands down my shorts and wrapped around my goolies to keep them warm, plus kicking the toes of my boots against the goalpost to stop frostbite setting in. My teammates always moaned at me for the number of penalties I'd give away. And I must admit I'd be frightened to death when a potential goal scorer was heading towards me. I'd just close my eyes, ready for the impact and kick out wherever I'd last seen the ball, only to hear a cry of pain, having usually kicked the player instead and given away another penalty. But I was still proud of the fact that I held the record at Rose Hill for being the first goalkeeper to let in 20 penalties – all in the same game!

Nightmare

There came a point when Martin went very quiet on me, which was something I'd never witnessed from him prior to arriving at Rose Hill. The fact that we'd had a different upbringing from many of the kids incarcerated there wasn't to say that we were ungrateful for our lot. Happiness in its true sense of the word had never been an issue for us. We just got on and made the best of what life had on offer for us, grateful for the nice things that did come our way. And if the height of happiness was measured by, say, picking up a discarded piece of chewing gum, pulling it apart and sharing it with each other, then we were very happy.

Of course, Martin sometimes got frustrated about one thing or another, as I did. But he seemed to have become very sullen and quiet. And where once we had been able to talk to each other about anything, my brother seemed not to want to confide in me about what was troubling him. He even told me to "Feck off!" when I had gone on and on, asking him what was wrong.

This was very upsetting for me and I cried myself to sleep, wondering what it was I could have done, or if I had unwittingly said something to hurt him. But while I didn't know whether it was something I'd done, I knew for sure that he wasn't missing his mammy and daddy.

One weekend, Martin and I, along with 14 of the other boys, were chosen to camp in the orchards of Rose Hill. My brother had seemed a little chirpier and when I told him I thought he didn't love me any more, he threw his arms around me and told me he would love me forever, which made me cry tears of happiness.

It had taken an age to set up the camp, erecting two small toilets and six tents. We were helped by a silver-haired, muscular man wearing a sleeveless psychedelic shirt, short khaki trousers and leather sandals, who introduced himself to us as The Skipper. He seemed very jovial and touchy-feely, tickling the boys as they held up the main tent post, deliberately making it collapse before we were able to hammer in the wooden pegs to hold the guy ropes fast. We had great fun throughout the day, bringing us some small respite from our mundane daily lives.

On the Saturday evening, we sat around the campfire singing songs, accompanied by the Skipper on his banjo. A few of the songs were already known to us and a couple he had taught us for the first time, including "Dublin's Fair City", with the Skipper singing the verses and us loudly joining in on the "Alive, Alive Oh" chorus.

Mr Butterworth came into the camp later in the evening and served us up some fairy cakes and diluted orange juice, before sitting down by the fire and telling us a ghost story. It was about a young village boy who, heading home one night, had seen the Devil peer over the church wall, smiling at him. He ran off home, screaming the whole village awake.

Then the boy, along with his parents and a large group of villagers, set back off along the dimly lit lane to the church, where a goat had suddenly peered over the wall. Laughing at the little boy's obvious mistake, the villagers headed back to their homes. As the boy dragged his heels behind them, he took a quick peek over his shoulder, to see the figure of the Devil standing beneath the huge oak tree in the grounds of the church. But his fear of being ridiculed for a second time that night stopped him from calling out. And he ran home as fast as his legs would carry him.

Martin and I shared a tent with two other boys, McCormack and Flynn. We agreed to keep the battery-operated Tilley lamp switched on, which had given out a very dim orange glow – enough to be able to find our way out of the tent if we needed to go to the toilet. I climbed into my sleeping bag, zipping it right up to the top before pulling the drawstrings tight inside of it. I could only see darkness.

"The Devil won't come here tonight, will he Martin?"

"If he does, he won't be botherin' us for sure."

His answer wasn't that much of a help and then some fecker had to start making wooing noises.

"Shallup or I'll be wooing yah with me fist," warned Martin.

Lying in the tent and tucked right down inside the warm sleeping bag, I felt relaxed and safe. Even so, I lay as close as I could be to my brother, listening out for the slightest sound. I could feel a strange sensation inside my head, similar to sitting on a swing with my eyes closed as it gently rocked back and forth, before my heavy eyelids closed. I'd often wondered afterwards, had something been slipped into our orange juice?

This would certainly have explained my intense drowsiness and the dream-like quality of what happened next...

I remember waking suddenly and hearing a strange, low sound close by. Inside my head, I could see fleeting, ghostly images, which at the time, I'd been unable to make any sense of. I was awake and yet I felt the images I was seeing were unreal. There were people in our tent. They were speaking in low tones. Mr Butterworth led me by the hand, out of the tent and through the orchard, to the wooden huts used whenever the remand centre had an overspill of kids. I remember laying on one of the beds. I was naked and he was asking me to do something. But I couldn't understand what he was asking me to do, and then I began to panic. I could hardly breathe because he had put something in my mouth and he was pressing himself into me.

Another man was kneeling in front of me. I was only able to see the top half of him, which was bare. He suddenly lifted my legs and put one either side of him before pulling me forwards towards him. Mr Butterworth was now standing behind him and telling me it was fine, as I felt the man pushing himself inside me. Pushing and pushing. And then I suddenly woke up inside my sleeping bag, from where I could see someone kneeling behind Martin and holding him still.

In the dim light of the tent, squinting through half-open eyelids, I made out the grey form of Skipper. He was naked from the waist up and kneeling just a foot away from me. He had my brother in front of him and I could see Martin was up on his knees, with the bottom half of his pyjamas down around them. I froze as I saw Skipper holding onto my brother's hips and pulling him backwards and forwards, backwards and forwards, repeatedly, before suddenly stopping. Moments later, he released his grip, letting my brother drop onto his sleeping bag. And in the blink of an eye, the image was gone.

The following morning, Flynn and McCormack were at each other's throats, arguing over whose undies were whose. I noticed the zip of my sleeping bag was completely undone to the bottom, though I knew for sure I had zipped it right up to the top the previous evening.

"Are yah okay Tommy?" Martin was awake and out of his own sleeping bag.

"I had a bad nightmare is all," I told him, unable to make sense of the images flickering through my brain. "Der's some blood on the back of yer pyjama bottoms," I said, noticing the red smudges as my brother stood up.

"Piles," he said. "I'd been squeezing me head on the bog all the morning. Look at them two eejits!"

"I don't crap me undies like you, Flynn, these are mine!" McCormack had managed to pull the cleaner pair of undies from Flynn's grip, before kicking the skid-marked pair across the ground to land at Flynn's feet.

"I'm not wearing them shitty things," said Flynn, taking a kick at the dirty undies and stubbing his big toe on the ground in the process. He hopped around, howling in pain, causing the three of us to howl with laughter.

Skipper cheerfully bade us a good morning and dished out a breakfast of sausages, beans and toast, which we ate around the campfire. By the late afternoon my head had cleared and I thought no more about the nightmare I'd had during the night.

Later that day, those of us who had been camping were taken to the pictures in the two Bedford vans to see "The Sound of Music". I loved the film, especially near the end when each member of the Von Trapp family, having planned their escape from Nazi-controlled Austria, sang "So long, Farewell".

I still remember the tension I felt as, one by one, each family member left the stage, leaving the little girl on her own to sing the last chorus. How my heart had drummed, as I screamed inwardly for her to hurry up and go to her family before the Nazis realised what was going on.

My favourite song from the film was "Climb Every Mountain". The lyrics were so powerful in the sense that they gave me hope and a reminder that there were better things beyond Rose Hill. And in some small way, it became my burning ambition to search out the rainbow that could lead me and Martin to our dream, which was to be free.

That little rat, Paul Seager, got to sit on Mr Butterworth's knee again. The crawling little fecker. It seemed to us he could get away with almost anything and not get told off. The squeaky-voiced, giggly blond git! Too afraid to sleep on his own in the dark, he'd often let one of the older boys in the bed with him. On many occasions, he and his little circle of secretive friends would be chosen to visit places outside the home, staying tight-lipped and refusing to mention in conversation where they'd gone, even when Martin and I had grabbed Seager in the bogs and had threatened him with the dire consequences of not giving up his secret to us. But he wouldn't say a word, so we were none the wiser as to why he and his friends always got first dibs at everything.

Our Little Secret

Mr Samson picked a group of us to join his Christmas Eve choir to sing carols at the local community centre for the elderly. Martin wasn't chosen because he sounded like a foghorn. When Mr Samson had asked him to sing solo, Martin told me he had deliberately sung out of tune, just so as he didn't have to sing to "smelly auld fogies".

Anyway, it made a change to have learned all the words to a carol, instead of making them up as we went along, as we used to do when we were out carol singing in Hulme.

A few weeks before Christmas, Mr Butterworth informed us of the upcoming nativity play, saying those who were interested in taking part should give their names to him. I don't know why I put my name down to be the Virgin Mary, I just did. The following day when the four of us – me, Williams, McGuinness and Seager – had gone to the gatehouse lodge to audition, I was confident of having a good chance, considering the opposition I was up against.

"It's the Virgin Mary we're looking for, not a gollywog," explained Mr Butterworth to the weeping black boy, Williams. "Sorry lad, you can play one of the Kings, they can be any colour. As for you McGuinness," he said to the plump Irish lad, "you haven't a hope in hell's chance of getting any talking part with that accent of yours. Let alone fitting into any of the costumes. Look at you lad!"

"Sure, wouldn't Mary have been fat after havin' a baby?" argued McGuiness. "Me mammy was blown up like a big balloon for ages, so she was. An' I'll be sittin' down so no one will notice me much?"

"Well, for one, the Virgin Mary came from Nazareth, not a potato field somewhere in Ireland. Secondly, I would have thought the size of your head would be a giveaway. You can be the donkey, along with Miller. Sort it out between yourselves, who's the back and who's the front end."

With those two eejits out of the way, there was only me and Seager in contention for the part. We only had the one line to say and he couldn't even get that right. When the angel came down from Heaven to tell him the surprise news, "You're going to have a baby", all he had to say was, "How can this possibly be?" but he couldn't remember all the words. And even when he did eventually get the line right, he just wasn't convincing enough. He was no better at holding the baby Jesus, perching the plastic doll with the cracked face on his knee like a ventriloquist holding his dummy. And he paid no heed to it at all. Whereas I'd been an attentive mother and had held the baby Jesus close to my bosom, shushing it now and then to make it more convincing. I even put on my best girlie voice and added a few extra words to my line, having known (though not understanding) that a woman must be shagged before she can find a baby under a bush. So I said, "But how can this possibly be? I've never been shagged before."

A belt around the ear was surely all the punishment I deserved, but my effort to impress Mr Butterworth had all been in vain and that maggot, Seager, ended up getting the part. I couldn't understand why I always missed out. I knew life wasn't fair but just for once it would have been nice for something to have gone my way.

But then, for the first time in my life, my prayers were answered. Seager went off to face the magistrates and never came back to Rose Hill. Mr Butterworth took me down to the Gate Lodge, telling me on the way that he had a nice surprise waiting there for me. When we walked into the music room, my eyes lit up at the sight of the pale-blue Virgin Mary costume, consisting of a baggy white flannel dress and a blue head shawl like the nuns wore, only this was a much lighter blue.

"Do you still want to play the part of Mary?"

"I do that sir. Please, sir."

"Quieten down lad. We don't want the world to know what we're up to."

"I'm just excited, sir."

"There are other lads who want to play the part as well."

"Oh." My face dropped.

"Do you remember the little secret we had between us? When I cuddled you? In my office? I gave you the little bag of sweets afterwards?"

"I didn't tell a soul sir, honest," I lied. Though I'd forgotten all about it by this time.

"I know. And that's why I am going to give you this one chance. It's just that, we don't want the other boys getting jealous, do we? And this is our secret too, do you understand?"

"I wouldn't say a thing ta anybody, I promise yah I wouldn't."

"Well, let's see how it fits then. Take your clothes off and see what you look like in the costume."

As quick as a flash I stripped down to my socks and underpants, before I noticed the small grey cine-camera he was recording me with.

"Take your pants off as well," he ordered. "Come on." He noticed my hesitancy and smiled at me. "There's nothing to be shy about. Come on, quickly."

I obeyed and slipped them off before getting into the costume.

"Come and kneel up on this." Mr Butterworth tapped the piano stool, which he'd moved slightly away from the piano. I picked up the hem of the costume and knelt with my bare knees on the stool as he fiddled around with the camcorder, which he placed on the table further away from me. Then, putting his hand up the front of the costume he gently felt around my goolies. It was so quick, it took me by complete surprise. It tickled. And when he asked me if I liked him doing what he was doing, I told him "Yes" and he carried on until my mickey went stiff. Then, still fiddling with me with the one hand, he moved behind me and a moment later I felt him pushing himself inside me.

I didn't know whether I wanted this to be happening to me. My first thoughts drifted back to the time we'd been camping out in the orchard and I realised that what was happening to me now had also happened with him and the strange man in the hut, and had not been a dream after all. Like then, he wasn't hurting me. In fact, Mr Butterworth was being gentle towards me, and I liked him playing with me more than I disliked it. I felt a strange, thrilling sensation explode through my whole body. And then it was over.

I told no one, not even my brother Martin. I felt sly for not telling him, but my guilt for that was far outweighed by the fact that I felt special and didn't want to share that feeling with anyone else – including my brother. The nativity play went off without a hitch and I kept to the proper script without adding any extra words to my line. The carol concert was also brilliant, though it didn't go off without a hitch.

When we finished singing the last Christmas song to the old fogies, Santa Claus made his appearance, to the sound of boos from some elderly folk. I got talking with two old Irish fellas, Sean and Michael.

"Do yah see Father Christmas there, son?" said Sean. "Him with the big belly an' the even bigger head. An' there's not even a pilla under there, I tell yah lad. He's a fat, greedy rat is what he is, isn't that right Mick?"

"He is dat! A fat feckin' greedy bastard of the worst kind for sure," agreed Mick.

"What's he done?"

"What's he done? Jaysus! Did yah hear that Mick? Come closer, so the whole world can't hear us."

I bent my head closer and got a whiff of Sean's whiskey breath. "That blue-nose auld fecker sittin' in that chair over there has a way with all the women, if yah see what I mean?"

"Sure, we can't even get one eye in, let alone the two, with all his womanising," added Mick.

"Could yah do us a favour son, there's two shillin if yah will."

"Ok." I held out my palm to him.

"I'll give it ta yah after the favour. I've just met yah, I can't be trustin' complete strangers."

"What's the favour?"

"Go wait in the line. An' when yah get ta sit on the feckin' rat's knee, tell him 'Charlie Whiting sent yah over just ta let yah know you're a blue-nosed fecker if ever he'd set eyes on one.'"

"Who's Charlie."

"He's another rat we don't like. Will yah do that for us son an' make two old Irish codgers happy old codgers?"

"Sure."

It only took a short while for my turn to come around and I hopped up on Santa's knees, giving him a big smile before delivering the message. "Charlie Whiting told me to tell you, you are the tightest blue-nosed bastard of a Santa he's ever set eyes on."

"Did he now?" raged Santa. Springing to his feet and letting me drop to the floor, he rushed across the hall and took a swipe at another old fella, knocking him straight off his chair.

Looking in the direction of Sean and Michael, I saw the pair of them up on their feet, throwing thumbs-up signs at me. But as I headed towards them to get my two shillings, Mr Samson stopped me in my tracks, then hurried the whole choir out of the church hall and away in the vans.

Torn Apart

The short drive in the police car to the Manchester courts was a quiet one, with Martin and me sitting in the back, contemplating what fate might have in store for us. The police had handcuffed us, just like they used to do to Daddy when they came to the house to arrest him, only Martin and I were handcuffed to each other.

The previous day we'd been informed out of the blue that we were up before the beak in the morning and would not be returning to Rose Hill. This obviously meant another place had been found for us, though no one had been willing to tell us exactly where that was. I couldn't understand what all the secrecy was about, considering we were inevitably going to find out once we got to wherever it was we were going.

Glancing at Martin, whose hands were clasped tightly together with his fingers interlocked, as if he were in silent prayer, I wondered what he was thinking. I'd noticed the change in him not long after our arrival at Rose Hill. But he still had his infectious laugh and had joined in many of the sports we played, especially his beloved football, with the same passion to win at all costs, which in some way was the difference between us.

We both had an inborn will not to be broken. Beaten, yes, sticks and stones and fists and feet could break our bones, but they could never break our spirit. And yet, despite this, I noticed the sparkle had left Martin's eyes.

He suddenly gazed at me with a serious, almost tearful, look on his face. "Whatever happens ta us Tommy, I'll never forget yah. Yah know that, don't yah?"

"Course I do Martin. I'll be gettin' on yer nerves all the while, yea'll be wantin' ta get rid of me for sure."

"I'd never want that."

"I was only coddin' yah. Anyway, we're probably goin' ta end up in Nazareth House, with the others."

When we arrived at the court we were taken in through a side entrance below the courtrooms. We had once again slipped our skinny wrists out of the handcuffs and handed them back to the policeman. He was not impressed with our escape act, pushing us into the small cell before slamming the heavy door closed and locking us inside.

Not long afterwards we found ourselves standing in the dock, like two wretched criminals waiting for our fate to be sealed. The haughty, long-nosed woman glaring down upon us from her high perch had a look of distaste written all over her crabby old face. On each side of her sat another old dragon. The one on the left, with the small head attached to a long skinny neck (which reminded me of a shrunken head on a pole), gave us the once-over, before nonchalantly dropping her gaze to the pile of paperwork in front of her. The other dragon seemed to take an age to pinpoint our location, as her rat-like eyes peering out through her spectacles continued to dart to and fro before homing in on us. She was probably helped by the sound of our giggling, caused by Martin given me the nudge and blurting out, "Will yah get a look at the mop!" He was referring to the obvious thick, jet-black, shiny wig sitting on top of the old woman's head.

For someone who had never set eyes upon us until that very day, Mr Mann, the social worker, seemed to know an awful lot about our family. He'd gone on as if he'd been a friend of the family for donkey's years, telling the court everything there was to know about us. This included how our Mammy and Daddy, both being alcoholics, had abandoned the whole family late last year, leaving us to fend for ourselves.

This had really got up my nose, because that part was a big lie: we'd always had to fend for ourselves, even when Mammy and Daddy were at home.

He even mentioned each family member by name, telling the three old dragons, who had hardly moved a muscle since we'd peered out over the dock at them, how all our siblings had happily settled in their placements. "With the exception of Martin and Tommy," he said, "who are beyond control, especially when they are together."

"I see by the files, the children have already been made Wards of this Court?" said the Judge, casting a suspicious eye over us. "And are therefore already under the care and protection of the local authority?"

"That is correct," agreed Mr Mann. 'They were both made Wards of the Court in late August of last year."

"Then why hasn't a suitable and more permanent place-ment been found for them? They are, after all, very young children."

"No one will take them."

"That isn't a reason!" snapped the crabby-faced Judge, finally coming to life. "If every establishment declined their charges because they didn't want them, we'd have thousands of children running amok on the streets." The thought of such a scenario might have been the reason for the sudden shocked expressions on her two companions' faces.

"I meant, Martin and Tommy are unable to deal adequately with normal social relationships and are, at times, disruptive. The local authorities deem them to be beyond the scope of their normal care and protection practices. If you look at their records you will see that both boys have amassed 180 charges of grand larceny – and that's just since the application to make them Wards of Court last year."

I was unable to understand the reason for the shocked gasp that rippled around the courtroom, given I'd heard the word "grand" being mentioned. I always thought that meant something good, as in, "Isn't it a grand day!" or "That's a grand-looking horse yah have there." So, it baffled me as to why all eyes were on us, with almost every head in the courtroom shaking in dismay when the words Grand Larceny cropped up.

Mr Mann went on to tell the court that suitable places had finally been found for the both of us, near Liverpool. All that was now needed was the Order of the Court to have both of us placed in the care of the Liverpool Local Authority. This was soon agreed.

"Martin will be resident at St George's Approved School in Freshfields. And Thomas will be resident at St Vincent's school in Formby," said the Judge. This was the moment we learnt we were going to be separated "for our own good" and sent to different homes.

"Yah feckin' lesheens yah! Yah poxty auld witches! May the cat eat yah an' the divil eat the cat!" We cursed the three auld women, calling them every name under the sun, but they just ignored us, and got up out of their chairs and walked out of the courtroom.

We had people pulling us in opposite directions as my brother and I clung tightly to each other, kicking and screaming and biting at any skin that came into contact with our teeth. But it was all to no avail. There were just too many people pulling and tugging at us. And though it took them a long time to get us apart, they eventually managed to tear us from each other's grasp, and all we could do was use our voices to reach each other.

"Martin!"

"Tommy!"

"Help me Martin! Help me! Get off me, yah feckin' bastards yah!" But he was gone. They'd taken my brother away from me. They'd ripped open my chest, grabbed at my heart and squeezed it so tightly that the pain was unbearable.

How could they? How could people who say they only want the best for the child and to make that child happy do such a thing? I was broken. I felt lost and unable to see how I could ever live without Martin. He wasn't just my brother, he was my best friend, my life, the only person I could turn to and trust and believe in. And these bastards stole him from me and me from him. I would never ever forgive them.

Monster Mother

Mr Mann hadn't spoken to me since leaving the M26 service station. I think he'd been miserable because of his swollen lip, though he hadn't said as much to me. He probably blamed me for his injury, but it hadn't really been my fault, though it was no less than he deserved, considering he was too tight to buy me a breakfast.

When the lady peering over the counter at me had asked what she could do for us, I'd ordered sausages, eggs, beans and toast, with black pudding and plum-peeled tomatoes, and a glass of Tizer. But Mr Mann had laughed at me, like I'd just told him the funniest joke in the world.

"Sausages, bacon and eggs, with toast and beans and black pudding? You're having a laugh, aren't you?"

Well, I hadn't noticed myself laughing when I'd blurted out my order. Nor could I, for the life of me, see what was so hilarious about wanting sausages and eggs and beans and toast and black pudding and plum-peeled tomatoes, swallowed down by a cool glass of Tizer.

When he'd composed himself, the tight-fisted old git ordered two mugs of tea and nothing else. The lady behind the counter offered me "on the house, sweetie!" her last rock cake on the stand and I exaggerated my sincere gratitude to her for her kindness, just to embarrass the tight-arsed social worker.

On the house? Jaysus, it must have come *off* a feckin' house! It was like biting into a brick. Just the one bite and I felt the pain shoot up through my teeth until I was sure the lot of them were going to fall out on to the table.

"I'm not eatin' this shite." I blindly threw the cake in temper and watched as it flew over Mr Mann's head, before hitting a workman on his temple as he'd sat chatting with some workmates a few tables along from us. Jumping to his feet, the red-faced man headed in our direction.

"I should ram this doon yer fackin' throat Jimma!" screamed the fuming Scottish fella, holding the rock cake up under my nose.

"I'm sorry about this," said Mr Mann. "I'm sure it was an accident, wasn't it Tommy? The boy is upset about —"

"An' me name's not Jimma, yah big blue-nosed twat yah!" I shouted.

"Whaaat!"

"Me Daddy says yer all blue-nosed homos, the lot of yah!"

"Did he!"

I think Mr Mann was just as surprised as I was when the workman's fist collided with his gob, knocking him off his chair and to the floor.

"Yea should be scalping that little shite of yours!" raged the workman, taking one last look at my smiling face before marching off out of the service station, with his laughing workmates following behind and patting him on the back.

I watched as Mr Mann, breathing heavily, dragged himself up off the floor and back onto the chair. "You're going to have to change your attitude, or this is the kind of problem you will keep getting," he advised, wiping the napkin across his swollen, cut lip.

I shrugged and looked away, unable to fathom out why he was warning me about my attitude when it was him who'd got the smack in the gob.

As Mr Mann's soft-top racing-green MG sped along the motorway, I had to put up with listening to the crackling radio spewing out songs such as "Bits and Pieces", "The Crying Game", "Anyone Who Had a Heart" – all serving as reminders of my emotional pain and rubbing salt into my wounds.

Heading into Formby, he drove the car off the main road, in through the open gates and up along the narrow driveway leading to St Vincent's Approved School.

"You'll be taken good care of here," he said, suddenly breaking the silence, his insincerity all too obvious from his avoidance of eye contact with me.

Pulling up outside the wooden entrance doors, he squeezed his large frame out of the tiny car and plodded around to the passenger side, opening the door for me. I got out and followed him to the entrance. As I looked up at the tall red-brick building, it crossed my mind to make a run for it. But it was only a fleeting thought. The fact that I was now on my own was the reason not to run.

"You can have the privilege." Mr Mann stepped to one side whilst pointing to the brass doorbell set into the wall.

Hardly a word out of him throughout the journey, and now he was giving me the privilege to ring a poxy doorbell. Young as I was, I had seen and done and been through more in my life than most kids of my age – including ringing feckin' doorbells. Sure, I'd rung many a doorbell, running off before they were answered – that was a game, not a privilege.

"I don't want ta ring the doorbell." I wasn't letting the likes of him have the privilege of giving the likes of me the privilege of ringing a feckin' doorbell. "Ring it yerself if yah like." He ignored my scowl, pressing his podgy finger on the button before taking a backward step, waiting for the door to creak inwards.

"Ah! Good afternoon, Sister Ignatius." Mr Mann almost genuflected to the giant of a nun standing in the open doorway.

Jaysus, I've never seen a nun as tall as her. She was 6ft high at the very least in her open-toed Jesus sandals. Her suspicious eyes peered out at me through black-framed bifocal spectacles, giving me the once-over while her huge, shovel-sized hands rested firmly on her wide hips. For some strange reason, her wide, unblinking eyes reminded me of big white gobstoppers, with a black spot in the middle of each one.

"This is Thomas, Thomas Rhattigan."

"It's Tommy," I corrected.

"Well, hello there, little Thomas." Sister Ignatius held her huge hand out to me. And like a feckin' big eejit, I took it. "Yea'll be looked after here – if yah behave yerself it'll be grand." She squeezed the living daylights out of my right hand, bringing me halfway to my knees. "Do we understand each other?"

"Yes, Sister."

"That'll be Mother Superior." She gave my sore hand another hard squeeze for good measure. "Ah, yea'll soon get the hang of it. They all do," this powerful curse of a woman, disguised as a God-fearing Catholic nun, sneered down on me.

I soon discovered Sister Ignatius never smiled, or perhaps it was just that I'd never had the pleasure of seeing her smile. That stern scowl on her face seemed permanent, as if it had been frozen in time – perhaps because of the sudden shock of seeing her reflection in the mirror for the first time. She was always suspicious of me and had a habit of staring straight into my eyes for the slightest sign of a guilty secret that I might be hiding from her. This only caused me to feel even guiltier, which in turn made me look guilty.

I was never able to understand the wisdom behind the scale of corporal punishment she'd dish out to us daily. Two strokes of the cane for minor indiscretions, such as being out of bounds or back-chatting the nuns. Three strokes if heard (or snitched on) for using foul language or being caught fighting or stealing. Four or five strokes for being caught playing with yourself or another boy. And six of the best for taking the Lord's name in vain. As for me, I always got six of the best, regardless of whether I deserved four or five or less.

"Pants down! And those underpants, too. Lord in heaven's name! When was the last time yah changed them dirty things?"

I recall the very first time I'd been sent to her for calling Johnny Johnson a bastard, after he came back to school from being a page boy at his parents' wedding, and how she'd recoiled in horror when she caught sight of my soiled underwear.

"Yesterday, Sister Ignatius," I lied.

"Yesterday?" she turned her nose up at me. 'Sure, don't yah use toilet paper ta clean yerself with? Yah dirty little divil yah."

"It's too hard on me hole, I mean me bum, Sister."

"Too hard indeed. You should be grateful yah have paper ta wipe your dirty little self with. There are children out in the world who'd be eatin' that stuff – the paper I mean! Pull them things back up. I can't be walloping yah and lookin' at that filth at the same time."

It worked! Before I'd gone in there to receive my punishment, John Priestley, who was waiting outside the office to see the witch, had let me in on his secret: deliberately skid-mark your undies so she'd make you pull them back up. Admittedly I might have overdone it a little. But it did do the trick and stopped the cane from drawing blood.

"Just the dirty underpants."

She made me touch my toes before tapping the cane on my bottom, sizing up her target. Then, as she raised it high into the air, it always amazed me that she would whisper a prayer under her breath.

Can you believe it? Lord forgive me! I wanted to ask the question, "If caning boys' arses wasn't a bad thing, why are yah asking the Lord for forgiveness?" But I was thrown by the fact I'd counted eight strokes instead of the usual six.

"You gave me eight of the best, Sister," I said, before asking politely if there was the possibility of her giving me a credit note for those two extra strokes – which I could use on my next visit to her office.

"What?" her face suddenly turned a shade of purple.

"Like one of them IOU notes yah get in the shops, sister."

"I'll give yah a credit note!"

"Thanks Sister."

I couldn't for the life of me understand what I'd said that was so wrong. But it had obviously upset the Mother Superior. She went berserk and began swinging the cane wildly at me. I could hear it whooshing through the air and past my ears as she flailed it around like a drunken cavalier in a sword fight. Running around her office, ducking and dodging her onslaught, she still managed to catch me a couple of good whacks on my back before I'd opened her office door and made good my escape, with her chasing after me along the corridors like a wild banshee.

It was no wonder I'd been so joyful when, nearly a year after my arrival at St Vincent's, the nuns announced they were leaving for good.

Too Close for Comfort

"This way Mother Superior. That's it, bring the little boys in closer to you," coaxed the local photographer-cum-journalist assigned to write a short editorial on Sister Ignatius's imminent departure from St Vincent's. "Closer, closer," he urged, as he clicked away with his camera. "That's it, that's it. Oh, what angels."

Angels? He wouldn't be saying that if he'd eyes in the back of his head to see 12-year-old Danny O'Connell dipping his thieving hands into his camera bag and stealing the small camera and packet of Woodbine cigarettes.

"Once a thief, always a thief!" Sister Ignatius would constantly remind us all. Of course, it was an accusation none of us could honestly disagree with. It wasn't as if we hadn't attempted to do the right things, according to all the self-righteous religious garbage we were taught by her and her coven, day in, day out. But when you spend a long while praying to the Lord for something good to happen and you receive feck all in return, it's only human nature to look for an alternative way of getting what you want. And so we would steal it first, and then ask the Lord for his forgiveness afterwards.

Sister Ignatius reluctantly complied with the wishes of the photographer as his camera whirred and clicked at the beautified images of the saintly nun, with her muscular arms clasped around the shoulders of the two crying orphans – the very picture of sadness as they hugged the Mother Superior one last time. Had anyone looked closely, they would have seen panic written all over the children's faces as she pressed them tightly into her pious bosom. Motherly? She feckin' certainly wasn't. Superior? I'd go along with that. Pious? Even Lucifer himself stood a better chance of entering the gates of heaven than that evil woman.

Every time I clapped eyes on her, I got twinges in the cheeks of my backside. A backside she had so often beaten black and blue, seeming to relish every moment. The only other time I'd had contact with her in the 11 months I had been in St Vincent's was either at Mass, Benediction, or religious studies in the classroom – her emphasis on the three R's being religion, religion, and more feckin' religion. It was such a wonderful notion to think God might have given her that face as a penance for beating little children's arses. Just as it was wonderful to know, after a year of physical torture from her unnaturally large hands, Sister Ignatius was finally leaving us, along with the rest of her unholy coven of nuns.

"Go on Tommy." Sister Benedict suddenly thrust the large shining brass crucifix into my hand. "Go and make the presentation ta the Mother Superior." She attempted to nudge me forwards, but I wouldn't budge.

A skeleton of a nun, with her black habit hanging loosely over her bony body, it wasn't surprising Sister Benedict was usually mistaken for one of the scarecrows in the school's three-acre vegetable field, where she would sometimes stand, with her head bowed in silent prayer.

"I don't want ta give her anything," I said.

"Mother Superior wants yea ta be the one."

I bet she feckin' did. "Well I don't want ta be the one."

"Ah, go on now." Sister Benedict gave me another nudge. "It's an honour."

"Not for me it's not. And I don't want the honour anyway."

"Don't be showin' yourself up now, look! Everybody's gawkin' at yah."

"They can gawk all they like, I don't care."

"Ah, there's a good fellow." The auld witch suddenly gripped a handful of my hair on the nape of my neck and twisted it, her momentum pushing me forwards in the direction of the rostrum.

Wanting to faint, I exhaled every ounce of breath I had left in my body and stopped breathing. I prayed silently to Jesus to please let me faint in a heap. But he still turned a deaf ear.

Gasping for breath, I was frog-marched to within a foot of the rostrum, where Sister Ignatius stood, at least another two feet taller than usual, with her gobstopper eyes glaring down at me. She had her favourite whipping cane in her left hand and I could only assume she was either taking it with her as a trophy, or she was going to present it to me as a souvenir.

"Hello Tommy." Her grotesque grin leered down at me and I suddenly had the strangest feeling, as if everything around us was moving in slow motion, like those special effects you get in the films. There was a stillness in the air, as the crying boys suddenly stopped crying, the cheering boys suddenly stopped cheering and everyone looked in my direction.

Even the birds in the trees had suddenly stopped singing, as though they'd all wanted to share in this special moment with me. Then a thought suddenly sprung into my head, almost like a revelation from the Almighty himself. I looked down at the Mother Superior's big toes protruding over the edge of the rostrum and I swear to this day, I heard a divine voice telling me, "Beat the feckin' living daylights out of them feet with that crucifix."

"God bless yah, Tommy." Sister Ignatius leant over the rostrum and in one foul movement snatched the crucifix from my raised hand – saving herself from being a cripple for the rest of her life. She then grabbed my cheek between her massive forefinger and thumb and squeezed as hard as she possibly could. "I'm going ta miss yah Tommy."

"Miss me arse you mean."

Her saintly smile suddenly deteriorated into a toothy snarl, while the photographer's camera kept clicking and whirring away, unaware of the battle of wits being played out to the bitter end between the pair of us.

She promised to make me cry one day and had been unsuccessful, to date. This was now her final moment, her final opportunity to squeeze a tear out of me. "Cry you little fecker!" I could almost hear the words on the tip of her tongue as she squeezed my skin to its limit. But she failed to squeeze one teardrop out of me. And I remember thinking, not her or anyone else will ever force me to shed a tear ever again.

I was proud of that moment. Proud of retaining my dignity and of pushing myself through the pain barrier, just for the hell of it. I was proud, too, of the fact that everyone was looking our way, witnessing the final battle between us.

Then they were gone. Sister Ignatius and her holy army of battleaxes turned their backs on us and walked off, as if we had never existed in their lives. And perhaps to them, we hadn't. Cheek squeezing aside, there were no handshakes, no goodbyes, no blessings. No thank yea's for letting us beat yer backsides black and blue. They were gone. And a new era was about to begin.

Drill discipline

The crying boys were still crying. The others stood around in small groups, discussing the departure of Sister Ignatius and her coven and what that might mean for us. With the initial excitement now over for me and the cheek of my face still smarting from the vice-like grip of Sister Ignatius's shovel-sized hand, I felt indifferent to it all.

There were no fond memories jumping out at me. I could not in any way relate to those strange, distant people who would have us believe they were married to God and yet seemed to have sold their souls to the devil. And though, in fairness, I couldn't tar them all with the same brush, they had all seemed to have one thing in common: their indifference towards the children of St Vincent's Approved School.

The school was formerly a lunatic asylum, which says it all really. It wouldn't have surprised me in the least if Sister Ignatius had been a former patient here, prior to it being taken over by the Catholic Church and the Nugent Catholic Care Society, who were paid and trusted to care for their charges, but who miserably failed to do so. And just as insignificant as we had been to these so-called Sisters of Mercy, they, in turn, were just as insignificant to most of us.

Besides, I was too preoccupied with watching Paul Lyons scaling the dizzy heights of a 30ft sycamore tree and willing him to fall to be paying much attention to what was going on around me. The last time he'd fallen he'd spent two weeks in hospital, with a broken leg, a broken arm and a fractured collarbone. When he came back to the school, they'd laid on a small welcome-home party for him, with jelly, blancmange and sponge cake. I was wondering whether that sort of thing would continue under the new regime and hoping to find out soon enough.

"Right, we can cut out the crocodile tears for starters," snapped our new headmaster. He seemed slightly baffled, looking to his right and then to his left, before peering over his shoulder, as if he'd lost something or someone. And then we saw him.

You could almost hear a pin drop in the instantaneous silence, as all eyes fixed on the large, bespectacled fella zipping up his flies having just exited the boys' outside toilet block.

"It's Sister Ignatius dressed as a man!" someone guffawed, taking the words right out of my own mouth.

It was just uncanny. Barring the gold-framed spectacles and the lack of a nun's habit, everything about the tall fella seemed to fit in with the Mother Superior. As we stood watching his large figure loom towards us across the tarmac playground, his shovel-sized hands almost convinced me they were one and the same.

The giveaway came as he walked up to stand alongside Mr Lilly and the rest of the staff, bidding them good morning with a fat, pinkie-faced smile.

"Ah, Mr Sweet, there you are," said Mr Lilly. "Can you get this rabble into four lines of 12?"

"Right you lot!' Mr Sweet bellowed, like a Sergeant Major ordering his troops. "I want you to form four even lines of 12 along here. Come on, come on, quickly does it, we haven't got all day."

We formed one line of 27, one line of 13, one of six and one line of one, making 47. Paul Lyons was still up the sycamore tree.

"I said four rows of 12!" screamed Mr Sweet, standing with a large hand on the shoulder of 13-year-old Billy "Skunk" Smart, who was standing on his own. "Not very popular then, eh lad?"

"No sir," said Billy, breathing his foul breath all over the unsuspecting new master, who staggered backwards, gasping for fresh air.

When he'd gained his composure, Mr Sweet walked back to the line of 27 and counted the first 12 boys as he walked down the line. "Right, the remainder – that's you lot – move over to the next line." He repeated this line by line until he came towards the end of the fourth line.

"How are we doing, Mr Sweet?" enquired the increasingly impatient headmaster.

"45, 46, 47 – we seem to have a lad missing, sir." Mr Sweet retraced his steps back along each row, carrying out a second head count. "Definitely one lad missing, sir."

"Will you get this ragtag of a mess into some orderly fashion," snapped the agitated headmaster, glaring at us as we stood slovenly in line, nattering to one another.

"Atten-tion!" Mr Sweet barked, suddenly bringing his knee right up to his chin before slamming his foot back down onto the tarmac surface and standing as rigid as a wooden board, with his big arms straight down at his sides and his thumbs pointing to the ground.

We could only stare at him in bewilderment, not having seen the like of it before.

"Obviously there has been a lack of discipline around here," said Mr Lilly, shaking his head in dismay. "It seems life has been a little too easy for this lot. Mr Sweet, get this shambles ship-shape and show them how to come to attention and stand easy on command."

"Atten-tion! Staaand at ease! Bring those knees right up high lad. Higher! Arms straight down by your sides. Push those thumbs right into the ground. Not literally into the ground you idiot. I was speaking metaphorically. *Metaphorically.* Don't give me any of your backchat lad. Now get back up on your feet."

For the next half-hour, we were drilled in the art of looking like planks, which wasn't too difficult for us. And as we were all competing against one another, it made it that much more spectacular once we'd got the hang of it. Though it didn't come off without its casualties. Brian "Donkey" Carey (so called because of the way he elongated certain words, along with his hee-haw laugh) was standing a little too close behind Paddy Gavin, so, when he brought his knee up and acciden-tally kneed Paddy up the backside, the Irish lad swung around and chinned Donkey, knocking him senseless with the one punch. To be fair, there wasn't much sense you could knock out of Donkey, considering he had a mental age of six – so we'd been told by the nuns. Paddy had been so quick, none of the staff saw what had happened, and assumed Donkey had fainted in the heat.

Timothy White didn't fare too well either. Trying hard to outdo Mr Sweet, he brought his knee up too high and chinned himself, causing a tooth to cut his lip in the process. And now he was crying even more loudly than he'd been just prior to the nuns walking off.

The hair of the lad from Scunthorpe had just started to smoulder. I only knew the lad as Noddy, named because of his head shaking like one of those nodding dogs you see in the back of a car. Once, I had attempted to have a conversation with him about football, but it was so difficult to tell whether he was agreeing with me or not, I didn't bother talking to him any more.

Hurrying down along the line to Noddy, Mr Sweet began whacking his smouldering head. Unaware of what was happening, Noddy screamed his innocence, swearing blind it wasn't him who'd stolen the photographer's camera and cigarettes, stopping short of snitching on O'Connell.

Fifteen-year-old Michael Clarkson was the boy standing behind Noddy when his hair began to smoulder, so he was the number one suspect. Clarkson tried to convince the headmaster it was either caused by the heat of the sun or it was 'spontaneous combustion', which he'd read about in a book. But once he'd been strip-searched in front of us, the petrol lighter fell out of his undies.

"Name!"

"Michael Clarkson."

"Michael Clarkson, what?"

"Just Michael Clarkson."

"Sir! Michael Clarkson, *sir!*" hollered Mr Lilly, his face almost purple with rage. "Say it!"

"Sir! Michael Clarkson, sir!"

"Outside my office after we've finished here. I'll deal with you then."

Brute Force

We remained standing like planks while the enraged headmaster turned to the retained staff and questioned them about the missing boy. None of them had a clue about him. And why should they? We were only numbers to them. I was number 26, which had been stamped into every article of clothing I possessed. The same went for my toothbrush, small round tin of pink, powdered toothpaste and my shoes.

Turning back to us, Mr Lilly walked up and down each line. Searching out each individual face in turn, he demanded to know who the missing boy was – more importantly, *where* the boy was. "You've all suddenly lost your ability to speak, have you? Well, we will just have to stand here and wait until one of you decides to talk. We'll stand here all day and night if necessary," he threatened. But his threat was always going to fall on deaf ears, and we remained silent.

We weren't particularly bothered if we had to stand on parade all night. In fact, it sounded like a novel idea, serving to break up the monotony of our daily lives. It wasn't as if we'd other plans, like going out for the evening to the cinema or the boy scouts' club. And as intelligent as he wanted to make us believe he was, he should have known better than to ask us to snitch on one of our own. Not because we weren't snitchers – we were. But the idea of snitching right in front of your own peers was out of the question and asking for big trouble.

As it turned out, we all snitched in unison, as our innately guilty consciences forced our eyes to automatically look up in the direction of the tall sycamore tree next to the toilet block, where Paul Lyons could be seen sitting on the large overhanging branch, a sour look on his face.

When I say our innately guilty consciences had forced us to give Lyons away, that is only half the truth. The other half is that none of us could stand the little shit-bag. He was a thief of the worst kind. Yes, we were all thieves in our own right, granted. But Lyons was worse than a normal thief in the ordinary sense of the word. He stole the most valuable thing from right under our very noses: the limelight. Our Limelight.

"What in heaven's name is he doing up there?" Mr Lilly had turned to look behind, following our gazes.

"Sir!" My hand shot into the air.

"Well?"

"He's sitting up there, sir," I volunteered, which immediately got a chorus of laughter from the other boys. Their reaction to my answer confused me a little, since that was precisely what Lyons was doing.

Paul O'Brien, who was standing directly across from me in the next row, shook his head at me and mouthed the word "Wanker" while simulating the motion with his hand. But I ignored the moron, because he had no room to talk. He'd been caught red-handed (so to speak) on so many occasions, it prompted Sister Ignatius to broach the subject at morning assembly, when she'd informed us all about the consequences of masturbating and going blind. In a completely spontaneous reaction, we had all looked in the direction of 70-year-old Sister Margaret, who'd been almost blind for years.

It seemed I had an ally in Mr Lilly who, like me, obviously didn't see what was funny about the information I'd just given him. Hurrying along the line, he eyed me up and down for the briefest of moments.

"One of the smart boys in the school, are we?" He pulled out his little black book and pen from his jacket pocket.

I smiled modestly, glad he'd noticed some of us were not complete imbeciles.

"Name?"

"Paul Lyons, sir," I replied.

"And the boy up the tree?"

"How do you mean, sir?"

"The name of the boy up the tree is how I mean!"

"Paul Lyons, sir." Jaysus, I'd only just told him.

"Not your name, you blithering idiot. I meant the boy up the tree!"

"That is his name, sir."

"Comedian, are we?"

"Sorry?"

I didn't see his fist until it made contact with my chin, knocking me senseless. I was stunned by the power and nastiness of his attack, and the laughing boys were no longer laughing, stunned into silence. Corporal punishment had, as far as I knew, been an acceptable part of the system, as was a clip around the ear from time to time. But this! It was nothing short of physical brutality, something I had grown accustomed to, having a father who could dish it out, but I hadn't expected it from a headmaster. And for what? The fat bastard had asked me a straight question and I'd given him a straight answer. All I wanted to do was to make a good impression. Surely, he must have seen me clapping when Sister Ignatius had announced her departure?

My face hurt. I could see the small throbbing lump just below my right eye. Lilly was staring straight into my eyes, with his smug smile stretched across his nasty Nazi face, waiting, I assumed, for the tears he usually saw from the likes of me. Well, he was in for the longest wait of his life – for eternity, for all I cared. He needed to understand, time was of no consequence to me. Time was meaningless. I got plenty of practice waiting for time, as the mundane days rolled by, from one boring week to another, and so on. An eternity was how long he would have to wait if he wanted to see one small teardrop spill from my eyes, caused by the consequence of any action made by him upon me. I'm not talking about the tears caused by someone giving me a poke in the eye, or when the cold wind blows into them. I'm talking about real, emotional tears caused by an assault from him or any of his thugs.

I ignored the pain and stared defiantly back into his evil eyes, which told me nothing more about him than his actions had already revealed. I just wanted him to look into my dry eyes for a little while longer, so he could see there were no tears.

Small as I was, my tears were my only weapon against the likes of him, Sister Ignatius and all the other child beaters. The lack of tears diminished their superiority, perhaps even questioned it. And if I had been older and stronger, I'd have certainly fancied my chances against this pot-bellied pig. I'd have bitten his podgy nose right off his face. I'd have gouged his squinty little brown eyes out of their sockets and played a game of marbles with them! I'd have torn off his Nazi moustache and shoved it down his gutless Austrian throat, followed by his trilby hat and feathers. It was safe to say I hated the bastard already.

"Your name."

"Rhattigan."

"Ah yes. The Mother Superior made mention of you." I watched him jot down my name in his little black book.

I really must have had a big impact on Sister Ignatius for her to have mentioned me in dispatches. She'd obviously lost her own battle of wits against me and wanted it to continue, in one form or another. No wonder she'd looked at me for the last time with that knowing gloat in her swollen gobstopper eyes. I wondered what she'd told this bully about me. Insubordinate, mischievous, non-compliant, has a good whipping arse.

"Yea've spelt me name wrong." I point out the mistake to the Führer. "It's spelt Rhattigan with an H after the R."

"What?" The incensed headmaster suddenly raised his hand as if to strike me again, and I stared back into his angry eyes, waiting for the pain. But I was saved by the intervention of the shocked gasps from the two female domestic staff, who were obviously unaccustomed to witnessing this level of physical violence.

"It doesn't matter how it's spelt," hissed Lilly. "I know who you are. And I'll be watching you." He eyeballed me back and, no longer holding out on any hope for jelly and sponge cake, I lowered my gaze, which he might have assumed was an act of surrender. But in truth, my survival instincts had kicked in.

The Boy with the Swagger

As a true believer in using any strategy that will give me an advantage, the Element of Surprise will always come second to the Don't Get Caught By the Enemy strategy. Both are among the most useful tactics I learned when being led into battle during the long, hot, summer holidays in Formby, when we had too much time on our hands and little all else to do except play games.

A veteran of many campaigns in the pine forests and on the sandy dunes of Formby beach, I always planned my defensive tactics for any eventuality, so that I was fully prepared in the event of the enemy throwing a surprise attack at me and my platoon. And when I say enemy, I don't use the term lightly. They might have been war games to an outsider looking in, and of course no one got seriously maimed or killed, but if we were taken prisoner we were totally at the mercy of our enemy.

Torture was an acceptable part of the game, especially when attempting to extract information from a prisoner. Some of the gentler forms of persuasion included being stripped naked and tied to a pine tree, before being whipped with a thin branch, or having stinging nettles rubbed up your legs and around your balls, or newts forced into your mouth. But on occasions I'd witnessed other forms of torture that had gone beyond the call of duty, which were usually carried out for the sexual gratification of the captors. This was as good a reason as any not to get captured – unless, of course, you wanted to.

There was an unspoken code of honour amongst us, so whatever happened on the battlefield stayed on the battlefield. Silence was another tactic we used for our own survival, as was knowing your enemy and what that enemy could do to you, then looking for the best strategy to either avoid them or put them out of action.

Although we were young, we were knowledgeable enough to know that everything and everybody has a weak link. Find the weak link and you find the best way to get at that person. And that had been a significant factor a few months earlier, when new boy Johnny Woods had swaggered into St Vincent's. He wasn't tall or muscular or of a real size to have any of us shaking in our boots, but there was something different about 13-year-old Woods which we had all sensed. Besides the large indent and tissue scarring to the left side of his forehead, he seemed very confident and too self-assured for my liking. Looking at him, I didn't think his confidence was just a front, yet it certainly wasn't normal – not for a new boy coming into a place like St Vincent's for the first time.

Petty thieves, robbers and arsonists we were, but we were certainly not overly confident or as self-assured as the new boy seemed to be. Why was he so cocksure? That was the question on my mind, which was answered on the evening following his arrival.

During that early evening, Donkey was having a bath, while Cruickshank, Butler, Collins and I were hanging around outside the cubicle. As usual, we were taking it in turns to have our bath, while the rest of us kept an eye out. Safety in numbers was another good tactic to stop the likelihood of becoming prey to the older boys looking for a gobble or a bum, which we'd managed to avoid up to this point. To be fair, I don't know if any of them would have tried anything on Donkey. He was such an ugly fella, I had wondered if God had completely run out of ideas when he'd made him. With his copper-coloured skin, rounded shoulders, a slight hump in the middle of his back and a thin layer of fine hair covering most of his body (including his face), he looked uncannily like the large picture of Neanderthal Man hanging up on the classroom wall.

We went quiet when Woods strutted into the bathhouse and walked past us towards the showers without acknowledging our presence. Not long afterwards, Dave Banana-Knob McGuire, one of the hard nuts and longest-serving resident in the school, walked in and told us to "Fuck off". We did so without hesitation, leaving Donkey to scramble out of the bath and follow us, stark naked, back up the corridor to the dormitory. Apparently McGuire had taken a shine to the gold St Christopher hanging around Johnny Woods's neck and decided he wanted it. And when McGuire wanted something, he usually got it.

So it had been as much of a shock to us, peering out from the doorway of our dormitory, as it must have been for McGuire, when he staggered back out of the bathhouse a minute or two later, with a pained expression on his face and tears welling up in his eyes, whilst clutching his groin area. For us, this was an indication that his usual tactic of threatening to bum his victim senseless unless he got what he wanted hadn't worked on Woods.

"I slipped on a bar of fuckin' soap," growled McGuire, feeling it necessary to threaten to do to us what I assumed he'd threatened to do to Woods if we so much as breathed a word about his mishap.

A little while later, Woods emerged from the bathhouse. He threw a smug glance in our direction as he walked past us with his nose stuck up in the air, as if he were sniffing out a fart. And that's when we saw the source of his swaggering self-assurance. A pair of brass knuckledusters! No wonder he was so full of it, with confidence boosters like those.

Not one to miss out on an opportunity and knowing how devastating such weapons could be against our enemies, I followed Woods to his dormitory to see if I could somehow persuade him to befriend us. But my attempt at friendly persuasion was greeted by a persuasive thump in the pit of my stomach.

"Get knotted," said Woods, turning his back on me as he slipped on his clean shirt.

Knowing I stood no chance of parting Woods from his knuckledusters, I walked off, winded and feeling a right prat for even trying. But I had every intention of finding a way to get my own back on him.

Understandably, most of the boys kept their distance from Woods, the older boys letting him do whatever he liked, provided he didn't step on their toes, leaving Woods to go unhindered on his bullying rampages against the younger and more vulnerable of the boys who were forced to answer to his every whim.

Having already had a small taster of the damage he could do, I made it my goal to avoid him at all costs. Not that he'd ever bothered me since our first point of contact. But in such a close environment, avoidance was a very difficult thing to maintain and I was sure our paths would inevitably cross. And that is precisely what happened a few weeks later, when I heard from one of his goons that Woods was looking to have words with me.

I hadn't a clue as to whether those words were going to be in the form of an amicable sit-down chat, or whether I had annoyed him in some way, and he was looking to introduce me properly to his knuckledusters. The thought had even crossed my mind that he might have become tired of the same old clique around him and, against all the odds, he wanted to initiate some new blood into his gang. This wouldn't have been of any interest to me, as I preferred to keep myself to myself and avoid the same old trap, where one favour deserved an even bigger favour in return. But having said that, I was always willing to get to know the Devil a little more…

I suppose, in some way, I was already in my own gang with Donkey, David Cruickshank, William Barnes, Norman Butler and Peter Collins. We were a complete bunch of misfits with nothing in common, other than the fact we seemed to get on well with one another. I don't recall how we'd banded together but, bearing in mind the old saying "there's safety in numbers", our survival instincts might have played a big part in this. In any event, it was evident we were going to be stuck with each other for a long while to come.

One Sunday afternoon, I came to a decision. Rather than wait for Woods to come along unexpectedly and catch me off my guard, it was in my best interest to make the first move and pay him a visit. He wasn't too difficult to locate, because wherever 12-year-old Jimmy Clarke was to be found, Woods probably wasn't too far away.

My search took me to a small parcel of land known as the grotto. Just slightly smaller than our football pitch, it had been sectioned off into separate plots for the more green-fingered boys, who would buy their own packs of flower seeds to grow there. This was the place I loved the most. It was my escape from the real world, especially at the height of the hot summer months, when the area was carpeted in a sea of coloured blooms – pansies, wallflowers, carnations and gladioli – with their fragrance filling the air.

I hated the reality of my life. There was nothing in it that captivated me, so I was forced to use my imagination to escape from the box I found myself living in. Within the boundaries of the grotto, it was easy for me to find peace and tranquillity. I would lie deep amongst the flowers and watch the gliders from the local Royal Airforce base dancing across the deep-blue, cloudless skies, allowing me to dissociate myself briefly from my past and present.

Even in such a peaceful place, there was still fierce competition amongst us to see who could grow the tallest sunflower. For a while, those majestic golden giants were left to grow tall, until some sly, jealous little fecker came along and hacked down the tallest ones until eventually there were none left.

"What you want, Rat-e-gun?" Clarke and his mate Robinson were standing guard outside the door of the run-down stone potting shed, which stored the old rusty gardening tools that were no longer used. Tucked away in the far corner of the allotments with wild ivy covering most of it, the shed was completely hidden from prying eyes.

"Yeah, what do you want, Wall Talker?" Robinson chipped in as I ambled up along the cinder path.

The name Wall Talker came about after I had been deliberately kicked in the face by a lad called Brian Walters while I was lying on the grass one afternoon talking with another lad. I've no idea, even to this day, why he'd decided to hurt me. I'd never had anything to do with him up to that point.

In one corner of the grotto was a small man-made cave, just three or four feet in depth, with a weathered grey stone statue of the Virgin Mary at the entrance. Shortly after the attack, I'd gone there and had begged Our Lady to give me the power to be able to deal with this sly 12-year-old bully, who was too afraid to put his dukes up in a fair fight, preferring instead to attack someone when they least expected it. And from that day, he became my nemesis. I loathed and despised him with a vengeance, but despite my regular curses and prayers for him to drop dead on the spot, he remained alive – and kicking.

It was Clarke and his other mate who'd spread the rumour they'd seen me talking to the grotto wall. And when my own explanation, that I'd been praying, was met with derision and hoots of laughter, I was formally christened Wall Talker. And at the same time I'd learned a valuable lesson: it was best not to defend myself against the name-calling and the lies told about me.

"At least I get more sense from talkin' ta a feckin' wall than talking ta yea pair of bum-bandits," I hit back to the potting-shed sentries.

"Yah what?" Clarke suddenly raised the stick in his hand, like a baseball player ready to take a strike.

I always made sure to keep a safe distance when getting into confrontations. It was an instinct that had served me well on the streets of Manchester. And I knew these two snide bastards would just as easily have beaten me with their sticks as they would have whacked out at a fly.

"What's going on?" Woods suddenly opened the shed door and peered out. "Tommy! Come in." He gestured for me to enter his den.

Tommy? Now I knew he must be after something that he couldn't get without my help.

"Fuck off you two."

"But what about Wall Talker?" protested Clarke.

One glare from Woods and they were on their way, muttering under their breaths as they reluctantly pushed their way past me.

Potting-Shed Showdown

Slightly apprehensive, I walked into the musty-smelling shed and watched as Woods closed the door behind us.

"Can't be too careful," he said as he slid the inside bolt home, causing me even more apprehension. I was getting the feeling he was about to do something he shouldn't be doing and obviously didn't want to get caught doing it.

"No," I agreed, swallowing nervously as I grinned back at him while quickly scanning the interior of the shed for a handy weapon, just in case he was having any ideas of giving me a good beating. Sweeping the interior of the shed with a quick glance, I felt spoilt for choice at the abundance of rusty garden tools resting up against the shed walls. I especially noted the small pitchfork just off to my left, which was well within easy reach if anything were to kick off.

A small, dust-stained window was the only source of light, filtering in through the layers of old cobwebs hanging off the frame. In one corner, the mummified remains of a giant harvest spider still stood guard over a couple of cocooned, dried-up blue bottles, as if time had suddenly stopped still on them.

"Wanna fag?" Woods pulled away a brick from the wall to reveal a small hidey-hole, from where he pulled out a packet of 10 Woodbines and a box of matches.

"I can't," I said, sure he'd detected my sigh of relief to see he hadn't pulled out something to hurt me with.

"Relax Tommy, Jaysus." There was that smile again. "Sit down here, I only want to talk to you." Woods patted the large, rusty cast-iron roller, which used to take two of us to pull back and forwards across the football pitch, until all the divots in the ground had gone from the previous day's match.

Sitting on the edge of the roller, I watched Woods light the untipped cigarette and suck inwards before swallowing all the smoke and then exhaling it out into the air.

He sat on the rickety old wooden chair, facing me. "Is it because of your health? Or you've never done it before?"

"I've never done it before."

"Have a drag?" He offered out the smoking cigarette to me. "There's always a first time for everything." He smiled for a third time. I noticed, too, the slight tremble in his hand as he held the cigarette out to me.

Oh bollocks, why not? I knew smoking stunted your growth but there were lots of boys in the school who didn't smoke and were much smaller than average for their age. Licking my lips, I put the cigarette into my mouth and took a long drag, swallowing the smoke in one gulp, as I had seen Woods do.

The immediate effect was an awful feeling of suffocation, followed by dizziness, followed by spluttering coughs as the smoke came out of my nose and mouth. It was a weird sensation to see everything suddenly spinning around so fast in front of my eyes, and I found it difficult to focus on any single object without it spinning out of my line of vision. I managed to regurgitate and spit out the bits of tobacco in the back of my throat, as I handed the cigarette back to the amused Woods.

"Here." He offered out the glass bottle of coke, from which I gratefully took a big swig before handing it back.

"Look what you've done to my fag," he suddenly moaned. "You've put a d-a on it."

"What?"

"Duck's arse. You've wet the end of it." He showed the wet end of the cigarette, where the paper had split, leaving strings of tobacco hanging out from it.

"I'm sorry," I said, wondering if this was the end of our newfound relationship. But Woods didn't seem to mind and broke off the damp end of the fag, flicking it into the far corner of the shed before taking another drag. Then, when he began to tell me about himself and his family, I realised the fella was completely nuts.

He spoke about his father, with just a fleeting mention of his mother, who'd apparently run off with a sailor the day after his eighth birthday. His father was a fighter pilot, shot down and killed in 1945 just as WWII was coming to its end – which would have made 13-year-old Woods at least 21 years old. Apparently, his wealthy granny owned a stately home in Birmingham, with acres upon acres of land and a zoo, complete with crocodiles!

"I got this," he said, pointing to the scar on the side of his face, "when I was feeding them."

Ah, Jaysus! I was locked in a potting shed with a lunatic.

He went on to tell me he'd been sent to St Vincent's Approved School because he'd attempted to elope to Gretna Green with his 14-year old cousin, Maggie, after he'd fiddled with her private parts the previous day, getting her up the duff! Luckily for them, her father was a tank commander, so they were able to drive his tank and head in the direction of Scotland and Gretna Green! Alas, the fleeing lovebirds were cornered by the police on the M1 and he was arrested. The lying fecker!

"What about your parents then?" he asked me.

Now, how could I beat that story? "Ta be honest, I never knew my parents that much," I said. "They went off on one of their usual Polar expeditions to Greenland when I was five and they got lost somewhere in the North Pole. No one has heard from them since."

"Perhaps they were eaten by grizzly bears."

"I suppose it's better than freezing to death," I said.

As an awkward silence descended, I was conscious of him studying me, which made me feel a little uncomfortable, thinking my blackheads must have been more noticeable than I had originally thought when I'd washed my face that morning.

"I like you," he said suddenly, taking me by surprise.

"I like you, too," I lied, hardly able to tell him I hated his guts and would, if I were able to, have kicked 10 tons of shite out of him the minute he turned his back.

"I really like you."

"I really like you as well."

"I mean, really, as in really."

"I mean, really, as in really, too."

"Really?"

For feck's sake! What sort of game was the loony playing? "Really," I repeated, promising to myself, if he said "really" once more, I was getting that pitchfork and showing him just how much I really, *really* hated him. But then, to my horror, he stood up in front of me and pulled down his trousers and pants, revealing his semi-erect penis, before kneeling up on the rickety chair and sticking his spotty arse out to me.

"You bum me first, and I'll do you after. Or shall I go first?" he said, peering nonchalantly over his left shoulder at me.

Jaysus, Mary an' Joseph! What was I going to do? I wasn't shoving me mickey in that pimply hole for sure! "There's someone coming," I said, jumping up off the roller and hurrying the few short steps to the bolted door.

"I never heard anything." Woods was peering out of the small window while fiddling with himself.

Luckily for me, I'd experienced these situations before and had always managed to get myself out of them without too many problems. So, it only remained for me to find a way to leave quickly before it was too late. As things turned out, his two idiot sidekicks, Clarke and Robinson, had made their way back into the grotto and were heading in our direction. We could hear them talking as they drew closer to the potting-shed door.

I breathed a heavy sigh of relief when Woods, after struggling to pull his pants and trousers back up, finally opened the shed door. But not before I was forced to give him a peck on the lips and agree to meet up with him in the bathhouse later that night, to continue our little tryst.

"What do yah want to see me about?" asked Dave McGuire. I had found him sitting in one of the two tatty, straw-filled leather armchairs in the recreation room. A small, windowless affair, the room was also furnished with a small dropleaf table and four hard chairs. A built-in cupboard, overflowing with an assortment of board games and jigsaws with their pieces either missing or packed into the wrong broken boxes filled one corner of the room, while a row of five shelves stacked with records and a battered red and cream record player took up the opposite corner.

"Woods," I replied, above the background noise of the sixties pop band Traffic, with Dave Mason singing about the time he had a hole in his shoe that was letting in water.

"What about the twat?"

Swearing McGuire to secrecy, I told him about what had taken place in the potting shed and the hurriedly arranged rendezvous in the bathhouse planned for that night.

McGuire stayed silent for a short while, as he mulled over the information. "So, he wants to bum you. Why are you telling me?"

"I thought you wanted to get him back for whacking – I mean, when you slipped over that time in the bathhouse. When you went to have a word with him…"

"Keep the gob down," hissed McGuire, glancing across to the doorway. 'So, what's the big plan then? I take it you've got a plan?"

"Well, I've got a sort of plan."

Taking Down Woods

I am sitting in the front row of the circus ring. The place is packed with laughing people, as the dwarf clown rides the Penny Farthing around in circles. He throws a bucket full of make-believe water, made from silver paper, at unsuspecting members of the audience, who unwittingly duck out of the way each time.

He looks in my direction and heads across the ring towards me. I am determined I am not going to flinch and make a fool of myself, like the other morons. As he approaches with his bucket at the ready, I sit smiling up at him, before I'm hit, full in the face, with a bucketful of real cold water, which takes my breath away.

The whole place erupts into fits of hysterical laughter. I want the ground to open and swallow me up. But instead of showing any signs of annoyance, I stand up and begin bowing to the audience, letting them think I am part of the clown's act. I get a standing ovation, which really peeves the clown. I suddenly spot the large catapult underneath my seat and the large marble conveniently loaded into the leather sling. I take aim and fire, hitting the laughing dwarf at the back of the head, and he falls from the bicycle. The whole place is full of laughter and the audience are clapping loudly, waiting for the clown to get up and take a bow. But he doesn't get up and take the bow. Instead, the Ringmaster, kneeling at the side of the clown, suddenly stands up and pronounces him dead. The audience are now staring accusingly at me.

I am now riding the Penny Farthing up along Stamford Street, pedalling for all my dear life is worth, whilst the baying mob chasing me is getting closer.

At the other end of the street, I can see someone standing under a gas lamp. As I get closer, I see it's Sister Ignatius. She is levitating a few inches off the ground in her flowing black habit, screaming at me to get off the bicycle.

"Get them dirty pants down! Yah thievin' little divil yah!" she screams, as her long, thin cane whooshes through the air, catching me a stinging blow across the face. I topple from the Penny-Farthing, and she is above me, the cane held high, in readiness to beat the living daylights out of me. Forgive me, Father. Forgive me, Father. Forgive me…

"Wake up Tommy, wake up!"

I woke with the fear of God inside me, to see Donkey's hairy face peering down at me! "Jaysus, what's happened?"

"Ssssh," he whispered, as my head jerked up off the hard pillow.

Letting my eyes adjust to the dim grey light of the dormitory, I saw the large frame of Bunter Barnes blocking out the light from the window behind him, while Collins stood next to him, looking as excited as a child waiting to unwrap a present.

Speaking in a low, whispery voice, Donkey informed me that Cruickshank was dead to the world and impossible to wake up, while Norman Butler had pissed his bed again, so they wouldn't be joining us. I wasn't surprised nor too concerned about this setback, since McGuire had said he was bringing along his own back-up. But I was concerned that Woods might bring along his knuckledusters, which I'd heard he wore in bed. That was the deciding factor in persuading McGuire to get involved.

The plan was for me and Woods to meet, as arranged, by the entrance to the bathhouse and go in together. Once inside, Donkey and his team were to sneak in and overpower him from behind, whilst McGuire and his gang, already hiding in the bathhouse, would attack from the front. I'd been over this plan of action in my head, time and time again, and felt sure nothing could go wrong if we followed it to the letter.

Standing in the open doorway of the dormitory, I watched as Donkey and the others tiptoed off to take up their planned positions. I confess, it was a strange sight to see all three figures silhouetted in the dimly lit corridor, peering in through the small gap into the night watchman's room before creeping past it.

They met up with McGuire and his lot coming from the opposite direction and I watched as they all turned off along the narrow passageway leading to the toilets and the bathhouse. That was the first part of the plan accomplished.

Some moments later, Woods exited his own dormitory and headed in the direction of the bathhouse. I walked out to meet him, quietly sneaking past the night watchman's room, where I could hear loud snoring. We didn't speak to each other as we came face to face, before walking side by side along the windowless passageway with only a dim nightlight to guide us. I could see he wasn't wearing the knuckledusters and I was able to breathe a sigh of relief.

I don't know why I glanced over my right shoulder as I turned left towards the bathhouse, walking straight past the four toilet doors. But the sight of Donkey's body pressing up against the glass pane of a toilet door had my heart in my mouth. Of all the feckin' places to hide, the lunatic picked the half-glazed door to stand behind, with his face pressed right up against the glass! If Woods were to cotton on, my life wasn't going to be worth living. Fortunately for me, he didn't notice the goon and we continued our journey to the bathhouse, where we stood just inside the door in the dark, with only a tiny grey light from the night sky filtering through the small window.

Woods turned to face me and suddenly kissed me full on the lips, before shoving his hand through the gap in my pyjama trousers and groping around for my mickey.

"Touch mine," he whispered, giving me no choice in the matter as he grabbed my hand and planted it on his stiffy.

"Jaysus!" I was all hot and flushed. Where were those eejits? And where was McGuire and his gang? They should have rushed out of their hiding places by now! I'd been stitched up. Oh Lord. Woods had his lips puckered up, ready to kiss me again. "Faint!" I said to myself, but immediately had second thoughts, thinking he might think I was getting down on the floor, ready for him. I could throw a fit, like my brother Martin used to do. I could drop down and writhe on the ground with froth coming out of my mouth. But would the lunatic Woods be able to see in the dark to know I was having a fit? Or would he just think I'd come over all excited?

I could make a run for it and pay the consequences later. I wasn't having them big lips touching mine again. Ah Jaysus, he kissed me again. Feck this, I decided, I'm going to have the fit. At least with my legs kicking all over the show, he'd have his work cut out to get that mickey of his anywhere near me.

I was saved by Barnes and Collins, who suddenly rushed in behind us. One of them pushed Woods further into the dimly lit bathhouse and I picked myself back up off the cold tiled floor and stood alongside them, to find we were now facing McGuire, King, and Jones, with Woods piggy in the middle. Gone was his usual cocky self-assurance, as he stood with his head bowed, like a guilty prisoner awaiting judgment.

It was a strange feeling seeing someone lose so much power and belief in themselves, just by not having a weapon on them – in his case the knuckledusters. I suppose it could have been likened to Samson, when he'd woken up one morning to find Delilah had scalped him, causing him to lose all his strength with the shock of it all.

I admit I did feel a little guilty seeing Woods standing alone, apprehensive and doing nothing. Oddly, I had no feelings of jubilation. Even if I'd wanted to tell McGuire I'd changed my mind and the plan was off, he wasn't going to listen to me. And so, walking off quietly, with Collins and Barnes following close behind, I made my way back out of the bathhouse and past the toilet block, where I could still see the form of the big eejit, Donkey, standing behind the toilet door with his face pressed up against the glass. I was tempted to leave him where he was, but Barnes had already tapped on the glass, making him aware we were leaving.

With Donkey lurching after us, we silently sneaked back past the night watchman's room, which was still filled with his usual loud snores. Donkey couldn't resist taking another peak in through the gap in the door. Then, to my horror, he quickly tiptoed inside, coming out a few seconds later with a packet of biscuits, which he shared with us as we quietly hurried back to our dormitory. When we got there, I had this sudden thought and hurried back along the corridor to Woods's dormitory, where, making my way across to his empty bed, I followed my natural instincts and put my hands under his pillow to feel the two knuckledusters lying there. He wouldn't be needing those any more. I snatched them up and tried them on for size. A snug fit. I turned to leave, bumping into Donkey, who was standing right behind me. The fact that my heart had almost jumped out of my throat had stopped me from screaming with the fear. And, hard as it was, I resisted my instinct to beat Donkey half to death with the knuckledusters.

Safely back in our own dormitory, I disposed of the two knuckledusters out of the window, throwing them into the thick shrubbery below. Back in my bed, I felt an overpowering sense of relief that I had come out unscathed from the night's events. I don't remember closing my eyes or drifting off to sleep. But in my mind was the knowledge that, for many of us, tomorrow would be a new dawn.

Woods never spoke to me after that day, though oddly enough he did seem to be on much better terms with the two older boys, McGuire and King who, I was told later, had bummed Woods into submission. His cocky swagger and aura of self-assurance were no longer his trademark.

Victorian Values

Several months had passed since the new regime had taken over the approved school and it pained me to admit that I was missing the nuns. Given the choice, I'd have had them back. At least they ignored most of the things we got up to, unlike the staff we now had, who watched our every move.

There had been many changes to our lives since the nuns had left St Vincent's. Not least, the reinstatement of those great Victorian Values, which, the headmaster constantly reminded us, helped to shape our Great British Empire. This was a bit of a liberty coming from an Austrian!"Privileges are no longer an automatic right and will be earned from now on!" he'd announced, when he brought in his new house-points system. 30 house points was the equivalent to 30 pennies or two shillings and sixpence, which was our weekly pocket-money allowance. Lose a point, lose a penny. Lose 12 points, lose one shilling. Lose anything over 20 points and you also lost privileges for the week. This didn't amount to much anyhow – swimming, walks, cinema every six months, and our annual summer camping trip to the Lake District.

And while we had once rolled out of our beds at 7.30am, throwing our piss-stained sheets into the laundry baskets before sauntering off to the bathhouse to change out of our wet pyjamas, we were now woken at precisely 6am on the dot (save Sundays) by the loud clanging of the old brass A.R.P. bell. It was usually rung by Mr Sweet, moving from dorm to dorm and shouting like a Town Crier, "Wakey-wakey rise and shine! All the wet beds in a line!" or "Hands off cocks and on with socks!"

The only way to stamp out bedwetting was to embarrass the bed-wetter: this seemed to be the philosophy of our despot headmaster. So the bedwetters were made to form a long line in the corridor and throw their wet sheets and pyjamas into two separate laundry baskets, before having to march in single file, like a battalion of naked infantrymen, to the bathhouse, in full view of the non-bedwetters, who would take great delight in taunting us.

I was usually able to hold on through the night, sometimes having to force myself to do so. But if I couldn't, then I would consciously pee my own bed, rather than risk a meeting with the ghost of Sister Agnes, who'd apparently worked there when it had been a lunatic asylum. Rumoured to haunt the nearest toilet block to my dorm, she'd apparently fallen head over heels in love with the gardener and the pair of them were caught up to no good in the potting shed. The young gardener lost his job and she'd lost her life, drowning herself in one of the baths. No one knew which of the seven baths it might have been.

I remember, just a few days after my arrival, suddenly waking up one night with painful stomach cramps and needed to get to the toilet urgently. I'd scampered off along the corridors in the direction of the bathhouse, squeezing my cheeks firmly together. I just managed to get myself over the toilet seat before my bowels erupted.

I'd been on my eighth sheet of the small square pieces of hard toilet paper (shiny side down), when I'd been sure I'd heard someone, or something, scurry past my toilet door. I held my breath, sitting quietly and straining my ears for the slightest sound, hearing nothing but the distant drip of a toilet cistern. Exhaling deeply, I felt annoyed with myself for having let my imagination almost get the better of me. But just as I was on my last piece of bog paper, I heard a distinct low, ghostly murmur further down from me. It made the hairs on my head, and the odd one here or there, stand on end.

"Arrgh! Arrgh!" (or words to that affect) was the ghostly moan.

Throwing caution to the wind, I was out of the bathhouse, almost falling over myself as I hurried back along the corridor to my dormitory, where I'd hidden down under the covers of my bed, imagining all sorts of terrible scenarios that could befall me should the spook have followed me.

Children in general are quick learners. But children growing up in institutions such as ours inevitably had to be much quicker. We had to be on the ball all the time, trusting our instincts and learning to sense whenever trouble was around the corner. Just as importantly, we had to learn ways of avoiding it at all costs. Simplicity was the key factor to our survival and the simplest survival techniques I'd learnt were to wait, watch, listen and then act.

With none of us particularly keen to run the degrading gauntlet of the wet beds, we simply stopped wetting them. This had put a gloating smile on the headmaster's face, as I'm sure it did on the laundryman's. But then Carl Williams came up with the simplest solution: pee out of the dormitory window. We all followed suit and everyone was happy – until the day the gardener reported the sudden stench coming from the thick evergreen shrubs at the front of the building, which mysteriously seemed to be dying off.

Making preliminary investigations with his nose, Mr Lilly initially pointed to the possibility of a broken sewer pipe somewhere in the vicinity. A more thorough investigation from the water company, helped by the discovery of the untold number of poo-parcels, gave the game away. Faced with a ban on relieving ourselves out of the windows, some bright spark came up with another simple, but brilliant, idea. And peeing in someone else's bed became the next fad.

Bedwetting wasn't the only habit we had to change under the new regime. At 7am prompt, we would be scrubbed up, dressed and standing to attention by our made beds, waiting for Mr Lilly to come along on his routine morning inspection. Where once we had quickly made our beds before hurrying down to the dining room for our breakfast, leaving the fart-filled, urine-smelling stale air to eventually dissipate throughout the day, we were now under orders to have all the dormitory windows wide open to let in the fresh air, regardless of the weather.

Each of us had a bedside locker containing a second set of daily clothing, including a pair of socks and underpants, which we would change into every Wednesday. We kept our non-important odds and sods in the drawer and our more personal possessions on us, otherwise they would easily have become someone else's personal possessions.

Every morning we would hear Mr Lilly's squeaky shoes moving along the corridor to our bedroom, where he'd march into the dorm, sniffing at the air, before throwing his usual dismissive scowl around the room. He would instruct Mr Sweet to dock two points (that was tuppence) if our lockers were not straight or not exactly following the edge of the join between the floorboards.

"Morning sir." I gave him my usual insincere greeting, which he ignored sincerely, as always. He hardly looked at me. It was as if I was invisible as I stood to attention in front of him, reading his beady eyes for the first sign that he was not happy.

"Why is a button missing from your shirt?"

He found me wanting for a good answer to that tricky question and I sensed he knew that.

"It must have fallen off," was the most obvious answer. But the chances were that he would only see that as insubordination and dock me points. So I was going to have to come up with something special. "It isn't missing sir. I have it in me pocket." My turn to look smug.

"Three points, for insubordination," raged Lilly, slapping my pile of neatly folded clothing off my bed and onto the floor, "and two points for untidy clothes." He walked off, with Mr Sweet diligently following behind him, holding the large black register and calling out each name, along with the number of house points deducted, as he passed by each bed.

"Rhattigan, five points. Mullins, one point. Carey, one point. O'Connell, your pillow is out of line, one point."

I spent a while refolding my clothes to get them into a perfect pile on the bed, with my red tie snaking in and out between the front of each garment – just to give it that extra wow. But this didn't impress the headmaster. Having finished his inspection, he walked back over to me and pulled my pile of clothes off the bed again.

"Sir…" I wanted to ask the fat miserable pig to give us all a demonstration on how to fold our clothes properly. But Mr Sweet intervened with a quick knee to my thigh, giving me a dead leg.

I was unable to fathom what made Mr Sweet tick, or even what he wanted from me. Sometimes, he came across as a very sensitive and understanding person, while at others he seemed insensitive, frustrated and very angry towards me. I tried to keep on his good side and was rewarded occasionally with kind words of encouragement, along with a pat on the back. But most times he would either be bawling me out for the smallest of indiscretions, or he'd completely ignore me out of hand.

With his mood swings changing from day to day, it was almost impossible to second-guess his state of mind. If I had to liken him to anybody, then it would have to be both Doctor Jekyll and Mr Hyde: one moment considerate and sympathetic, then in the next breath, a violent, vicious thug. He hit me around the head quite often or kneed me in the thighs. I admit, at times I could be difficult to deal with, especially if I was in a bad mood myself. And I probably deserved the odd slap now and again. My father was always beating me for one reason or another, which I'd never dared to question. And although Mr Sweet wasn't as consistent with the violence as my father, he did seem to have a need to take his frustrations out on something or someone. Unfortunately for me, I was one of his targets.

At 7.30am we were all in the dining room ready for breakfast. This was another opportunity for Mrs Lilly (Matron) to get in on the act of pretending she cared about the children in her charge. Strutting around like a spring chicken in her high black stilettos, she gave an automatic "Good morning" as she passed each table, without so much as a glance in our direction.

We replied in our usual don't-give-a-toss incoherent murmurs, with some of us calling her uncouth names under our breath. Standing alongside her pint-sized, pot-bellied husband, she was a few inches shorter than him. I always smiled as I imagined how the pair would look if she'd stood alongside him without her towering high heels. He'd probably not even notice she was beside him, unless he looked downwards!

"Hands together," she called out. "For what we are about to receive."

"May the Lord make us truly thankful." Some of us would follow with the correct prayer, while others added their own words, such as "may the Lord have mercy upon us," or "the pigs have just refused".

We were divided into eight tables, with six to each one. Our usual cook, Mrs Collins, had been run over by her own car the previous week. Her husband was reversing out of the garage when he'd hit the accelerator instead of the brake as she'd been waiting for him. The news wasn't good. She wouldn't be back for a long while, if ever. She was a great cook and we'd always looked forward to every meal she made. But until she returned, or they found another cook, we had no choice but to make do with the food dished up by Miss Peggy, the wispy-haired Irish seamstress-cum-part-time-cook of sorts.

It was no coincidence the staff no longer tucked into breakfast or dinner with us, as they used to do before Mrs Collins' accident. And who could blame them, with the slops Miss Peggy was dishing up: burnt sausages, dried, oven-baked eggs on burnt toast, or on greasy fried bread. Not to mention the unwelcome garnish of curly silver hairs in the cabbage.

For the life of me, I just couldn't figure out how she was able to produce mashed potatoes as a watery substance with solid lumps, and the odd trouser button. And her waterlogged boiled potatoes were just as bad, having so many eyes in them, it was no wonder we all suffered from acute paranoia!

A strange-looking woman by any standards, Miss Peggy, or Piggy, as she was fondly known to us, was a rather large, lump of a lady. She was taller than Matron and unlike her, she hadn't a need to smother herself in make-up because she already had ruddy cheeks and the most wonderful, watery, bright blue eyes peering out from a thick set of dark brows. She'd suffered with polio from birth, which had resulted in a deformed left hand and knees that turned inwards, causing them to knock together as she waddled along, making every effort to squeeze her enormous, lopsided backside through open doorways. Other than that, she seemed perfectly normal.

That morning's breakfast was cheese on toast. Miss Peggy called it Welsh Rarebit, a sauce made up from dried cheese powder, which reminded me of yellow bile. Not mixed properly, it had lots of lumps in it, which we would have to break down with our forks and mix back in to the watery sauce before eating it. Admittedly it did have a slight, though very weak, cheesy flavour to it.

"Hands up for seconds." Doing his usual slow military march up and down the centre of the dining room's highly polished green lino floor, Mr Lilly peered from side to side, as 48 hands suddenly shot into the air.

"Please, sir."

"It's my birthday today, sir."

"It's your birthday every week, Hutchinson."

"I've been good all week, sir."

"It's only Monday, Gavin!"

Our frantic pleading fell on deaf ears, which wasn't that much of a surprise, considering he had his favourites. But we still attempted to get a second helping. Even if the food did look like puke, it was better than no puke at all.

A turn-up for the books for once – I was picked to have second helpings. Well, I thought I saw Matron point her finger straight at me, but I could have been mistaken. Hence my hesitancy. Could it have been for real? Or was my imagination running riot?

"Well, get on then!" The headmaster's wife pointed straight at me again, gesturing for me to hurry up. I was out of my chair like a greyhound after a hare, in case she suddenly realised she'd made a mistake and changed her mind. I made a wide detour past Mr Lilly in case this was a ruse enabling him to smack me around the head in front of everyone for something I'd forgotten I'd done. As I was passing him, I saw his arm come up so I took evasive action, flinching and ducking as I hurried past him – just as he looked at his watch. Glancing back, I saw him staring at me, shaking his head in wonderment.

An Unfair Fight

By 8am we were going about our assigned daily cleaning duties, spending the next hour washing and polishing the floors of the long corridors, the dormitories, bathrooms and toilets, the games room and TV room. Our work was then inspected by the deputy head, Mr Alston, who wasn't as fanatical as Mr Lilly when it came to Victorian values, usually turning a blind eye to most minor indiscretions.

The ARP bell always rang out at 8.55am on the dot, telling us we had five minutes to quickly pack away our mops, buckets and long-handled floor polishers, before forming a long line outside the entrance leading through to the school block. There were four classrooms and the office of head teacher Mr Keenan. We were divided into two main classrooms, with 24 of us in each room. We also had a woodwork room, used twice weekly, on a Wednesday and Friday afternoon, plus an art room that doubled as a music room.

Mr Keenan taught art and science. He didn't usually have any involvement with the day-to-day running of St Vincent's outside normal school hours. He did, however, come out on some outings, plus the summer camping trips, as well as organising the annual Christmas show, which we performed for the local community.

Short, though slightly taller than Mr Lilly, Keenan had unusually large, bushy eyebrows, which he liked to move up and down one at a time. And although I was impressed by this, I disliked him from the moment I'd set eyes upon him.

His greasy black hair had an unusual white streak running through the front, which, he told us, was a special birthmark passed down through his Scottish ancestors, who had once lived up in the treacherous mountainous ranges of the Scottish Highlands. These ancestors were, apparently, known among the Scottish clans as the fiercest of all the Highland warriors.

I only begged the question, "Did skunks come from the Highlands too, sir?" when I felt his warrior wrath as a hard slap across my face. But however superior or special he thought his streak of white hair made him, all I ever saw was the bullying streak inside him. Like most of the male staff at St Vincent's, Keenan, Marron and Sweet were always quick to throw their weight around to show us who was in charge. It didn't take much for them to lose their scant patience and lay into one of the kids with a cane, a few slaps and, on occasions, their fists and knees.

Mr Marron taught English, History and PE. Unlike Mr Keenan, Mr Marron played an active role in the running of St Vincent's and we saw him almost every day until the early evenings when we went off to bed. Standing at over 6ft tall, he was a slim, muscular man with short, curly fair hair and smelly breath (like Billy Smart but stinky). I guessed he was aged around 30, and always seemed keen to jump in and separate the many fights between the kids, throwing his own punches in whenever the opportunity arose.

Once a week, he would have the lot of us out on the football pitch, forming a tight circle around him. And there, amid the baying mob of boys calling out the names of the other boys they wanted to be paired off with, he would throw the boxing gloves across to two boys of his own choosing. Timing the seconds on his stopwatch, he gave them one minute to beat the hell out of each other.

It didn't bother Marron that one boy might be much bigger or tougher than his weaker opponent. In fact, it had seemed to me, as I looked at his smirking face, that he relished the sight of the blood, snot, and cries from the weaker boys.

One day he called out my name and threw the boxing gloves across to me. It wasn't the first time Marron had made me put on a pair of boxing gloves. The last time was when he had dragged me by the hair along to the assembly hall after I'd got into an altercation with another lad, twice as big as me. We'd been standing in line at the time, waiting to go into the school block, when someone had pushed me from behind, sending me forwards and causing me to knock into the other lad. He'd not been too pleased and had given me a mouthful. Mr Marron and Mr Sweet had heard the commotion and immediately ordered the both of us to the hall to sort out our differences. I'd refused to budge, but Marron had caught a handful of my hair and had dragged me along the corridors. Once we were in the hall, they physically forced the boxing gloves onto the both of us. But under threat of losing his privileges, the lad had refused to lay a glove on me. It turned out he was as good a thief as me and so wasn't particularly bothered about losing his pocket money.

But this time, out on the football pitch, I couldn't wait to get stuck in to my opponent, once I knew who it was. "Walters," called out Marron next, and I was elated. My heart was pounding as it pumped the adrenaline around my body. And in the blink of an eye, I had already planned my tactics as to how I was going to deal with this bastard. We were now on equal terms: a fair fight without his mates backing him up. There was nowhere to hide. And more importantly, it was in front of so many witnesses, so he wouldn't be able to make feeble excuses, or be able to say he'd been cheated one way or another. I was going to teach him a lesson he'd never forget.

Why did I dislike Brian Walters? He was a nasty, vindictive parasite, who spread lie after lie about me and snitched on me for any little thing, just to see me punished. He was always trying to show he was the best at everything: football, swimming, athletics, singing, the list went on. I had no idea why he had particularly honed in on me, setting me up as one of his biggest targets.

The first time I had encountered Walters, he had kicked me in the head for no discernible reason. The second time was during Mass one Sunday morning. Though modest by nature, I don't mind admitting I am a good singer and was sometimes told that I sang like an angel. Walters was also a very good singer, but I could hold my last note much longer than he could, as well as being able to sing much higher. That Sunday, as we were singing the "Ave Maria", I'd noticed all eyes were on the pair of us, as we went into vocal battle and suddenly changed tempo, harmonising against all the other voices in the chapel. I must admit, it had sounded beautiful and heavenly, sending a shiver down my spine. And when we hit the last high note, we'd held it for about 20 seconds. I think I could have gone on for a little longer, if the creep hadn't suddenly turned blue in the face and keeled over, allegedly due to an epileptic fit. I'd been more inclined to think it was a bit too convenient and he'd probably faked it because I was a much better singer, and he could not accept his defeat when it stared him in the face. And although he did go on to have more of these fits, I could never be convinced they were all genuine.

I hated him with a vengeance. I even prayed to God for terrible things to happen to him. Not for him to die, mind. I didn't wish for it to be as quick as that! I wanted him to suffer the pain and the anguish he had inflicted on me. I'd never done anything to hurt him and yet he seemed to be possessed by an urge to hurt me in any way he could.

I avoided him like the plague, while making sure I had nothing to do with his friends. He seemed to be silently smirking at me every time our eyes met, and I would always be the first to avert my gaze from his. I suppose I was afraid of him, but this was more from the fear of knowing what he could do to me while I could do nothing, because he always had his goons alongside him, ready to stick the boot in. But now my time had arrived!

"Your minute starts now," said Marron, stabbing his finger on the face of his stopwatch. In the background, the baying mob were calling out.

"Break his nose!"

"Gouge his eyes out!"

"Kick him in the bollocks!"

A cheer went up a split second after the sly bastard had boxed me one to the side of my head, while I was still looking at Marron's stopwatch, giving me no chance to have put up my dukes. And with my plan of action now in tatters, lost somewhere in the cloud of stars forming a new Milky Way inside my head, I felt two more punches in quick succession, before my survival instincts automatically kicked in and I tactically dropped to the ground to avoid further punches. Of course, Walters took this as my submission to him, and – big mistake – stood over my prone body with his arms raised aloft victoriously, leaving himself wide open to a sixteen-ounce boxing glove straight up into his privates. I'd got the snide little bastard!

My jubilation, on hearing the loud cry of pain from Walters, amidst the cheers and the jeers, brought a wide grin to my face. And as my brain kicked back into life, I got up on my hands and knees – big mistake – steadying myself to get back up on my feet, and not seeing the kick until my bottom teeth had split my lip wide open.

"Time's up!" Marron shouted over the gratified mob. Ignoring me out of hand, Marron viciously grabbed the front of Walters' jumper, pulling the bully towards him until he was standing on tiptoes like a ballerina. "Right, let's just be clear on the Queensbury rules here," said Marron, his nose almost touching Walters'. "No use of the feet, arms, elbows, head, or teeth." Then he glanced at me as I staggered to my feet. "And no punching below the belt." This was how he'd settled the matter, with no punishment for Walters' actions, nor sympathy for my bleeding split lip. Hurriedly pulling off my boxing gloves, I was sent off to the washroom to clean myself up, while he called another two names into battle.

The downstairs washroom had 48 sinks fixed along three walls. Above each sink was a number corresponding with the one written on each boy's small round tin of pink, powdered toothpaste, toothbrush, and plastic cup. I was boy number 26. Looking into the small wall mirror, I could see my throbbing lip was swollen and had a wide split about half an inch long. But it didn't look as bad as it felt, especially when it kept rubbing up against my teeth, which, fortunately for me, were intact. Bathing it as best I could, I had only the one thought in my head: I was going to get my own back on Walters – even if it killed me.

Gone With the Wind

We were in the assembly hall, standing at ease in four straight rows of 12, waiting for the headmaster to make his usual grand entrance. We never knew what would be on his morning agenda until he sprang it on us. But on this Monday morning, I had a suspicion he'd be wanting to have his say about little Frankie McGee, who'd been taken to the hospital the previous night after scorching his hole!

Ten-year old Frankie and his best friend, Tony May, aged 12, were always competing against each other in farting challenges. I had to admit I was among the many who were impressed with their trumping talents, amazed by how the pair of them were able to fart recognisable notes to songs we all knew – "Hitler Has Only Got One Ball" being a firm favourite. If I'd had to pick the better farter of the two, then I'd have to say Tony May just squeezed ahead because of his ability to fart in different pitch combinations, as well as hold beautifully timed pauses. But when it came to the elongated fart, then Frankie was by far the better of the two. And he held the record of seven seconds, the longest one to date.

It was around 10 o'clock the previous evening when we had gathered in McGee's dormitory for the farting competition between Frankie and Tony. There were some 30 of us packed inside and we had to peer over shoulders to get a clearer look as 14-year-old Johnny Hill, the oldest boy in the school, tossed the penny coin into the air and caught it.

"Heads," called May.

"Heads it is."

"You first," May invited McGee. And with a wide grin spread across his face, little Frankie had shamelessly slipped his pyjama bottoms off and hopped up onto his bed, before laying on his back and bringing his knees right up around his ears to expose his bare backside.

"I'm lighting up now," warned Johnny Hill, flicking the lighter into life and bringing the dancing yellow flame a little closer to Frankie's bottom, until it was about an inch away from his hole. "Okay, it's lit."

Whoosh! It was the weirdest thing I had ever seen in my life. The fart had ignited, sending out a two-foot long flame lasting a few seconds, which singed Hill's eyebrows and lashes before he could jump out of the way. In the process, Hill had dropped the lit petrol lighter between Frankie's thighs, causing him to leap off the bed, yelping in pain. This in turn started Donkey off into one of his hee-hawing fits of hysterical laughter. And with that, everyone scarpered back to their beds, as little Frankie had staggered off in pain to the night watchman's room.

Half an hour later, we could hear the chatter of voices coming up from the other end of the corridor, with a loud Mr Lilly throwing question after question at poor Frankie. Slipping out from my bed, I saw McGee strapped onto an ambulance chair just outside the night watchman's room, and he wasn't looking happy.

"Does the lighter belong to you, McGee?"

"No, sir."

"How did it get into your bed?"

"Someone must have put it there, sir."

"While it was alight? Do you think we're blithering idiots, McGee?"

"No, sir."

"So how did you manage to burn your skin and not your pyjama bottoms?"

"I wasn't wearing any sir, I was hot, sir."

"Were you playing with it?" Matron cut in. "Under the covers?"

"I'm not a wanker, Matron!"

"The lighter, you fool," snapped Mr Lilly.

"Can I go to the hospital, sir. It's hurting."

The incensed headmaster instructed the ambulance men to take McGee away, but not before promising, "I'll deal with you tomorrow." But as we hadn't seen Frankie this morning, I could only assume he was still in the hospital.

"Ah-tennn-sion!" cried Mr Sweet as Mr Lilly finally made his grand entrance, slow marching into the assembly hall, his podgy hands behind his back and a look of disdain on his face. This wasn't helped by our slapdash way of coming to attention, before singing out our usual lethargic and somewhat insincere, "Good Morning Mr Lilly" greeting.

He looked cheesed off as he stood silently glaring out at his audience for a moment or two, before telling Mr Sweet to stand us easy.

"Stan-at-ease!" screamed Mr Sweet, and we automatically followed his order half-heartedly, forcing Mr Lilly to shake his head in frustration.

"Right you lot," bellowed Mr Sweet. "We'll do it again! Ah-tennn-"

"Not now," said the headmaster, with a wave of his hand. "Can we get on with the music?"

We spent around five minutes listening to a classical violin concerto, written by a German composer called Johann Sebastian Bach, who was born 300-odd years earlier. And for that short spell of time, I was able to leave this miserable world, listening to the violin's emotional voice calling out to me, lifting my spirit free. Every morning, we would have to listen to a piece of music from the headmaster's vast classical record collection, which he would play on the old gramophone set up in the assembly hall. It was my favourite time of the day, besides bedtime. I enjoyed listening to the music and I wasn't the only one. After a few months, a good few of the lads could recognise many classical pieces, from Bach and Beethoven to Chopin, with Rimsky-Korsakov's "Flight of the Bumblebee" being my favourite piece of all time. It was so busy and hectic, I could close my eyes and instantly fly off to anywhere my imagination allowed me to go.

"Spontaneous human combustion." Mr Lilly suddenly brought me back to reality. "Is there someone amongst you who can tell me what this is?" He cast a sly eye over us, probably expecting some bright spark to shoot their hand high in the air and answer the question. Unsurprisingly, there were no volunteers willing to risk his wrath, even if they knew what it meant. "Spontaneous. Human. Combustion." He repeated the words in a slow, deliberate manner. "I take your silence to mean none of you has a clue as to what I am talking about?" The deafening silence continued.

"Putting it in much simpler terms: burning from the inside out. That's precisely what it is. And this stupid, idiotic stunt that McGee decided to pull could have proved fatal. He could easily have burnt to a cinder. Gone, in a flash." Mr Lilly clicked his fingers to emphasise the quickness of the flash. "In all my years of dealing with delinquent, imbecile children, such as those I see standing before me, I have never, ever, come across such a ludicrous and dangerous thing to do to oneself. Setting one's backside alight! What's the joke, Williams?"

"Nothing sir. I was only coughing sir."

"You'll be more than coughing if you don't get that smirk off your face. Right now!"

"Sorry, sir."

"Where was I?"

"Gone in a flash, sir" offered Williams, clicking his own fingers to emphasise the flash.

"What?" Lilly's face went a deep red.

"The flash sir? When McGee lit his fart."

"Flatulence! He lit his own flatulence!"

"I thought it was a fart, sir."

"Outside my office. Now!"

Lilly went on to tell us a weird, though fascinating story, about an old lady who had been found sitting in her chair next to the fireside in her front lounge. Well, *she* wasn't sitting in the chair, but her ashes were – a big pile, by all accounts. Luckily for her, the police forensics had been able to identify her by her feet. Remarkably, these were all that was left of her amid the smouldering ashes, and the only evidence to show she'd existed. Apparently, her feet were still in their Hush-Puppy shoes, which were in perfect condition, with no signs of burning or scorching on them.

"And that," concluded Lilly, "is the consequence of spontaneous human combustion."

He didn't go as far as to tell us whether this was caused by the woman sitting too near the fire and letting a fart drop. Or whether she, like McGee, had deliberately struck a match to one of her own farts. So we were none the wiser as to how she had suddenly burst into flames. But McGee had been lucky that his flame had shot outwards and not inwards. The thought of striking a match near a fart that could suddenly burst into flames and burn you to death from the inside out made my skin crawl.

That Sunday Feeling

Another weekend was upon us. And just like the previous weekend and the one before that, along with all the others before those, this one would pass without leaving any fond memories from which I could derive some comfort. I'd been used to living within a large family in Stamford Street. There were 15 of us in total (when my parents were there), though at times this number would increase to around 20 or so, with aunties, uncles, and cousins popping in for a visit and staying for days, or weeks on end. Nanny Gavin, a first cousin of ours, seemed to have been a permanent fixture, until she upped and left the house one day, never to return. We never questioned this. In fact, we had never questioned any of the goings-on in our house because it had been an acceptable part of our lives. That's how it was. Uncles, aunties and cousins, some of whom we'd never set eyes on before or afterwards, came and went. Living with my family and living under the roof of St Vincent's were oceans apart.

Looking from the outside in, perhaps my siblings, particularly the older ones, might well have seemed to the stranger's eye to be indifferent to one another's presence. I suppose that would have been understandable, considering our age differences and the fact of having to deal with the personal issues going on in our individual lives. But we were nonetheless a very close family, living up to the adage that blood is thicker than water, with no doubts about the love and compassion we had for each other when it mattered most. This was in complete contrast to life at St Vincent's Approved School, where indifference and knowing who your friends were became the key to keeping relatively safe. I use the term friends loosely because, in truth, although I had my own small peer group who I was comfortable with, I did not have anyone at the school that I would, or could, call a true friend.

Not too far from St Vincent's, there was a slate plaque in one of the front gardens of a house we would often pass on our many walks to Formby beach. And I would pause to read the inscription, which served as a reminder to me of how volatile, cold and lonely this world can often be.

True friends are like diamonds,
Precious and Rare.
False friends are like Autumn leaves,
found everywhere!

Simplicity was always the key to my life. I didn't need to be educated to know what life was about. I saw it, I felt it, I lived it day to day. And just as I expected to achieve nothing from my life, I didn't expect to give it anything in return. Mr Lilly would have us believe our lives were mapped out for us from the moment we were born. Once, he'd angrily told us in assembly, "You are all born thieves," and he likened us to "leopards that will never change their spots". This was after someone had nicked Matron's new bicycle, which had been found the following day, sitting high up in one of the orchard's apples trees, minus both of its wheels. These had been found a few days later up another apple tree, minus their spokes and innertubes. I was not one for accusing innocent people, but after the theft, Michael Fleming made some powerful catapults from innertubes and bicycle-wheel spokes, which he sold to us and also over the wall to some of the local kids.

"A leopard never changes its spots" was a phrase I had heard mentioned lots of times and I didn't quite understand the logic behind this comparison. Why the leopard, when there were many other spotted animals to choose from? Skunks and snakes sprang to mind. The thieving hyena was another, which for me was a much closer comparison to us all, considering we were sly, thieving buggers who would laugh at getting away with the things we'd done wrong.

If I were to make comparisons with myself and other animals, spotted or otherwise, it would be based on its environmental instincts. And the environment I'd been born into had given me the instincts I needed to survive, by begging, stealing, and scavenging on the streets. I'd never once stopped to consider or realise that stealing someone's personal possessions was a bad thing, especially during the times I was being used by my father to help him steal. I only ever saw the results of the stealing: putting some food on the table and keeping him and Mammy in booze for a few days. And it did make me feel sad later, to know how personal and upsetting it is to have something you own taken from you. Even as young as I was, I could so easily have refused to help Daddy with his robberies, regardless of the consequences. But I didn't.

It did seem the powers that be were intent on letting all of us know there was no hope for the likes of us. Their real message, once a thief always a thief, was instilled into our "tiny brains" on a daily basis. But despite the leopard comparison, I believed I had changed over the past couple of years. And just as my environment had changed, so, too, had my instincts. I was bathed, clothed, fed and educated. And while I no longer had a need to use my stealing instinct to survive, I had to quickly sharpen other instincts to survive the cruel environment I found myself in. That said, I would still help myself to the odd jar of sweets from the local sweetshop.

One of the biggest changes in me was that I was no longer illiterate. I never thought it possible that I would ever be able to read or write. But I was learning new words every single day. And the joy of learning to pronounce a written word correctly as I read it remained as overwhelming as the joy I'd felt when I had first read the line "The cat sat on the mat" all on my own and without any prompting.

I wondered what Daddy would have thought of me being able to do that. Would he be impressed? Would he be proud? Probably not. Somehow, it would be all thanks to him. He'd probably let me read all the letters that came to the house, so he didn't have to get stressed out about them. I recall him being the only one in the family that I ever saw reading and writing. I was always fascinated listening to him reading out the letters like short stories and using such long words as Authority, Custody, Prosecution and Tosspots.

He once went up the wall about a pile of bills he'd received. "Nothin' good ever comes in through dat feckin' door, save for begging letters," he'd moaned. "The coalman, the milkman, the council – all after me hard-earned money. Can yah believe this? Seven shillings in rent arrears! They should be feckin' payin' us ta live in this dump. Der all at it! Ten shillings for being drunk an' disorderly. Drunk an' disorderly my hole! I was dancing, that was all!"

"After half-killing your cousin, Paddy Ward," Mammy reminded him.

"Half killing him? Jaysus, that gimpy-eyed eejit's been walking around half dead for years."

"An' yah kissed one of them coppers."

"It was a peck, was all. Everyone kisses everyone on New Year's Eve."

"Yah feckin' never kissed me!"

"Well, Paddy Ward was makin' up for dat!"

"He was bein' friendly, was all."

"Friendly my arse. He was feckin' stuck ta yer lips. Til I flattened the fecker. And look at all them homos who were kissing an' cuddling each other. Not one of them arrested. It's us, Lizzy, everyone hates the Irish."

"The copper that arrested yah was Irish."

"More reason why he shouldn't have arrested me, the feckin' turncoat." Daddy had thrown all the letters straight onto the open coal fire.

At St Vincent's we were relatively free over the weekends to do nothing, apart from Mass on Saturday and Sunday mornings. The part-time staff, all four of them, arrived at the school, while the full-time staff (barring the one on weekend duty) left the school behind them for two blessed days.

Mr Sweet was on weekend duty and in charge of the whole school. I couldn't stand the fat bullying bastard. Two weeks earlier, he'd belted me hard around the side of my head, causing my ear to ring. And, although the ringing noise had settled down to a softer tone, I could still hear it and it was so frustrating at times, especially when I was on my own, or trying to concentrate on reading my Janet and John book. Bedtimes seemed to be worst, with the silence only exaggerating the sound in my ear. But I learnt a simple trick, which helped me to drift off into a deep sleep. I just closed my eyes and imagined I was on a battlefield with the sound of big guns blazing around me. And before I knew it, the following morning had arrived.

The reason for the slap? We were out on one of our many expeditions to Formby beach and some eejit had decided to throw a skinny three-foot stick, no thicker than my finger, on to the railway track. We were immediately ordered to march back to the school, with Mr Sweet remonstrating with us about how that could so easily have caused a derailment of the train, with the loss of hundreds of lives. When we arrived back, we were made to stand on parade in the playground for three long hours, until the culprit owned up, or someone pointed out the would-be mass murderer. And when the first part of the miracle hadn't taken place, we were dismissed to the dining room for our tea and told in no uncertain terms that unless the culprit was found, it was straight up to bed without any association time.

"Get your hands washed and then to the dining room. And if there is any one of you wanting to have a little word in my ear, you've five minutes to do so," said Mr Sweet. "No one will know who you are." And some grovelling little shitbag went and pointed me out as the guilty party.

"Rhattigan! A word in your tiny ear." Mr Sweet had beckoned me out of the dining room and I jumped to his command, taking my plate of beans and toast with me.

"Why did you throw the stick onto the railway lines?"

"I didn't, sir."

"You were seen throwing it."

"Whoever said that is a liar, sir."

"There was more than one person who saw you."

"Then they are all lying. Sir."

I was expecting it to happen, but I didn't see it coming until the open palm of his podgy hand had already hit me across the side of my head, catching me around the ear. He was a big man and had once bragged about weighing in at 18 stone. So, there was a lot of power behind the wallop, which had almost knocked me senseless. Though not senseless enough to make me drop the plate of food, which I held onto for dear life as I fell to my knees. He'd gone on to berate me about the number of people I could have killed as a result and how I would have to explain my actions to Mr Lilly when he arrived back from his holiday in Rome.

I could do nothing to defend myself but stand there, staring defiantly back at him, dried-eyed and wishing the years would roll by to when I was 18 years of age, so I could come back here to pay him a visit – bigger and tougher than the bullying fat bastard.

I suppose I could have argued the fact that Mr Cuthbert had mentioned the stick had been thrown by someone behind him, and as I had been walking further up the group from him, this ultimately should have proved my innocence. But there was no point in even attempting to argue the toss with him, or indeed any of the grown-ups. Ultimately, someone was responsible for throwing the stick and with a couple of cowardly tosspots conspiring to point the finger at me (probably to protect one of their own mates), that was good enough for Mr Sweet. Fortunately for me, he'd forgotten to report the incident to the headmaster because I got away without further punishment.

A Proper Plank

I made my way across Formby Beach to meet up with Noddy and a group of the boys who'd been too scared to join in the usual war games, which I'd been playing just a short while earlier. As my men were stupid enough to get captured and were probably being tortured, I'd decided to abandon them. The boys had found a rusty bonnet of a car and were taking it in turns to sit in it and slide down the largest of the sand dunes. I asked Noddy if I could have a turn but he just kept nodding and said I would have to ask Martin Gore, as he was the boy who'd found the bonnet. So, I made my way to the top of the sand dune, where the fat eejit was standing.

"Hi Martin." I gave him a pleasant smile.

"It was Fatty yesterday."

"I was only having a laugh with you, Martin."

"Well it's not nice calling fat people fatty."

Ah, shallup yah fat lump of lard! is what I really wanted to say, but I held back from doing so, as I wanted to have a few turns at sliding down the sand dune in the old car bonnet. "You're not that fat, Martin." I added for good measure, "I've seen fatter people than you."

"Yeah? Like who?"

"The Michelin Man, for starters," I told him, after a pause. I couldn't, for the life of me, understand what I had said to upset him, but after that he refused point blank to let me have a go. And with a couple of his best friends standing at his side, convincing me he meant it, I gave up.

I'd been on the point of walking off, when I spotted the plank-sized length of driftwood lying a short distance away on the other side of the dune. It was about 7ft long and 2ft wide and wasn't all that heavy. So, I dug it out of the sand and hauled it back to the top of the dune.

Setting the plank at the edge of the sand dune, I sat on the wider part of it, before shouting across at Noddy, who was sitting inside the car bonnet ready to go down. "Last one to the bottom is a tosser," I yelled, before launching myself downwards. But my cry of "Geronimo!" turned quickly to a scream of agony!

The plank had flown down the dune at speed before coming to a sudden halt at the bottom of it. Unfortunately for me, though hilariously funny for the others, I kept sliding along the length of the driftwood and got speared by a large splinter of wood that had been protruding upwards. I attempted to get up on my feet, but was unable to, because my arse had become firmly attached to the plank. How deep the splinter was stuck inside me was anyone's guess, but to my relief the initial pain had subsided to a throb. However, every time I made the slightest move, I could feel the skin pulling away from the plank.

Feeling like a proper goon, I had to sit astride the length of driftwood as eight lads carried me up, down, and around the sandy dunes of Formby beach like an Egyptian Pharaoh being carried by his slaves. Only this lot were well and truly taking the piss.

"I knew you had a wooden head, but not a wooden arse."

"Did yah just drift together?"

"Always knew you were as thick as a plank."

Ha bloody ha. Idiots, the lot of them.

We stopped at the first house we came to and Mr Mears asked the old woman living there if she could telephone for an ambulance. She fussed over me like she was me auld Granny, bringing me out a large tumblerful of fresh, cold orange juice. I milked it for all it was worth, drinking slowly and making loud gulping noises, while the others looked on, all dry-mouthed and sweaty, having carried me for almost half a mile.

"Are you alright, mate?" was the first question one of the two ambulance men asked me. Was I alright? What a question! I'd a seven-foot plank sticking out of my backside!

"You look bored, fella," his companion quipped. "Board! Ha-ha-ha."

"I don't think the lad's twigged it, yet! Ha-ha-ha."

I couldn't believe it. The pair of them were taking the mickey! I pretended to cry, throwing out gulping, heartbroken sobs. The granny ticked off the pair of them and told me to complain about them when I arrived at the hospital. Of course, they were very remorseful, and I accepted their apologies after they agreed to give me half a crown to keep my gob shut.

There was a discussion, and lots of head scratching about how to go about detaching me from the driftwood without causing me any further injury. Then some bright spark of a nosy neighbour came rushing along with a saw in his hand, suggesting they saw it off me.

It was embarrassing enough to have all those people gawking at me as if I were a circus act. But I wasn't prepared for the moment I had to plant my feet firmly on the ground and stand there, like a bowlegged cowboy, astride a plank, while some onlookers held the weight of wood while discussing with the ambulance crew the best way to saw it off.

I was relieved when eventually they managed to saw off the plank from both ends, leaving me with a piece about a square foot still attached to me, along with the six-inch splinter. Mr Mears told me Mr Lilly would be waiting for me at the hospital. And on the way there, I reminded the two ambulance men about the half-crown they owed me, which they reluctantly paid.

Mr Lilly was indeed waiting at the hospital. I was hardly surprised to see his usual unconcerned, tight-lipped expression as he shook his head at me in dismay. But I was sure I detected a slight flinch when he saw the driftwood sticking out of my backside. This was a good sign for me and the thought suddenly jumped into my head that this was my big chance to show my courage and get my just reward.

The previous month, nine-year-old Dave Carole had broken his ankle in two places during our annual inter-house football competition. I can only assume he must have had a brainstorm if he'd thought for one second he could tackle Paddy O'Neill and get the ball off him. As mean as they came, Paddy was built like a brick shit-house and running into a brick wall would probably have caused fewer injuries than running into him.

When Carole had hopped into the assembly hall wearing the plaster-cast boot, Mr Lilly had called him out to the front to talk admiringly of how this brave young man had not uttered one single word of complaint, or shed a single tear when being treated at the hospital. What a load of old cobblers. The minute it happened, he'd been on the ground screaming and writhing all over the field like he'd been gunned down under a hail of bullets. As for no tears, the baby had cried bucketloads, so wouldn't have had a tear left in him by the time he'd got to the hospital. He also got a bag of mixed toffees for his trouble.

So, there I was, lying on the examination table, with a doctor and a nurse leaning over me, having a good gawk.

"We'll have to cut your trousers off," said the doctor. And before I even had a chance to acknowledge him, the nurse had obliged, expertly cutting them off in seconds, before cutting my undies off, too. I think they were slightly caked, but to my relief, she said nothing.

"Can you hold my hand, please?" I asked Mr Lilly, who ignored me.

"Come on, Grandad," coaxed the nurse.

"I'm not −"

"You can stand over this side, with the doctor." She stood out of Mr Lilly's way, leaving him no option but to come reluctantly to my side and hold my hand.

"Okay, Thomas. I'm just going to give this a little pull. Just to see if it will come out."

I looked straight up into Mr Lilly's eyes, making sure he could see me grit my teeth tightly.

"Can you feel any pain as I'm pulling?"

"Yes, I can," I said in a soft voice while pulling a pained expression, though I couldn't feel a thing, with the injection they'd given me having already numbed my backside. "But you can pull it straight out, if you like. I'll be brave."

"Right, I'm going to pull it out now."

I felt a slight twinge and the skin pulling, as the doctor took out the large splinter of wood. But I remained silent, as planned, looking up at Mr Lilly with my best suffering facial expression – the sort you would be expected to pull if in great pain – squeezing his hand tightly for added effect.

"There we are. It's out – two stitches ought to do it, nurse." The doctor had gone before I could even thank him.

Hardly any blood and two stitches later, I was discharged from the hospital, wearing blue and white-striped hospital-issue pyjama bottoms which the nurse had loaned me. She'd thrown my cut trousers and undies into a paper bag which she'd handed over to me, and I gladly took them, knowing the half-crown was safely tucked inside my trouser pocket. But outside the hospital, Mr Lilly suddenly snatched the bag off me and dumped it into a nearby waste bin.

"They're me favourite trousers!" I told him, promising I'd sew them back together myself if I could only keep them.

"Blithering idiot," he called me, forcing my hand off the bag and threatening to give me a good wallop and six of the best when we got back to the school if I didn't let it drop straight back into the bin.

The following day, after we'd finished the morning assembly, without a solitary word about my bravery, Mr Lilly ordered me to come along with him to his office. A large, inviting box of Black Magic chocolates lay on his desk. Jaysus, I must have been convincing, was my first thought. And I'd already set my brain in motion, trying to work out how and where I could hide such a big box of chocolates without the others seeing it and suddenly becoming my friends.

"Here." The headmaster pushed the box across the desk at me.

"I wasn't that brave, sir." A little bit of modesty goes a long way.

"What?"

"Yesterday, sir. When I was in the hospital?"

"Brave?"

"Yes, sir. When the doctor pulled that massive piece of driftwood out of me hole – bum, sir. An' you held my hand, 'cos I was in so much pain."

"Lump of wood? It was a small splinter, lad. And those funny faces you were pulling, what were those all about?"

"I was holding back the pain, sir."

"Gurning more like. Well, the less said about that the better. As I was going to say, before you interrupted, take these to Mr Mears. He's waiting outside in the van to take you along to Mrs Biggins' house. She was the kind lady who telephoned the ambulance and took care of you until they came. Run along now."

Special Friends

"What can I do for you, Rhattigan?" asked Mr Sweet.

"I've come to see if I've any pocket money, sir." I wasn't hopeful.

"Pocket money? Let me see." He pursed his lips as he ran a fat finger and a keen eye down the page of the house points ledger. "Hmm, just as I thought. You have the same as last Saturday."

"I didn't get any pocket money last Saturday, sir."

"There's a surprise." He threw me a wry smile.

Saying nothing, I closed the office door and walked off along the corridor.

"Rhattigan!" Mr Sweet's fat face was peering out from the doorway of his office. "Here, quickly. I want to have a word with you."

As I entered his office, I noticed him flick the catch of the Yale lock, which didn't bother me and I just assumed he wanted to talk to me without being disturbed.

"Sit there." He gestured to the other chair near to his desk.

I sat facing him, wondering what he wanted a word with me about. Perhaps he'd found out that Donkey and I were loosening bricks on the exterior side wall of his office, which was hidden from view by tall green shrubbery. The fact that we'd either got no pocket money at all, or just a few coppers, had prompted us to take drastic action. And so, we'd meticulously planned our daring mission to dig our way through the outside wall into his office and rob the petty cash tin.

We'd worked out that any Friday was going to be the best time to do the robbery, because it was the day when all the pocket money and petty cash was brought in from the bank, ready to be paid out on the Saturday. We'd only been able to scrape out the dry, loose mortar around the bricks when there was no one in the office, so it had taken us a couple of weeks just to loosen and remove two bricks, only to find there was an inner wall behind the outer wall. We'd worked out that, at the rate we were going, it would take us at least two or three months to remove enough bricks from both outer and inner walls so we could crawl through into the office.

"What is your problem?" asked Sweet.

"What do you mean, sir?"

"You always seem to be in some sort of trouble?"

Because you're all bullying bastards and you are always picking on me, sir! "I don't know, sir."

"You don't seem to make too many friends either. What's that all about then?"

"Don't know, sir."

"Is it because you can't make friends? Or that you just don't want to make friends?"

"Don't know, sir."

"You don't seem to know very much, do you?"

I know more than you, fatty! "No sir." I gave a nonchalant shrug, though inwardly I was ecstatic that he hadn't discovered the hole in the wall. Donkey and I had covered our tracks well and had replaced the bricks back into their original position before re-pointing the gaps with damp soil. The only way anyone would have been able to spot something amiss was if they went looking for it. And to look for it they had to know about it. And the fact that no one could possibly know about it meant they weren't looking for it, which put us in the clear!

Never let the enemy know what you know or what you are thinking, was my motto. That way, you don't have to explain yourself to anyone. I found it much easier to shrug and say "I don't know" when I wanted to avoid people attempting to get inside my head. Granted, it made me look a bit less intelligent, but people are less expectant of dimwits, which was just the way I liked it.

"You know, Rhattigan, I don't believe you are as bad or as stupid as you're made out to be." The corners of his mouth suddenly creased to form a slight smile, which was a first for him.

"I don't mean to be bad, sir."

"I believe you."

Uh? Where was this going? "Thank you, sir."

"So, if I gave you your pocket money right now, do you think you can be a good boy for me?"

"Yes sir!"

"Okay. Let's see how good a boy you can be for me." He suddenly put his dimpled hand on my bare knee and rubbed it up along my skinny thigh.

He seemed slightly nervous and I noticed a strange look pass over his face, while his eyes seemed to glaze over as his warm, sweaty hand continued to rub up and down my thigh. I felt my heart racing and an unusual thrill run down my spine, as his hand slowly crept up inside my trouser leg and fondled my goolies. I was unable to comprehend what was taking place and felt confused that it was happening. Even more confusing was the fact that I was doing nothing to stop it, as well as getting a stiffy, as I did when Mr Butterworth had done the same thing to me at Rose Hill.

"There. You see, you can be a good boy, can't you?" Sweet suddenly stood up and unzipped his trousers.

"Yes sir."

I knew what was going to happen. As well as my dim recollection of that night at summer camp with Mr Butterworth, I'd seen it happening many times between the boys at St Vincent's. Only a few days earlier, when I'd pushed open the door of what I thought was an empty toilet, I saw Tony Palmer chewing on Dave McGuire's banana-shaped mickey. A few of the older boys had tried to persuade me to let them bum me, or give them a gobble, or toss them off, but I had always resisted their advances. But now, as I watched Sweet pull out his long mickey and put it to my lips, I closed my eyes and automatically opened my mouth for him.

"That's a good boy." He moaned softly as he pushed himself deep into my mouth, moving his body in and out. And then, after what seemed like a minute or so passing, I opened my eyes but couldn't see much because his large hairy frame was pressed up to my face. I had to put a hand out to prevent myself from almost choking as he began to roughly push himself to the back of my throat.

"Just suck." He stopped moving and held a hand to the back of my head. "That's it."

He immediately began to make strange groaning noises and I had to stifle the laugh I felt rising inside me.

"Keep sucking." He pressed my head firmly into his groin and moaned even more. And that's when it suddenly dawned on me, those ghostly moans I'd heard going on in the toilet block had nothing to do with the spirit world after all. As the wave of salty liquid spurted into my mouth, I gagged and felt the tears welling up in my eyes. Sweet held my head tight into him for a few more moments before releasing his grip on me.

"This is our secret, just between me and you. Do you understand, Rhattigan?" he said as he did up his flies.

I could only nod in agreement as I attempted to swallow the taste away.

"Here." He plucked half a crown out of the money box and placed it into my hand. "You and me can be friends from now on. Do you want that?"

"Yes sir."

"And if you keep being a good boy for me, we'll get on like a house on fire, you understand what I'm saying?"

I nodded, not having the faintest idea of the consequences of my submission to him that day.

Allowed out on Saturdays to go down to the local sweetshop, I hurried out of the main gates of St Vincent's, managing to catch up with Donkey and the rest of the gang piggy-back riding along the road. Squinty Cruikshank was on

Donkey's back and Norman Butler was riding on the back of Bunter Barnes. Stuttering Pete Collins was a few yards behind them, galloping on an invisible horse and neighing loudly as he vigorously whipped it!

I was toying with the idea of telling the others about what had just taken place. But the thought was only a fleeting one. And in any case, the biggest lesson learned to date was that secrets shared were no longer secrets. Also, if I did open my gob and tell them what had happened, I was worried that they, too, would look for a way into Sweet's affections, such was our desire to be wanted and loved.

"Pete! Pete!" I called out to the horseless jockey whacking his own buttocks. Readying himself for me, Collins crouched down so I could jump on to his back and we galloped after the others.

Sting in the Tale

Every Saturday afternoon without fail, half the boys from St Vincent's would cram inside the local confectionery shop, wanting to spend all their pocket money in one go before they either lost it or had it stolen from them. That was if they hadn't already lost it or paid it out in protection monies. The other half congregated outside the shop and waited, pushing and shoving, until all the happy customers emerged with their sweets.

Mrs Appleby, grey-haired and miserable looking, stood on the other side of the counter, her eyes darting from one pair of thieving hands to another. She always held her walking stick aloft and would bring it down on anyone she thought might be pilfering from her. A big sign in the shop window, which, oddly enough, only ever went up on Saturdays, warned:

ALL CHILDREN MUST HAVE THEIR SPENDING MONEY IN THEIR HANDS BEFORE ENTERING THIS SHOP!

This, according to her, was to give us no good reason to be putting our hands into our pockets until we'd paid and were back outside.

Old Mr Appleby was always at the other end of the counter, weighing up the orders from the large jars of loose sweets on display. He was always cheerful and rightfully so, if the rumour was true that he had fixed the shop scales to give us fewer sweets per ounce, to compensate for the likelihood of us stealing their goods.

Rhubarb and Custard sweets were my favourites, with white Bon-Bons coming a close second. I helped myself to a jar of each and squeezed my way through the mob, pushing back outside amongst the other group waiting to come in.

Luckily for me, I'd quickly spotted the Panda car and the two policemen standing by it before I had pushed myself right out into the open, where I could have been caught red-handed. I pondered how I was going to get out of this one, and there were only two options open to me: either to slip back inside the shop and put the jars of sweets back on to the shelf, which probably would be the best thing to do, or take my chances and make a run for it.

As I wasn't particularly bothered about doing the right thing, the only viable option was to make a run for it. But then another thought suddenly sprung to mind, prompted by the sighting of the ginger-haired idiot and biggest snitcher, Michael Burke.

He was standing just a couple of feet away with his back to me. Leaning over the shoulder of the unsuspecting moron, I dropped the jar of bon-bons into his hands, which automatically closed around it, bringing a wide smile to his face. The smile immediately vanished when I gave him an almighty shove and he stumbled out into the open. As the two coppers closed in on him, I took my opportunity to walk off up the road unnoticed, with my jar of Rhubarb and Custard sweets tucked up under my jumper. The jabbering snitch, meanwhile, attempted to convince the two coppers that it was someone else who'd handed the sweets to him, though he hadn't seen who the culprit was. As if they were going to believe that!

Crossing over the main road further on up, I noticed the police car set off in my direction. I dropped the jar into the grassy undergrowth and stood watching as the cop driving the car gave me a quick once-over. I could see Burke sitting in the back with his freckly red face pressed right up against the window. He peered sadly across at me with his grotesque tearful face and I waved him on his way with a wide grin spread right across mine. Hanging around at the edge of the farmer's field, waiting for the rest of the gang to get their sweets, I didn't feel an ounce of remorse about Burke: he had snitched on us all so often and he had got what was coming to him.

Taking our usual slow walk along the edge of the ploughed field, we made our way along the wide pathway running along the back of the Approved School. This path was out of bounds to us, with a loss of a week's privileges for anyone caught down there. But every Saturday we would take the shortcut and climb over the flint wall, dropping down into the vegetable gardens where, keeping low, we would make our way past the large greenhouses to the century-old brick-built stables, which were being used to store all sorts of old garden machinery.

Inside, we sat around and shared out a selection of our goodies before hiding the remainder of our loot in our usual place, behind some old rusting machinery.

"Ouch! I've been stung by a fuckin' wasp!" cried squinty Cruickshank, holding his bare leg just below his short trousers, where we could see the sting already causing the skin to swell.

"Look, there's a nest of them." Donkey pointed towards a large pile of old fruit boxes. "Most of them look half dead, they're all dopey." Whoosh! The idiot started swatting the odd wasp with an old bamboo cane.

"Don't hit them," I warned him, "or yah'll have the whole lot after us."

Too late. "Ouch! Ughh! Ahh!" cried Donkey, the last out of the shed, as the swarm of supposedly half-dead wasps chased after us. Fortunately for the rest of us, Donkey didn't follow us, but instead ran off in the opposite direction, leading the wasps away so we could make our escape, with only Bates and Cruickshank getting the odd sting.

A little while later, as we sat around in the recreation room, we could hear a low sobbing approaching along the corridor, before the overpowering whiff of TCP hit our nostrils. Donkey suddenly appeared in the doorway, aided by Matron. He seemed lost in a world of his own, as he walked painfully into the room. And if I hadn't already known he'd been attacked by a swarm of wasps, I'd probably have assumed from the state of his red, swollen face that he'd spontaneously burst out in either chickenpox or acne.

He cried out in pain as Matron gently sat him down on the wooden chair.

"Keep an eye on him," she said. "And if he gets any worse, or you think he might be going into shock, let somebody know right away." She talked to the room, and not to any individual, leaving it to everybody to take on the responsibility. Not that anyone was likely to have been paying much attention to her.

It reminded me of the tale my Uncle Oliver had once told us, on one of his many visits to Stamford Street, when some of us were arguing about whose turn it was to bring up the coal from the cellar. "There were four soldiers called Anybody, Somebody, Everybody and Nobody. There was an important task to be done and Everybody was given the task to do it. When asked why the task hadn't been carried out, Everybody blamed Somebody when Nobody did what Anybody could have done." The moral of the story: make sure you ask someone specific to take responsibility.

Not only had Matron not done this, she hadn't even explained to us precisely what sort of shock we should be looking out for. I couldn't imagine him looking any more shocked: did we look for lightning to come out of his fingertips? Would his hair stand up on end? Were we allowed to touch him if these things happened? I'd heard you could die of shock if you touched somebody who was dead or dying of shock.

"If he looks different, or you think he is acting unusual, just let a member of the staff know," Matron instructed the room before trotting off in her high-heeled shoes. Since looking different and acting unusual came naturally to Donkey, I couldn't see how this would give any of us reason to be alarmed.

Within a minute of Matron's departure from the recreation room, everyone else drifted off outside. I did feel sorry for Donkey and sat with him for a minute or two. But my attempts to pacify him were doomed to failure. I asked him if he knew how many times he'd been stung by the wasps and he responded by upping the noise. I eventually got fed up with the sound of his constant Donkey sobs, even though he hadn't a tear in his eyes, and I left him to wallow in his own self-pity while I went out to the playground.

No Smoke Without Fire

The next morning, Donkey was still smarting from the wasp stings, though his face didn't seem as puffy. And the blank expression in his eyes seemed to be back to its normal state. The sobbing had also stopped, so things were looking up for the lot of us. It had been so bad on the Saturday night, Paddy O'Neil had rushed into our dormitory, swearing on his mother's and father's lives, including all his other family and relatives, that if we didn't shut his gob up, he was going to throw Donkey out of the window.

There was nothing else we could do but take desperate measures, we put a folded blanket underneath each back leg of Donkey's bed. And then, lifting the front legs off the ground, we managed to slide him quietly out of the dormitory and down along the polished corridor into the bathhouse, leaving him, and everyone else, in peace. It hadn't been too difficult to convince the morning staff that, although he had no memory of it, Donkey had pushed the bed down to the bathhouse of his own accord.

It was my idea that led to Donkey setting fire to the stable block. I'd suggested to him he could have his revenge on the wasps by smoking them out of their nest. This, I thought, would make them dopier than they already were, which, in turn, would make them a much easier target for Donkey to whip to his heart's content.

"Okay. Light the match and put it to the end of this," I said, holding up the oily old piece of hessian sacking I'd found over in the corner of the shed. Donkey lit it and I blew out the flame, then handed the smouldering sacking to him. "Gently put it down between them boxes and quickly scarper back outside. It should only take a few minutes ta smoke the feckers out, if there's any still in there."

Having waited outside for a short while, Collins and I stayed put while Donkey went back into the stable block to see what was happening. Moments later, we could hear the whooshing sounds of his cane cutting the air, along with the sound of his demented, gleeful laughter. Walking to the open doorway, we stood looking in as he whacked out at the slightest thing that moved, prodding, slashing and then stamping his foot down on his prey.

"Ouch! Yah bastard!" he suddenly yelped in pain before dropping the cane, stung on his whipping hand. We were in stitches as we watched him frantically flailing his hands and feet about, while a few wasps chased him in a circle. Then the gormless idiot accidentally kicked one of the boxes housing the wasps' nest.

"R-r-r-run!' Collins stuttered the warning as a swarm of wasps flew out of the smoke like a squadron of Spitfires coming out of the clouds. I didn't wait for a second warning, taking flight up along the old pathway in the direction of the football pitch, with Collins just a few yards behind me.

We lay down, hiding behind the trunk of a large tree, waiting for Donkey to appear. But when there was no sign of him after a couple of minutes, we decided to go back and see what had happened to him. Probably killed by the shock of being stung all over again, was my first thought.

"W-w-what's that sm-sm-smell?" asked Collins.

"It smells like petrol. Shit! Donkey, yah dopy eejit yah! Don't strike a match! Ah feck!"

We saw the yellow flame flash out of the open doors, before Donkey came rushing out and up along the path towards us. "I set them alight," he laughed gleefully. "I got them all!"

"Jaysus, yer hair! We'd better get away from here before someone catches us," And, for the life of me, I couldn't get the picture of an orang-utan out of my head, as Donkey, with all his hair singed and now a lighter shade of ginger, hurried alongside me. We made our way up along the length of the boundary wall, which, fortunately for us, was hidden by the trees and high undergrowth.

Once we had made it nearer to the school block, I told Collins to sneak out of the undergrowth and join some of the other lads playing in that area, before taking Donkey further along. And once we'd moved past the classroom block, we slipped out unnoticed from the cover of the trees and started kicking around a discarded football.

"Jaysus Donkey, yea'll have ta get rid of them singed hairs, otherwise you're going to get sussed. Keep yer head down and follow me," I ordered.

With Donkey almost tripping over my heels, I made my way into the building and hurried along the narrow corridor to the nearest stairway, heading straight up them. "Will yah stop the laughin' for feck's sake! If yer caught ye'll probably be jailed for the rest of yer life," I warned him. "Go to the bathhouse and I'll meet yah there in a minute."

I stood watching as he lurched off like an excited ape, probably with no thoughts at all as to the seriousness of his situation. And why should he? He hadn't the capacity in his brain to know the difference between wrong and right. Most people treated him as a bad person, when all I saw was a sad, kind and gentle lunatic.

Off in the distance I could hear the sirens getting closer and guessed it must have been the fire brigade, which could only have meant the fire must have taken a good hold of the wooden boxes piled up inside. With little time to spare, I rushed into the night watchman's room and grabbed his shaving kit, before heading back along the corridor to the bathhouse.

"There's loads of smoke," said Donkey, pointing out through the small window at the large plume of black smoke streaking across the damp sky.

"That must be the old oil from the machinery. Here, stick this around your neck." I handed him the towel and then turned on the hot water, rubbing the shaving brush into the soap before slopping the foam I'd made all over his face. It took me a matter of a minute to run the shaver up, down and around his face, shaving off all his facial hair, with him only giving out the once, when I slightly nicked his top lip and he thought he was going to bleed to death.

"Close yer eyes."

"Why?"

"I need ta shave them brows off."

"Why?"

"Cos they're singed is why."

A sight for sore eyes would be an understatement. With his eyes squeezed tightly shut and his lips pouting, if I'd had to guess what the missing link might have looked like, I wouldn't have had to look much further than Donkey. The poor fella. He had nothing going for him. And yet he was funny and warm, and very rarely had a bad word to say about anybody. It seemed most of the people at the school scorned his simplicity. But if the whole world had been as simple as him, what a wonderful world it could be.

"Let's get a look at yah!" I'd trimmed his hair with the razor, perhaps overdoing it a little. "If anyone asks about the patches, just say your hair fell out, okay?" Jaysus! The sight of him! Well, they could accuse him of being an ugly fecker, but not for starting any fire – now there was no evidence. "Come on. We'd better get outside before we're missed. You go, while I put this lot back where they came from." I swilled and dried off the shaving kit before returning it back on the sink unit inside the night watchman's room.

Mr Lilly wasn't impressed with us, as we stood to attention in the assembly hall the following Monday morning. As far as he was concerned, we were going to stand there for a long while, and in silence, until the culprit or culprits owned up to setting the stable block alight. So, it looked as if we were going to be standing on parade forever.

Granted, the majority of the lads in the approved school looked a bunch of complete idiots, but Lilly treating us like the idiots we may have looked like, by telling us he was already aware who the culprits were and how he was just giving them an opportunity to own up before he named them, was even more idiotic. And if he seriously thought we were idiotic enough to believe him, then he was a bigger idiot.

His squinty eyes scanned the sea of nonchalant-looking faces staring back at him and then paused on mine for the briefest of moments, causing my heart to almost jump up into my mouth. I was sure he was about to say something to me, but instead his gaze moved past me to settle on Donkey.

"He's looking at me," whispered Donkey from the side of his mouth.

"Just ignore him," I whispered.

Jaysus, I couldn't believe what I was seeing. Donkey had stuck his head right out from his shoulders and was gawking at the headmaster in such a peculiar way, with his dark eyes staring out from beneath his hairless, furrowed brows. I was on the point of bursting out laughing and wanted to avert my gaze, but I just couldn't help looking at the expression on Mr Lilly's face.

"Who is that creature?" he asked Mr Marron.

"Carey, sir," said Marron, recognising Donkey without any difficulty.

Mr Lilly shook his head in bewilderment, before letting his gaze continue along the line. "Right!" he clasped his hands behind his back and rocked on the heels of his shoes. "All privileges are lost for two whole weeks."

"Ooh!" was the communal shocked response.

"Never mind, ooh. You can blame the culprit or culprits, who obviously believe they are man enough to set fire to buildings, but not man enough to own up to it. Now, I am willing to accept this could have been an accident. After all, accidents can and often do happen. So, come on! If it was an accident we can deal with it right now and get it over and done with, without further ado." The biggest non-believer in accidents ever happening now wanted us to own up to one.

I recalled how he'd once given me six of the best when I'd hit the large glass lightshade above the snooker table with the snooker cue and the whole unit came crashing down, splintering into hundreds of tiny pieces all over the show. "I didn't mean to do it, sir." I'd told him it had been a complete accident, explaining how I'd only raised the cue to hit Brian Walters on the head with it because he was making fun of me.

"How can you not mean to do something you did?" he bellowed, before whipping me with the cane and stopping my pocket money for two weeks.

"Sir." My arm shot up in the air and all eyes, including Donkey's, suddenly fixed on me.

"I might have guessed you were behind this." The headmaster glared at me. "Behind what, sir."

"The fire, lad."

"I didn't start any fire sir."

"You've just admitted it."

"No, I didn't sir."

"Don't answer the headmaster back," snapped Marron.

"But I only wanted ta ask a question sir."

"About what?"

"Well, sir. Why do we all have ta be punished, sir?"

"Because you're all tarred with the same brush, that's why!" Lilly went red in the face.

"But what if it wasn't any of us, sir?"

"Are you suggesting the stable block set fire to itself?"

"No sir. I meant, it could have been any of them boys from the village, sir. They're always climbing up on the wall and calling us names and threatening to set the school alight. It could only have been them, sir."

"I've seen them, sir!" Johnny Priestley suddenly threw his hand in the air and backed up my lie. This seemed to be the cue for lots of the other boys to stick up their hands and swear blind they'd also seen, at one time or another, these imaginary boys of mine. On the wall. Climbing over the wall. Stealing our vegetables from the garden nursery. Stealing our footballs, and so on.

"And they are always smoking fags, sir," I added for good measure.

"Shut up!" Incensed, the headmaster stormed out of the assembly hall without playing one of his classical records. A first for us.

Heaven and Hell

As we lined up for classes, Mr Marron went about picking the boys he was going to take to Southport for swimming lessons.

"Me sir! Please sir!" We raised our hands and jostled each other in the hope he would notice us. But I missed out again. I'd already won a certificate for swimming 25 metres some months back, and I'd been looking forward to pushing on for the 50 metres, as well as the life-saving certificate. But it didn't look as if it was going to happen any time soon.

"Rhattigan, Cuthbert and… O'Connor, you're on today's work-party," Mr Sweet suddenly informed us. And although I was disappointed not to be going swimming, I was happy to escape woodwork lessons. Not that I minded doing woodwork. And we all got on well with Mr Palmer, the woodwork teacher. But given the choice, I'd rather have been outside sweeping up dead leaves, or tending to the rabbits and the chickens in the pets' corner, instead of making sorry-looking wooden fruit bowls and tiny wooden stools with seats made from coloured canvas strips to take home to our Mammies and Daddies. Sure, you couldn't even sit on them without your knees touching your ears! The stools were a complete waste of time, unless you were a midget. And I'm sure most of us hadn't seen a bowl of fruit in our lives.

While the lads not going swimming or on outside work duties marched off to the woodwork class, Cuthbert and O'Connor were sent to the front of the school to sweep up the falling leaves from the long driveways. I followed Mr Sweet out through the side door of the school block and across the yard, to the pets' corner, where I began the task of cleaning out the hens and feeding them, before moving on to the three rabbits.

We had eight large hens, a huge, sex-mad cockerel called Dick, and three tiny bantam hens and a small cockerel called Buster. They all shared the same space and, unlike us, got on well together. There was the occasional fight between the two cockerels when Dick, who strutted around the place like he owned the whole show, attempted to hump the bantams. Not that he could stay perched on their tiny backs for more than a second before they would collapse under his weight.

The moment anyone climbed into their pen, Dick would charge, flapping his wings and pecking at your feet and legs. I had tried to make friends with him, attempting to hand-feed the vicious sod while he did his usual war dance around me or whoever else dared to trespass onto his land. But the ungrateful bird was having none of it and would peck at my fingers. I'd usually give him the odd boot up the backside and he'd run off for a good think about it, before charging in for another go.

"You like looking after the animals, don't you?" I'd not been aware of Mr Sweet, who was leaning on the large wooden gate, watching me.

"I love them."

"It's a good thing to be loved, isn't it?" he said, giving me a rare smile.

"Don't know," I shrugged.

"What about your parents? I see you haven't been home to visit them, why?"

"Don't know." I shrugged again. "Because they don't want me, I suppose. I'm not bothered though."

"Why not?"

What a stupid question to ask. For starters, why would I want to go back home to a mammy and daddy who couldn't care less about me? Why would I want to go back to a squalid, dark damp dump of a house, where the only sounds of laughter and songs came from the drunks who sang and laughed, and pissed themselves to their hearts' content to escape from the reality they didn't want to be living in? Why would I want to walk back into that life, not knowing where the next meal was coming from or when it would come? Or the next set of clothing? Or the next beating, or worse? What I missed about home – my brothers and sisters – had very little to do with my parents.

"Don't know."

"Here." He offered me a small pack of Spangles. And without questioning why he was giving them to me, I took them out of his outstretched hand and quickly shoved the pack of fruit sweets into my trouser pocket.

"Have you spoken to anyone about that Saturday?"

"No sir. You said it was a secret."

"It is." He smiled again. "Our secret. So, it seems nobody loves little Tommy Rhattigan, then?"

"Jesus and Mary love me."

"Come on, I want to show you something. It'll only take a couple of minutes, you can finish what you're doing later."

I followed Mr Sweet through into the small room at the side of the pets' corner, where we stored our work shoes and football boots. He unlocked another door leading into a narrow corridor, before re-locking it.

I had a feeling he was going to do to me what he'd done a few Saturdays before and I wasn't looking forward to it. The first time was horrible and had me retching. I didn't want to do it, but what could I do if he wanted me to? He'd been a lot better towards me for a while and I'd rather it stayed that way. Before we had our little secret, the vicious bully, a right bastard to all of us, used to always single me out. Therefore, I was prepared to do whatever it took to stop things going back to how it had been before.

I was so weary of my life there. I hated having to wake up every morning to be bossed and pushed around by the tough-nuts of the school, who basically ran the whole show and would think nothing of giving you a good beating merely for saying the wrong word or looking the wrong way at them. I was tired of having to put an arm around my plate to protect my food in case some greedy fecker decided he wanted it. I was tired of not being able to trust anyone who approached me with their friendship. Or those offering me their protection – so long as I did something for them, which was usually for their sexual pleasure, "just the once".

And then there was the name-calling. Sticks 'n' stones can break your bones, but words can never hurt you, goes the saying.

Well they feckin' can! And they did. Piss the Bed. Wall Talker. Homo. Ugly bastard. The doctor slapped your mother when you were born. Your Granny is on the game. Day after day after day. Someone would always attempt to bring you down, one way or another. There was always someone wanting to prove he was bigger, tougher and better than you. And while I could always admit that I was weaker than a lot of the boys there, I was fortunate that I had my group of so-called friends (weaklings admittedly), who helped to keep one another relatively safe.

I had often wondered what it would be like to be dead. Father Tierney said when we die we would either go to heaven or hell, depending on how we have lived our lives whilst on this earth. Helping others, being obedient, and giving our lives up to God were just a few examples of how God would like us to be. That didn't bode well for the nuns!

"Heaven, as opposed to the burning flames of Hell, is a tranquil paradise, with no wars, or famine, or pain, nor want for anything," he'd preached to us. "It's a place where the spirits of the faithful departed can roam freely at their leisure. And if any of you manage to make it up there, you will find those dearly departed members of your families who glorified in the name of Our Glorious Redeemer waiting at the gates of Heaven with open arms to greet you." This, in effect, ruled out a big family reunion for me. And if Hell was as he described it, a good few of them would certainly be feeling the heat.

I wished I could be in heaven. Even though I hadn't always seen eye to eye with God, especially when he never answered my prayers, I was sure I'd be much happier there. But to be there would mean I'd have to be dead. How could I die? I couldn't kill myself. Father-bloody-Tierney put paid to that!

"It is an original sin to commit suicide," he told us. "And anyone that does won't be going to Heaven, for sure."

So, it looked as if I'd just have to wait patiently until the Almighty decided when he wanted to give me the call-up. There was always a catch!

I followed Mr Sweet into a small room full of old gym equipment. Closing the door behind us, he turned the small brass catch to lock it.

"Here, come and stand on this." He pointed to the long wooden bench running alongside a couple of the wooden horses and I did what he asked without any hesitation. I wasn't afraid or nervous as I stood, almost level with him, and he suddenly started rubbing his podgy hand on the inside of my bare leg and underneath the trouser leg to my groin area.

"You like that. Don't you?"

I felt slightly embarrassed as I nodded, because he could obviously feel my mickey was going stiff, like last time. I hadn't wanted it to happen, it just happened of its own accord.

"Love works both ways Rhattigan – I give you love and you give me love in return. And we both keep it a secret between us."

"Yes, sir."

He was so quick my trousers and undies were down around my ankles before I had even taken in the full impact of what was happening. He was fiddling with me and I was enjoying it. "Can I not swallow it this time, sir." I had anticipated his next move, hoping he wouldn't be angry at me and make me do it again. But I needn't have worried. He told me to turn right around and gently held me on the bench, telling me to reach out across to the vaulting horse.

"That it. That's a good lad."

Doing as he asked, I leaned forwards across the leather top of the box. I could hear and feel his warm quick breaths on my neck, as he started to rub his fingers around my backside, before poking a finger inside me. "Shhh. Relax, it isn't going to hurt." He tried pushing himself into me, but it was too big to go in. "Open your legs wider and relax."

I did what he'd asked and could feel him persisting in pushing himself into me, but it still wouldn't go in and he stopped for a moment. I looked out through the dusty glass of the small four-paned window, where I could just about make out the empty swings, unmoving in the stillness. I could smell dubbin, the waxy oil we put on the leather footballs to stop them from drying out. And then I could feel him slowly entering me. It felt uncomfortable, but he was being gentle, whispering to me about loving me and asking if I liked being loved by him. I nodded my acceptance of the love he was giving to me, even though I didn't understand what love really meant, or why he'd chosen to love me.

As he continued to move himself in and out of me, he was still playing with my mickey. But my thoughts were preoccupied with the big spider on its dusty web, which was hanging down in the top left-hand corner of the window reveal. It was dead of course, dried out and mummified, to my relief. I didn't know why I was afraid of spiders, to the point of hating them. It's not as if they had done me any harm. I felt brave enough to blow in its direction and see both spider and its web move as one in their everlasting dance of death, and I couldn't help but wonder how long it might have lain here undisturbed, until we had come along.

Mr Sweet was making strange noises, like last time, and I was holding myself back from giggling. And then I had this strange, thrilling sensation rising inside me, which I had never felt before. My knees buckled as the overwhelming thrill surged straight up from my goolies and through the rest of my body, causing me to involuntarily give out a loud sigh. He murmured a few words, which I didn't understand, before he pushed himself right into me, staying close and still for a moment or so, before moving away.

"Get yourself cleaned up," he said, and I pulled up my trousers and pants, while he opened the door to the storeroom and then unlocked the door leading back into the boot-room. Weak-kneed, shaken and a little dizzy, I scampered off to the outside toilets.

A Strange Kind of Caring

The second week of September 1966, we were up in the Lake District on our annual summer camp. We'd travelled up in the four vans belonging to the school, with the hired lorry carrying the tents and all the other camping equipment, following closely behind us.

I had a lot of different thoughts going on inside my head at the time and I was finding it difficult to make any sense of them, let alone describe them. My emotions seemed to be all over the place, and I just couldn't seem to concentrate on any given subject, which made it even more difficult to understand what was happening to me. I cried a lot, when I could get a private moment, never daring to cry in front of other people, which would have been a sign of weakness. There was no obvious reason to why I should be crying. I didn't feel sad. And yet the pain I felt in my heart when I was crying was truly agonising at times.

Despite my habitual frown, which made me look like a miserable sod, even when I wasn't, I believe I was as happy as I knew how to be. I laughed and joked around and I accepted, without question, most of the things that had happened and were still happening to me. I'm not saying things couldn't have been much better. But I was aware just how bad things could have been.

I still missed my brothers, and sisters. And there wasn't a day or a night when I hadn't prayed and asked Jesus to protect them from harm's way. I would get very emotional when I thought about the possibility of them getting hurt in some way, with me not there to help them. I never thought I could have survived so long without my brother Martin, who was always at my side. But having no choice in the matter, I'd simply had to get on without him, having to stand alone and fight my own battles in the best way that I could. And though these physical battles were few and far between, I did seem to get injured in most of them. I'd had to acknowledge the fact that the aggressive streak I carried on the streets of Manchester was never going to be enough to see me through in this place. So I'd had to learn to assert a more intense aggression about me, even if it was mainly bluff, so any likely bullies might have second thoughts about having a go at me. Most of my adversaries were psychologically and physically aggressive, with taunting and unfair use of their feet and heads meant to inflict maximum pain. Whereas I, on the other hand, was minded not to sink as low as them, preferring instead to use only my fists. I knew I still had a long way to go before I could match the others, but when I eventually got there, woe betide you, Brian Walters!

I would often find myself thinking about those many journeys I'd taken with Martin and the others around the towns and small villages of Manchester, where we got up to all sorts of mischief. I remembered one time we'd strayed too far from home and were unable to find our way back in the dark. When we happened upon an old stone barn, we'd decided to spend the night inside. It had ponged a bit, but we were used to stinky smells, so it hadn't really put us off making ourselves at home in the large pile of dry hay, where we'd soon drifted off into a deep sleep.

I awoke in the early hours of the morning to strange grunting noises, which I'd first assumed was one of the others, until I saw they were all awake and that we were in the company of pigs. All nine of them, roaming freely around the barn. Martin and I took a gander outside the open door, where we could see the back of the farm cottage, some 20 or so yards away. The aroma of fried bacon hit our nostrils as it wafted out through the open window of the cottage in our direction.

"I've an idea," said Martin. Jaysus, not another one! I stood watching as he hurried back inside the barn, coming out moments later, a rope around the neck of a pig happily trotting behind him.

"Yer not expectin' us ta tow that ting all the way home, are yah?"

"Don't be daft, Tommy, come on." He ambled past me with the pig following behind him.

"There's the door," he said, throwing a knowing nod towards the back door of the cottage.

"And?" I queried, looking at him a little bemused.

"Knock on it, then."

"I'm not knocking on there! We'll be kilt for sure."

"Ah, bollocks." Martin did the knocking, before taking a backwards step.

In a matter of seconds, the old door had swung inwards and we were confronted by a giant of a man. I didn't know how tall he was, but I'd say if Martin, Bernie and I had stood on one another's shoulders, we probably wouldn't have come up to his eyes. He was a frightening sight, with untidy, greyish-black hair and a bushy beard to match, as he stood gawking down on us.

"What's that you have there?" he asked, eyeing the pig.

"A pig," said Martin.

"I can see it's a pig," smiled the big fella. "Anyone that knows what a pig looks like can see that's definitely a pig you have in tow there."

"We found it, didn't we, Tommy?"

"Where? I mean, we did that. We were coming up the road last night…"

"Dis mornin' it was," Martin cut in. "We were walking along mindin' our own business when we saw the pig escapin' and we decided to catch it and bring it back, so we did."

"Well that was very kind of you," said the big fellow. "I suppose you'll be wanting a bacon sandwich as a reward?"

"We weren't expectin' a reward −"

"Yes please!" I shouted above Martin.

"Well you'd best come in then."

"Bernie! Nabby!" I called out to my brother and sister. "Where do yah want us ta tie the pig?"

"She never leaves the yard, so you can leave her where she is." The big man turned his back and walked into the kitchen and we followed.

It only seemed like yesterday when we were all together, laughing and joking, singing and crying and getting up to all sorts of mischief. I couldn't help but wonder if we would ever see one another again. I'd often conjure up all sorts of images in my mind's eye of what Hulme might look like now, and what, if anything, was now standing on the site where our home had once stood. Another house? A shop? A new road? Or was it still the empty space Martin and I had stood mournfully over, when we went back and found the surrounding streets were no longer there?

Thinking of my siblings always reminded me of how lucky I had been to have had them, even for such a short time. More so, because I had such fond memories to fall back on when I was feeling lonely.

I couldn't for the life of me fathom out what made some of the boys I was forced to live alongside tick. Some were so carefree in the cruelty they inflicted upon others, for no good reason other than to prove they could do it. I had only ever held my ground trying to protect myself, never once setting out to deliberately antagonise or inflict pain on any of my peers. And yet, here in this former lunatic asylum, now run by the Catholic Church and the Nugent Care Society (a charity – the abuse here was all free), it seemed inflicting cruelty upon a weaker opponent was accepted as the norm – not only by the kids, but by adults, too. Why? What makes a child want to be cruel to another child? What makes an adult want to inflict cruelty on a child?

I didn't have the answers. But I did know what it was like to be subjected to cruelty from my own father and I'm sure many of my peers at the school had experienced the same. But surely this could not be a reason for a child to want to inflict pain on another child. I would have thought it should be the opposite. And yet it was a fact of my life at St Vincent's, all part of the learning process. And by Christ, I was learning very quickly!

It was nearly a year since Sister Ignatius and her coven had left St Vincent's. The time seemed to have flown by much more quickly than the previous year. The nuns were now a distant memory, though we still had the odd one or two popping up now and again to join us for Sunday Mass. My reading and writing were improving all the time, though I'd still a way to go before I got on to the Janet and John books. But the fact that I was able to read and write some words had opened up a whole new world to me. I'd even learnt to spell a couple of words off by heart: Mississippi was my best and, even more impressively, I could spell it backwards, too. And then there was the other word, "bastard", which, on the odd occasion, I could call another lad if I had good cause to, by scrawling it in big letters across their schoolwork, without them knowing it was me.

I'd also noticed how I had unconsciously drifted further away from the companionship of my closest friends, like Donkey, Bunter Barnes, Stuttering Pete Collins and the others in the group. And although I still hung out with them on occasions, especially in our many war games on the beaches, I often had an urge to be on my own. I'd felt that way for a long while, though I didn't really know why. Perhaps I felt I no longer needed them, or the protection I'd had from the group, now that I had Mr Sweet as my protector. It could even have been an age thing. Some of the boys mentioned that Matron had told them it was "an age change" after they'd gone to see her about their personal matters. I too had noticed this age thing in myself, spotting the few dark pubic hairs sprouting around my private parts. And of course, I was proud of them, keeping a close eye on their progress and taking a hair count almost every day, with another two growing after about six weeks. I also began to experience wet dreams, which some lads still thought meant pissing the bed! And I'd spend ages in the toilet flogging the bishop to bring about that thrill feeling I got (though taking an age) when Mr Sweet was playing with me.

My time with Mr Sweet could never compare to what had taken place at Rose Hill Remand Centre, with Mr Butterworth and the stranger. There was no affection or promises then. Nor did I feel any more special to them than any of the other boys. With Mr Sweet, it was different. He told me I was special to him and he was keen to show me, at every opportunity he could get, with repeated warnings never to mention what was going on between us, to anyone. Otherwise he would have to stop loving me and I'd also be in serious trouble.

As big as he was, it was truly amazing how he could be such a different person when he was being gentle with me. This was in contrast from the slaps, knees and the punches he used to give me to get his message across – and which he still did to the other boys. Besides letting me have my full pocket money each week, despite being docked most of it from my weekly points chart, he brought me in the odd bag of sweets, or a small toy. More importantly, if I had any problems from any of the other boys, all I needed to do was tell him and he'd have a quiet word in their ears, without mentioning the fact that it was me who'd snitched on them.

I had willingly committed to giving myself to him, in return for him treating me differently from the others. Though I did sometimes feel guilty because I didn't have anything to offer him in return for the attention he gave to me.

Camping with the Devil

We reached the Lake District by mid-afternoon. Not surprisingly, it was raining, just like last year. Not that it bothered us, though the grown-ups – Mr Alston, Mr Sweet, Mr Keenan and the headmaster – seemed rather pissed off about it.

Rain or shine, I loved being in the Lake District. I'd been looking forward to coming back since the previous year, when I cried as we left. I always felt most at home in that vast wilderness of the mountain ranges, which brought to the surface all sorts of emotions deep within me. And if I were given the choice, I would gladly have stayed there and become a part of the serene landscape.

Mr Lilly informed us he was to be the camp's skipper for the first week, with Mr Alston taking over the helm in the second week, when he would be leaving to go off on his holidays to Rome. He told us he'd planned many exciting hiking trips and adventures for us. Though how exciting these really were remained to be seen. The most exciting thing that could happen would be for him to topple off the side of a mountain and give us all some peace! He went on, taking us through the usual boring safety rules and all the dos and the don'ts, which he read from a book on camping. And then we spent the rest of the day setting up the campsite in a field surrounded by high mountains.

First to go up were the 11 army surplus tents, eight of which slept six boys in each. The remainder were for the staff, with Mr Lilly having one for himself. Next, we pitched up the huge marquee, which seemed to take an age, before we finally hammered home the large wooden peg securing the last guy-rope. Finally, we erected the four toilet tents, which were always kept about 200 yards downwind from the main campsite. These would be emptied every day by the four lads picked for that day's toilet duties.

The school's brass ARP bell rang out, echoing across the fields, to let us know it was teatime. We had sausages and beans, with a special treat of greasy fried bread, all washed down with a pint-sized tin mug of hot sweet tea. Once we'd eaten and cleared up, we sat around the large campfire, wasting a few precious hours singing boring songs, such as "Old McDonald Had a Farm", "Ten Green Bottles", and "One Man went to Mow". Then Mr Lilly began to tell us one of his boring ghost stories about a mysterious man. If he'd wanted to scare us to death, it didn't work. At least not for me.

I'd been fast asleep in our tent when Paul Riley woke the lot of us up. He was crying for his Granny, who'd died a few weeks earlier.

"I wish you'd feck off and join yer Granny!" snapped Terry Pritchard, one of the four school prefects.

I climbed out of my warm sleeping bag and went over to Riley, kneeling on the ground next to him.

"What's the matter with yah?"

"I want my Granny."

"She's in Heaven."

"I know. But I miss her."

"She's dead, yah daft bastard," snapped Pritchard.

"I'm scared," said Riley.

"Ah, take no notice of Pritchard. He's all mouth."

"I mean, I'm scared of the ghost."

"What ghost?" He had me looking around the tent.

"The one in the haunted lift."

"The liftman in the story?"

"Yeh."

"I wouldn't be botherin' about him," I said. "Mr Lilly makes these stories up as he goes along. Anyways, we don't have a lift in the field, do we?"

"I never thought of that." Riley, seemingly calmer, climbed out of his sleeping bag.

"Where are yah going?" I asked.

"The bog."

"Careful the Bogeyman don't get yah!"

"Fuck off Pritchard!" snapped Riley.

"Come on, I'll watch out for yah," I offered.

It was almost pitch black, with just a flicker of light from the moon peering through the swiftly moving clouds. Somewhere in the distance, I could hear some sheep bleating, along with the noise Riley was making as he took a pee up the back of the tent, which gave me the urge to go myself.

"What's that?" Riley suddenly called out, causing me to jump and pee down the leg of my pyjamas.

"What's what?" I hurried around to the back of the tent.

"Them!" He pointed a finger into the darkness. "Them pair of eyes!"

"Jaysus, it's the Devil, run!' I let out a girly scream as the large set of evil green eyes headed towards us.

Riley, the coward, pushed his way past me. But in his rush to get away, he managed to trip over one of the guy-ropes. Stepping over his prone body, I scrambled in through the small opening with Riley close behind me. "Is it the Devil?" I whispered to him.

"I don't know. I've never seen the devil til tonight."

"Did yah see them huge green eyes – Jaysus!" I felt my heart suddenly jump in my mouth as something big pushed firmly against the side of the tent. "Sssh, he's just outside!"

"What the feck's goin' on?" Pritchard had suddenly woken up.

"Sssh! It's the Devil!" I whispered.

"Do yah think I'm feckin' stupid or somethin'? Yah pair of – what's that noise outside?"

"The Devil," said Riley, as we heard the heavy snorts outside the tent.

"He followed us," I said.

"Who followed you?" questioned Pritchard.

"The divil. That's who."

"Why?"

"I didn't tink ta fecking ask him!"

"I want me Mammy!" Pritchard whimpered like a baby who'd just had his doll snatched.

"Shush the feck up. Or he'll know we're in here," I warned.

The other three boys in the tent were now awake and wanting to know what was going on.

"The Devil's outside the tent!" cried Pritchard, creating a panic.

"Gather around me," I advised. "It's safer in numbers." And the lot of them immediately huddled in their sleeping bags around me, as we listened to the strange snorting noises outside the tent.

My thoughts were racing through my head to recall the sins I had committed since being sent to St Vincent's, especially any sins big enough to warrant a visit from Lucifer to a tent in the middle of a cow-patted field. To be honest, I didn't class my wrongdoings as sinful, not in the true sense of the word. Admittedly and unashamedly, I stole sweets from the local shop, as well as the odd things from my fellow peers. But what young lad didn't have these natural instincts? It was like breathing or fiddling with yourself. I was actually finding it difficult to fill up my weekly confessional sins quota and had resorted to making most of them up for the priest.

I recalled that George Mullins and I had recently thrown the ancient recreation room telly, with its annoying throbbing sound and ghostly black-and-white screen, out of the bathhouse window, just to get a new one. In colour! But I was sure the Almighty wouldn't have classed that as warranting his wrath. And as I drifted off to sleep, I felt happy in the knowledge that if the Devil did happen into the tent during the night, he was likely to get one of the other sinners nearest the entrance.

It was very early morning when I awoke, to a slight damp chill inside the tent, along with the smell of old canvas, boot dubbin, bad breath and farts. A quick look around told me we were all accounted for.

Outside, there was a mad dash of screaming, bare-chested lunatics, rushing from their tents and scattering the wary sheep in their wake, as they headed in full flight across the dewy turd-trodden field to the stream, a few hundred yards away from the campsite. All this to be the first loony into the freezing cold water.

It goes without saying that I was the last one out of the tent. I could have outrun the lot of them in my bare feet, if I'd been minded to. But I didn't care which fool got to the stream first. Taking in a deep breath of what should have been healthy Lake District air, my nostrils were hit by the smell of shite. I let my nose and eyes follow to where the stench was coming from and spotted the dinner-plate sized cowpats at the side of our tent. This led me to conclude, either the Devil does cow-sized turds, or our visitor last night might well have been a cow. Not that I was going to let on to those idiots.

"Rhattigan."

"Sir?"

"With me, after you get back from washing," ordered Mr Sweet.

"Yes, sir."

Mr Sweet looked much stockier in his string vest, khaki shorts, long grey socks and size-12 hiking boots. His face also appeared much redder in comparison with the rest of his pale white skin.

Mr Lilly made a sudden appearance from his own tent. Unlike Mr Sweet, the Führer had constantly tanned skin, which was no wonder, considering he and Matron were always jetting off on one holiday or another. I couldn't help laughing inside as I stared at him. He reminded me of a little overweight boy scout, standing there in his khaki short-sleeved shirt and those ridiculous tight leather shorts he brought back from a visit to Germany, telling us they were called Lederhosen, a traditional piece of clothing worn by most German men. No wonder they lost the war!

Making my way across the field to the stream, I wasn't going to be fooled by the mist floating on top of the water, which looked like the steam from a hot bath. Stark bollock naked and all red-skinned with the cold, the others frolicked around in the stream like water babies. But my big toe wasn't going any further than the little dip I'd intended for it.

"Yah bastard!" I managed to shout out, just as Collins rushed up from behind and pushed me in.

My body was numbed by the cold shock, but oddly enough I felt warm inside, instantly becoming oblivious to my surroundings as I deliberately stayed submerged beneath the clear, cold water. I was overwhelmed by a sudden sense of wellbeing as it wrapped itself around me.

What peace there is to be found in silence. For me, silence was the only lifeline I had, preventing me from sinking deeper into the chaotic, confusing, uncaring existence I so longed to escape from. I was a cared-for child, but I was not cared about. I was tagged with the number 26, which was stamped everywhere bar my forehead – on all my "institutional" possessions. I was told when to sleep, wake, eat, shite, talk, stand, sit, wash, dress, undress, bend over. And I did it all without question, taking all the knocks and the beatings, and all other forms of abuse thrown at me, simply because I refused to let anyone take control of my emotions. Alone, in the silences, was where I felt safest. And whilst I could hear a distant voice calling out my name, I was ignoring it, in favour of the exhilarating feeling now coursing through my body.

"Tommy!"

I was hauled to the surface by Collins. "Are you alright?" he asked, without his usual stutter!

I gasped in mouthfuls of air as I looked up to see him and Donkey kneeling over me, surrounded by a group of other naked lads, as I lay at the edge of the stream.

"What's wrong?"

"Y-y-you were d-d-drowning!"

"I was swimming underwater, was all."

"You looked drowned to us," said the skeletal form of Dougie Bones Taylor, getting a nod of agreement from the others.

"What does someone look like that's drowned?" I asked.

"Dead, I suppose," he answered, after a brief pause.

"Well I'm not dead," I informed him, as I stood up and wrapped my towel around my waist. "Which is more than can be said for you, yer walking skeleton."

What Lies Beneath

I loved the stillness of those early mornings, watching the light dew dancing in the air, with the sunlight turning the hundreds of spiders' webs into a spectacular show of glimmering, diamond-like droplets.

This was the fifth morning I'd set off with Mr Sweet to fetch the milk. It would usually take us around 10 minutes to get to the small stone barn, where the farmer would leave the milk for us to collect and we'd leave the empty churns behind for him to refill. Mostly we walked in silence, except for him telling me to stop annoying the rabbits, or to catch up whenever I lagged back.

Only when we were in the barn, away from prying eyes, did he take a keener interest in me. As usual, there were no words spoken as I automatically pulled down my shorts and pants before leaning up across one of the stored bales of straw, and he pushed himself inside me.

I was not happy. It wasn't that I didn't want his attention – I did. But it did seem, since we came camping, I was not getting anything back from him. It was all over and done with so quickly, I was beginning to think all he wanted was to use me for his own pleasure, without giving me any in return. Back at St Vincent's, he'd touch and fondle me, and whisper kind words to me, in return for me letting him do what he wanted to me. I was confused. He'd told me love was a two-way thing when I'd first given in to him. But I wasn't feeling any love as I listened to him grunting and groaning and making no attempt to share his feelings with me.

"Squeeze your cheeks together," he whispered in his usual quivery voice, before gripping me by my hips and pushing himself further inside me, which always felt uncomfortable. Not that he cared when I'd tell him.

It was always the same routine, him holding my hips and pulling me tightly to him. And then, when it was over and done with, I'd pull my underpants and trousers back up, with him warning me each time not to say a word to anyone, otherwise I'd be in big trouble. Then we carried the milk churn between us, out of the barn and back to camp.

After breakfast, we piled into the school vans and headed off in the direction of Grasmere, to visit Dove Cottage, the home of William Wordsworth. I was surprised to see how dark it was inside his house and had wondered how Wordsworth could possibly have managed to find inspiration writing in a dump like that. Then, when I walked outside and around to the gardens, to see it fall away into those awe-inspiring, breathtaking views of the lakes and fells, it was easier to understand why he had called this place "the calmest, fairest spot on earth".

After a dinner of fish and chips, we were split into four groups. While the other three groups visited different places of interest, we were taken fishing by Mr Lilly. The small fishing lake was only a short walk from Dove cottage. We were each given a small fishing rod by the young fella running the little hut a couple of yards away from the water's edge. Mr Lilly paid him a shilling for the hire of each rod and an extra shilling for a small plastic container full of live maggots, to be used as bait.

"Enjoy the afternoon," said the fellow, with a smirk on his lips and a quizzical look in his eyes. I wasn't sure whether he was laughing silently at Mr Lilly in those stupid leather shorts of his, or at us, standing at the lake with our rods dipped in the water, expecting a fish to swim over and attach itself to the rod.

Mr Lilly took a large maggot out of the bait container and showed us how to attach it to the fishing hook, before he cast it into the lake. A couple of the sadists copied him, but most of us weren't interested in handling the squirmy things, especially now, after Sonny O'Connor had just told us about his auld granny being found dead in her bed, eaten alive by maggots.

"Here we go!" Mr Lilly was all excited, having just got a bite on his line and reeled in a fish no bigger than the maggot in its jaws. He unhooked it and threw the fish back into the lake, telling us we were not allowed to keep any we caught. Jaysus, this was boring!

I'd spent over an hour standing on the one spot, like a garden gnome around a pond, looking down at the surface of the water, where there wasn't even a ripple. A little lad of around six was standing a few yards away and off to my left, with his father. He was using a fishing net on a long cane and was catching the little feckers by the dozen. I'd had enough. Taking a few steps away from the edge of the lake, I took a run up and launched my rod into the air like a javelin.

"Sir! Rhattigan just threw his fishing rod in the water, sir."

"No I didn't Owens, yah big liar."

"Then how did it come to end up there?" The headmaster pointed to the rod sticking up out of the water.

"I had to let it go sir. I think a whale, or something bigger, must have grabbed the hook. It nearly pulled me in sir."

"A whale?"

"Or something bigger, sir."

"There are pike in the lake," said the little lad's father, who had walked over to us. "Some of them are enormous." He stretched out his arms to emphasise the size.

"It must have been one of them things then." I was saved!

"You can get in there and retrieve the rod, pronto," snapped Lilly.

"It's too deep, sir. I might drown." Not that he'd be that bothered.

"Oh, it isn't that deep," said the lad's father. "It's quite shallow for about 20 yards out before it drops down deeper."

"Oh. Thanks for that." Nosy bastard! Boots and long grey socks off, trousers rolled up and there I was, paddling in the lake. The rest of the morons looked on from the edge of the water, shouting their warnings about sharks, octopuses and crocodiles.

It took me a minute to make my way to the small fishing rod and I plucked it from the water. But just as I turned to make my way back, I felt something slimy slip past my right leg and I was suddenly frozen with fear. "Mr Lilly, Mr Lilly, there's a monster in the water!"

"Get out now, you idiot."

I was frantically searching the surface of the water closest to me to see what it could have been. I didn't see any shark fins, which was a relief. What was that? Jaysus! The long, slimy thing had just slipped between me legs! Sweet Mary an' Joseph! What was dat! I'd just seen the ugliest face (barring Donkey's) I'd ever seen in my whole life pop its head up out of the water and glare straight into my eyes. I'd only got a quick glimpse at the monster, but it was long enough for me to see it baring hundreds of sharp pointy teeth at me as it licked its big pouty lips…

Instinctively letting out a harrowing scream, I took off, as fast as my legs could carry me. I had always been a good runner, but I was sure this was the fastest I'd ever moved.

"Jesus, Jesus," shouted Owens, mockingly bowing his head to me, as the others laughed hysterically.

"Do not take the Lord's name in vain," said Mr Lilly, and he gave the Welsh git a slap around the back of the head.

"But he ran on top of the water, sir!"

"Shut up and get the fishing rods back to the hut," ordered the headmaster.

"You're funny!" smiled the young lad. His father agreed it was the funniest thing he'd ever seen in a long while. Me? I couldn't see what was so funny about running across the water for dear life and I gave the pair of them my best scowl.

Harsh Lessons

It had been four days since Mr Lilly left the campsite to go on his pilgrimage to the Holy Land, where he was, no doubt, seeking divine forgiveness for his multitude of sins. He'd told us he was going to Jerusalem to visit the place where Jesus once lived, and then on to visit the Wailing Wall, which, by all accounts, is the holiest place on earth. Apparently people flock there in their millions, from all four corners of the world, to pray and weep to this wall. It cheered me up no end to learn I wasn't the only wall talker around!

The evening before he left, we'd sat around the campfire singing that awful song "Ging Gang Goolie", which must have been written by a complete and utter lunatic.

Ging gang goolie goolie goolie goolie watcha,
Ging gang goo, ging gang goo.
Ging gang goolie goolie goolie goolie watcha,
Ging gang goo, ging gang goo.
Hayla, hayla shayla, hayla shayla, shayla, oooooooh,
Hayla, hayla shayla, hayla shayla, shayla, oooh.
Shally wally, shally wally, shally wally, shally wally

Oompah, oompah, oompah, oompah.

What a load of old bollocks!

But we made up for it with a few other songs, such as "Kumbaya" and "The Carnival is Over", two favourites of ours. Some boys also sang solo, including me, with the loudest applause for me at the end of my rendition of "Old Tige". The light was still good when we were ordered off to our beds, only to be roused from them a short while later by the sound of the ARP bell clanging in our ears.

"Right you lot!" We were now standing, in our pyjamas and bare feet, in the middle of the field. "You'll stand here all night if necessary, until I find the despicable animal among you who tampered with my bed," snapped the incensed headmaster. "I want a name."

He was referring to the apple-pie bed someone had made for him, complete with sheep droppings, which now plastered his toes.

I was always surprised that he seemed not to have learnt the simple and most obvious fact, that threatening us as a group was going to have very little impact. But he still threatened us with the dire consequences of our actions, as if we really cared. Perhaps we were all a bunch of "complete buffoons", but there was no way we were going to offer up a name.

I'd spotted the sheepish grins Harrison and Mullins were throwing one another, suspecting they were probably responsible and wishing I'd thought of it first. I would have added a few sloppy cow-turds to the mix.

It must have been about an hour later, as the light began to fade, when Mr Lilly, now holding a lit tilley lamp, spoke to us again, telling us we were a bunch of despicable excuses for human beings, as well as it being no wonder our parents had given up on us.

"Baa!" It was a brilliant impression of a bored sheep.

"Who said that?"

"A sheep." Donkey, standing in the front row, just a few lads along from the headmaster, had to open his big gob.

"What!" growled Lilly, taking the few strides needed to stand facing the idiot. I was taken aback by the headmaster's distorted, evil-looking features as they were lit up by the tilley lamp and the shadows danced across his face.

"Baa!" bleated Donkey again, grinning from ear to ear, like it was part of a game we were all playing. And for a split second, I believed Mr Lilly was going to belt him one. But to my surprise, he just exhaled deeply, shaking his head in despair before letting us know we were losing a full week of privileges when we arrived back at St Vincent's.

With three days left before the end of summer camp, I had to admit that, despite the expected minor clashes amongst us, it had been a relatively peaceful experience in the Lake District amongst my foes. It seemed odd that, whenever we were away from the approved school, the peer mentality automatically diminished to the point where we were able – if only briefly – to tolerate one another's company. The teachers had also refrained from throwing their weight around too much, though they'd still felt the need to be verbal. Stingingly at times. Now, with the headmaster gone, it was up to Mr Alston, Mr Sweet, Mr Keenan and the two weird fellas, Barry and Norman, from the local YMCA in Liverpool, who were retained each year to teach us all forms of survival techniques, as well as canoeing, tickling trout and map reading.

I didn't mind Mr Alston, the deputy head of the whole school. He was the only person I'd never had any issues with and he would let me use his office typewriter to write the odd letter to my brother Martin at St George's Approved School in Freshfields, two or three miles away from St Vincent's. Whether my letters were ever sent out was something I didn't know at the time. But I'd never received a letter back from my brother. Perhaps, unlike me, he hadn't learnt to read and write?

A very tall thin man, with a gaunt face, Mr Alston normally taught Religious Instruction and singing, teaching us all the new hymns as well as a few folk songs. I was always fascinated by his huge Adam's apple, which bobbed up and down when he was singing the notes to us. I'd also suspected he was tone deaf because he tended to sing out of tune and then have a good moan at us, telling us we sounded like a choir of strangulated cats.

Mr Alston could be very strict, but I never saw him physically hit any of the boys, unlike Mr Keenan. The complete opposite to Mr Alston and more like the headmaster, Mr Keenan was cold, indifferent and very intimidating. When telling us off, he would get up very close, almost touching noses, so you didn't see the knee or the hand coming until it made contact and you felt the pain.

Usually, I knew when a strike was coming a split second before it came, just by watching his eyes. Spotting signs of an imminent strike was a talent of mine, a gift, which I'd learnt when begging on the streets of Manchester. But I still needed to learn how to be quick enough to get out of the way in time.

I often wondered how these adults could be so cruel towards us. Why did they need to use such physical force against us? It was beyond me. We were, after all, defenceless children, even if we seemed different or came across as much tougher than the norm. This was hardly surprising, considering the kind of environment we were living in. Surely these people must have known their hard slaps, their fists and their knees did hurt and cause us pain – even if most of us didn't care to show it to them.

I wondered, too, how these people expected us to feel when they had hit us, having already psychologically demonised us to the point of us having no feelings of self-worth or respect for ourselves, let alone for them, or anyone else. We accepted punishments, we accepted insults, we took everything they threw at us, and we turned it back into bitterness and hatred. All this was a part of our normal daily lives and we expected nothing less.

We lived in a place owned and run by the Nugent Catholic Care Society, along with the Catholic Church. From the outside, they were charged with caring for and protecting society's most vulnerable young children, those unfortunate enough to have been born with dysfunctional parents who couldn't care a tinker's cuss. On the inside, it was run on a debauched ideology of Catholicism. We were sent to St Vincent's Approved School to be cared for and protected. Protected from what? And from whom? I hadn't a clue! Because no one had ever bothered to tell me.

I had always been happy and contented, in my own way, before coming to this cruel institution. And I certainly never needed any care or protection with my family around. I loved my brothers and sisters and cared so much about them, especially the younger ones. I would have done anything to protect them from harm. And I did everything within my own power to feed them, by begging, scavenging and stealing to put food on the table. And I know they would have done the same for me, if they'd had to. Yes, there were times when I had felt insecure and unsafe, but it was easy to run away and hide from trouble. Daddy was the one who'd caused most of our anguish, when he was drunk. But it was only a matter of keeping out of his way until he was sober again.

Here, in St Vincent's, I felt unsafe almost every single day. There was nowhere to run and hide. We were stripped of our dignity and our individuality in their quest to rid us of our unsavoury past. We were pushed and prodded, and fed with their God-fearing values and morality.

Here, we were taught to fear a majestic being who, on a whim, could strike us down at any given time of his choosing, if we didn't follow his way. But I didn't believe there was such a terrifying being such as God, ready to come down upon us in a thunderous cloud of fire and brimstone! I was more fearful of those so-called Christian teachers, nuns and priests, who deluded themselves in their rabid belief that what they were doing to us was for our own good.

Brought up as a Catholic, I had always believed God had sent his only son, Jesus, down to us in the form of a human being. He loved us and knew what it was like to be us. And yet, how could this be the truth, when the very people who preached to us about this merciful God were the very same merciless parasites without a moral value inside their hearts? Yes, we certainly were learning so much from them. Hence the reason why we hated them, hated each other and hated ourselves.

Climb Every Mountain

Today was the day we were hiking up a mountain called The Old Man of Coniston. I was disappointed to learn the previous year that, in fact, there wasn't an old man living up at the top after all.

We should have gone to Coniston a few days earlier, but the weather had put paid to that. I'd been really looking forward to our outing, remembering it well from last year, when we never made it to the top. It had started very hopefully: after a hearty breakfast of scrambled eggs on toast, swallowed down with a pint-sized tin mug of hot, sweet, stewed tea, we'd set off across the smelly pastures anew, hopscotching over the sundried cowpats and lumps of sheep turds. Dressed in our red anoraks, khaki short trousers, knee-length grey socks and red hiking boots, we headed across and up the steepening terrain in the direction of Coniston mountain and the old man, who apparently lived up it!

We had been about half a mile into the trek when some of the boys began complaining of tummy ache and within minutes, the whole lot (all 48) of us were on our knees moaning and groaning, before involuntarily filling our kecks.

By sheer coincidence, the only people immune from such a phenomenon were the staff...

With the awful stench following us, we marched like a battalion of mortally wounded soldiers, retching and farting our way back across the now smellier pasture to our camp, where we'd been ordered to jump straight into the stream running along the edge of the campsite, where, the previous day, we'd been taught how to tickle rainbow trout. But on this particular day, it hadn't been necessary to do any tickling, as the stunned fish had come up to the surface before floating off downstream!

It seemed there was no medical explanation for our sudden illness. Not that there had been anyone in the camp qualified enough to give an expert medical diagnosis. We'd just accepted the suggestion given, that mass hysteria was probably the most likely cause. The coincidence – that the only victims of this strange occurrence were the ones who'd eaten the eggs – never got a mention. But that was last year. Hopefully, this time we would make it to the summit without incident, hysterical or otherwise.

Piling out of the three vans, we moved off upwards, following the rough track originally used to bring the quarried slate down from the mountainside. We passed the skeletal remains of rusting mining equipment and the ruins of small stone buildings, standing solemn and mute as silent witnesses to a long-gone era.

We'd been walking for at least two hours and were looking forward to the rest Mr Alston had promised us once we were near the summit, which wasn't too far off. Mr Sweet was at the back, looking all red-faced and exhausted, while Mr Keenan was in the middle of the pack, telling two lads off for throwing stones into the water. I could feel the atmosphere changing slightly as we steadily made progress towards the top. Even with our red anoraks on, I could still feel a slight chill in the air. Looking out at the sparkling blue quarry waters and breathtaking views, I had a wonderful sense of freedom, and the sudden urge to take a running jump and fly across the valley. If only!

We eventually came to an area strewn with boulders and small chunks of slate. Mr Alston decided this was where we would have our break. Me, Donkey, Barnes and Pete Collins sat at the top of a huge rock, looking down on the others. As we tucked in to our lunches, we were joined by some curious sheep who also enjoyed some of our spam sandwiches.

Spud Murphy an 11-year old lad from Cork, had been going on about having a stone in his boot. Taking it off, he shook out the small stone and began to massage his sore foot. He seemed petrified of a scruffy-looking sheep, with its fleece hanging off it like an old beggar's coat, and we watched as it ambled over to him and started licking the inside of his boot. Taking an almighty kick at the creature, Murphy suddenly let out a howl of pain before falling to the ground.

"What's wrong with you, Murphy?" asked Mr Alston.

"I think I broke me foot, sir," winced Murphy.

"He kicked a sheep up the bum, sir."

"Let me have a look." Mr Alston, shaking his head, knelt on one knee in front of him. "You're right for the first time in your life, Murphy. You've broken your big toe, which ultimately should teach you not to kick defenceless sheep, especially without a boot on."

The three teachers had a brief discussion between themselves, before Mr Alston eventually informed us of their decision to cancel the trip to the summit.

Calling Murphy all the names under the sun, we let our feelings of disappointment be known to the teachers. Mr Keenan then had a word in Mr Alston's ear, and to our obvious delight, the deputy headmaster had a change of heart.

"Mr Keenan, out of the goodness of his heart, has agreed to accompany a group of you who would like to continue to the top. Those of you who don't want to go any further, stand just over there." He pointed to where Murphy was sitting, looking at his swollen toe.

Lazy buggers! There were nine of us left standing on our own. That was 38 boys who would never get to see the view from the summit, through their own choice. What was up with them? For just two weeks of the whole year, we were given the opportunity to see things we would never get to see in our mundane lives. And yet hardly any of them were interested in doing something different.

Perhaps they were afraid of change. In some ways I felt luckier than most, in the sense that I was brought up not having any expectations. And so, I didn't worry about where my life was taking me, or where it might end. I also didn't have any need to be concerning myself, or even caring about seeing my Mammy and Daddy again. I rarely thought about them and didn't feel I had anything to gain by being with them, except the freedom to roam the streets, which I didn't seem to miss so much these days. I also had no desire to ask the question, how much longer was I staying at St Vincent's? I was there, taking each day as it came, expecting nothing from the people caring for me, but making the best of whatever they gave to me. The best thing that had happened to me so far was learning to read and write. Not only had it opened up a new world up for me, I'd noticed I was increasingly on my own, preferring the company of a book, especially poetry.

So, onwards and upwards. The 10 of us, including Mr Keenan, continued the trek towards the summit. Our progress was steady, and a lot quieter than it had been when the whole group of us were together. Mr Keenan's mood also seemed to be less serious than it had been all morning, even when he kept having to tell Donkey off for lagging behind and to shut up with his baa-ing at the sheep. Donkey lurched forwards with his head down, before suddenly screeching out that awful campfire song, "Ging Gang Goolee".

The last part of the hike looked steep, with plenty of loose slate and stones, making the walk upwards slightly more difficult. But it was worth the effort to see the views of the surrounding fells and mountain ranges, which were even more spectacular as we neared the summit.

We finally made it! We were at the top of the Old Man of Coniston. We raced over to the tall cairn, where we added our own special rocks as a memento to the Old Man. Mr Keenan, reading from the little map, pointed out some of the landmarks to us, and we were even able to see the sea! As I stared out to the horizon, I felt an uplifting rush of emotions surging right up through my body, and I felt as free as I had in those days a few years earlier, when I was wandering the streets of Hulme and running through the heavy rain without a care in the world.

A light mist suddenly drifted in on us and within seconds we found ourselves engulfed in low cloud, with the temperature drastically dropping. Mr Keenan said we should be on our way, and though I felt disappointed to be leaving, I was glad to have made it to the top of the mountain at last.

"Hurry! Keep together! Keep moving!" There was urgency in Keenan's voice as he spurred us on our way. We turned and hurried back down the mountain in the direction we had come up, as the clouds thickened around us.

It was difficult to see ahead of us, but we could at least make out the grey shapes of the landscape closest to us, as we cautiously moved back down the loose surface. I was suddenly reminded of the smog in Hulme, though in Manchester it could sometimes be so thick it was almost impossible to see your hand in front of your face.

"Bastard!"

I was sure I'd just heard Mr Keenan swear under his breath.

"Damned bloody sheep!"

He'd just sworn again! At a sheep! He'd once given me six of the best for swearing.

"Are you alright, sir?" I heard Paul Matthews ask, as he and a few others grovelled around the prone figure of the teacher, who was now on all fours, looking for his glasses.

I rushed over, eager to be seen playing my part in his rescue, as they manhandled him back to his feet.

"I'm alright! Get off me!" he protested.

On seeing the opportunity, my usual instinct was to seize on it, and I'd finally seen a chance to satisfy my curiosity. Reaching my hand through the mix of arms helping Mr Keenan to his feet, I grabbed a handful of his hair and gave it a firm tug. It stayed on! We had all suspected he wore a wig, because his hair was too shiny, thick and stiff to be normal hair. But it was real. What a shame. I'd already planned to sling it into the mist.

"Get off me," he snapped again. "Just keep moving before this gets any worse. Are we all here?" He called out our names and we all answered, barring Donkey. "Carey?"

"He was ahead of us just a minute ago, sir," volunteered Matthews.

"I don't believe it! Right, follow me, stay together and keep moving."

It was a strange feeling to be racing against the sky, or being chased by it, as we were. We heard Donkey's faint voice calling out "Hello!" and we instinctively headed in his direction, wary that he could be sitting on the edge of the mountain, leading us all to our doom. I found myself saying a silent prayer in the hope that wasn't the case.

"Donkey!" Paddy O'Neil screeched his name.

"Who is it?" came the faint response.

"It's us! Yah feckin' eejit!"

"You can cut that language out!" warned Keenan. "Carey! Are you able to see anything in any direction?"

"Stones."

"Stones," Keenan muttered. "We're up a mountain!"

"Stones!" repeated Donkey.

"Lord help us. Stay where you are and keep making a noise. Sing a song! We'll come to you."

"Ging Gang Goolee Goolee Goolee Goolee Watchaa! Ging Gang Gooo! Ging Gang Gooo!"

We managed to outrun the mist and within a short space of time visibility was back to normal. The sun was shining on us. And Donkey was still Ging Gang Gooleeing!

"Where is the fool? Carey!" hollered Mr Keenan.

"Who is it?" Donkey's head suddenly appeared over the stone wall of a dilapidated stone quarry building, causing me to smile, as I realised why he couldn't see anything around him but stones when he'd been sitting inside that building.

Arriving back in camp, Mr Keenan called the small group of us together and thanked us for the professional way we had acted. He said he admired the way we had all worked together as a group to get ourselves safely down off the mountain, and even had some nice words to say to Donkey, who was about to give us another rendition of "Ging Gang Goolee" until O'Neil elbowed him in the side.

To be honest, I don't think any of us had a clue what Keenan was talking about. I didn't remember working with the others as a team. And I could tell, by the blank looks on the faces of the others, they were probably thinking the same thing. In truth, once I'd found out Keenan wasn't wearing a wig, I was only thinking about my own safety. But I was happy to take the plaudits Keenan was dishing out. He never uttered a word about falling over the sheep and calling it a bastard.

An Intriguing Find

Heading in the direction of Formby beach, we walked along the rough-stoned footpath that took us across a large expanse of overgrown wasteland, with a row of tall electric pylons running off to our left and across the fields as far as the eye could see. The path eventually ran alongside the edge of the nearby firing ranges belonging to the Ministry of Defence, which was sectioned off by high wire fences. Just inside the boundary fence, the large white signage written on the red metal backgrounds warned people to "Keep out. Live ammunition being fired!" It was quiet now, but sometimes when we came here, we could hear the loud pop-pop-pop of guns being fired.

We'd been given our usual two hours of free time to go off and play on our own, having to meet back up by the pathway once the whistle was blown. Anyone more than five minutes late or giving the excuse they'd not heard the whistle (meaning they must have been out of bounds) would lose house points.

Barnes, Donkey, stuttering Pete and I headed off across the beach and up along the sand dunes towards the pine forest. We hadn't made any set plans as to where we were going, or what we were going to do when we got there. We never did, preferring instead to keep going until something aroused our interest.

Being in the pine forest was like being in another world, with row upon row of tall trees standing in straight lines, allowing very little sunlight to penetrate through to the ground. Eventually we came upon a green-and-white-coloured caravan standing in a small circular clearing about the size of a tennis court. A few brief whispers between us and we decided to have a nose around. And with me leading the way, we got down on all fours and made our way along the edge of the forest. I loved the whole idea of creeping around like Red Indians looking for scalps, with no one but us knowing we were there.

It looked like the caravan had been abandoned for a long while, with the green we saw further back being the moss growing on the bottom of the van and rising upwards. There wasn't any door, at least, not attached to the caravan. It was lying further away amongst a large group of yellow gorse bushes.

Looking inside, we could see the interior had been completely stripped of everything, barring the piles of old cigarette butts and empty whiskey, vodka and beer bottles scattered about the floor, indicating it was probably once a drinking den. My attention was eventually caught by an unusual silver-grey object sticking up from the sand not too far away from the caravan.

"Look at this." I knelt on both knees and carefully studied it. I could see what appeared to be fins of sorts. And I started digging out the sand with my hands to eventually reveal the full object, which was about 10 inches long. "I think it's a bomb!" I was all excited and jumped to my feet, holding it aloft.

"Give us a look," said Barnes, suddenly taking it out of my hands. "It's a mortar bomb! Take cover!" he warned, before slinging it high into the air as the rest of us dived into the thorny gorse bushes for safety.

"Boom!" Barnes shouted above our own cries of pain as we were scratched by the thorns, and then he suddenly went into fits of hysterical laughter. "It's a dud!" he laughed. "All the insides have been taken out of it."

Dragging ourselves back out of the bushes, Collins and I gave Donkey a hand each and pulled him out as he heehawed in pain.

"How did you know what it was?" I asked Barnes, while Collins set about pulling out the couple of thorns stuck in Donkey's backside.

"My dad's in the army and he brought a couple of these back and stuck them by the fireside for show," he explained. "They take all the insides out, so they don't work any more."

We set off on our way, taking it in turns to throw the missile high into the air and watch it land in the sand as we made the explosion sound effects. We saw Armstrong and another two of the older boys, Adams and Dodds, lying on their stomachs at the top of a tall sand dune, peering over the top of it. And so, quietly and swiftly making our way to another tall dune off to their right, we gazed down in the direction the others were concentrating on, where we saw a man and woman kneeling in the sand. The man was behind the groaning woman, his trousers and pants down around his ankles and his backside going hell for leather. Looking over to Armstrong and his pals, I was slightly taken aback to see all three of them were tossing themselves off!

"Ooh!" the woman was groaning loudly, which got on my nerves, so I lobbed the mortar bomb into the air and watched as it landed close to the bare-arsed man.

The fella did a double take at the mortar before suddenly springing to his feet, attempting to make a run for it. But he tripped over his pants, which were still down around his ankles, causing him to fall flat on his face. The woman was now up on her feet. She seemed angry about something or other, letting the fella know, in a loud voice, what a big bastard he was. Then she hurried off out of sight. He had managed to pull his pants up, and hurried off after her.

Diving over the top of the sand dune and sliding to the bottom of it, I retrieved my new toy, before we made a hasty retreat, scurrying off in the direction of the main sands.

The tide was far out, leaving a vast expanse of hard, rippled sand between us and the sea. Despite the dangers of the fast incoming tides on Formby Beach, I usually tried to get out as far as I possibly could, just to get a closer look at the rusty, blackened remains of the shipwrecks that appeared now and again on the low tide. I especially liked to pay my respects to the Bradda (once known as the Jolly Frank). I'd learned about these wrecks after coming across a group of people standing out on the beach, listening to a fella talking of their demise. I think it was the Irish connection of the Bradda, along with the way the fella had described her sinking, that had captured my imagination.

A lump of dark twisted metal and a line of wooden spars are the only eerie remains left of the Bradda. She came to grief there in 1936, running aground in bad weather. The crew had fired off their flares and then resorted to lighting rags soaked in paraffin in their desperate attempt to attract other ships to their plight. But it was all in vain. When she listed, the crew were washed into the sea, with five perishing and one, Samuel Ball, surviving to tell the tale. For me, the place was a solemn, poignant spot to stand and reflect, and to offer up a prayer.

The distant sound of the football whistle told us our two hours of fun were up. Before heading back, I decided to take off my jumper and wrap the mortar bomb in it, before tying the ends of the arms together and slipping it over my shoulder like a bag, making it easier to carry back across the sand to our usual designated meeting place. Miraculously, for the first time ever, none of us were late.

"Right, lads," said Mr Marron. "Before we go any further, any toads, newts, or other live animals in your pockets or hidden down your pants, turn them out now."

"What about snakes, sir?"

"If you are referring to what I think you are referring, Seager, maggot would be a more appropriate word in your case. What are you hiding in your hand, Reilly?"

"Nothing, sir."

"I can see it."

"It's a toad sir, but it's a dead one."

"What do you want with a dead toad?"

"To bury it, sir."

"Well, go and bury it over there in the sand. Actually, let me have a look at it." Mr Marron left Reilly with no option other than to open his hand to reveal the healthy toad sitting contentedly in it. "It's alive," declared Marron.

"It's a miracle! It was dead when I first found it, honest sir."

"Well I'm sure it's very grateful for your miraculous touch. Now put it over there in the sand. That has cost you five house points." Marron took out his little black book.

"But why, sir? I haven't done anything wrong."

"Working miracles without permission will do for starters. Rhattigan?"

"Yes, sir."

"What are you hiding inside your jumper?"

"I'm not hiding it sir, it's just easier to carry like this."

"What's easier to carry?" Marron was eyeing my jumper.

"My bomb, sir."

"Your bomb?"

"Yes, sir."

"Don't get smart with me, lad."

"I'm not, sir."

"He d-d-does have a b-b-bomb, sir," said Collins.

"It's a world war two mortar bomb," explained Barnes.

"Let me see this bomb of yours." Marron wasn't looking totally convinced we were telling him the truth, though I did notice his sudden backward step.

Do Not Drop the Bomb!

Unwrapping the mortar bomb from its resting place, I held it up by its fins for all to see. I was amazed by the immediate reaction of Mr Keenan, who suddenly ordered the main body of boys to hurry off up the pathway, away from the apparent danger.

"Jesus Christ!" blasphemed Mr Marron (one rule for us and another for them). "Whatever you do, Rhattigan, don't drop that on the ground, do you understand? Do not drop that on the ground!" I noted a few more backward steps.

"It's not a real one, sir."

"Hold the bloody thing with two hands!" he bellowed, before he and Mr Sweet had a brief chat, too far out of my range to hear.

I wasn't too sure what all the fuss was about, or why I couldn't convince these eejits it wasn't a real bomb. I mean, I'd thrown it around a few times and nothing had happened, which proved it wasn't real. Mr Marron suddenly ran off up along the path at some speed. I watched as he stopped for the briefest of chats with Mr Keenan, before setting off again and disappearing out of view.

"Are you all right, Rhattigan?" Mr Sweet, keeping his distance from me, seemed genuinely worried.

"It isn't a real bomb, sir. Barnes told me his daddy has some at home and they take the insides out, so they can't explode."

"That's probably what this is. But we can't take any chances. Just stay calm and keep hold of that thing, there's a good lad."

"How long have I got to hold it for?"

"Not long. Mr Marron has gone to the nearby barracks for help. So, they'll be here in no time."

"What will happen if it explodes while I'm holding it?" I regretted my question the instant I'd asked, as images from the war films I'd watched flashed through my mind, with soldiers being blown to smithereens under mortar fire. I didn't think I'd want to live without arms and legs, which would have left me unable to defend myself from all the bum-bandits. Worse still, someone would have to take me to the toilet.

"It isn't going to explode." Mr Sweet was very reassuring, which only aroused my suspicions, causing me to wonder why I was made to stand there like a lemon holding the thing, if he was so sure it wasn't going to explode?

The more I thought about this, the more I suspected something iffy was going on. Mr Sweet seemed very calm under the circumstances, too calm as a matter of fact. This was certainly unlike him, considering he was always ready to explode into temper tantrums about the most trivial of things. So, what was going on? I could only think of one logical explanation: I was being punished for trying to sneak a bomb, albeit a dud one, back to the school.

A thought suddenly occurred to me. What if I did one of those rugby passes Mr Marron had taught us, and tossed the mortar across to Mr Sweet? Would he catch it and laugh, before throwing it back to me, giving the game away and proving I was right? Or would it explode, blowing both of us to pieces? It was not good, having all those confusing thoughts racing around in my head. And what if it just blew up Sweet? Could I live with myself knowing I'd killed him? Then again, seeing something like that happen in real life would give me something to talk about for a long time.

"They're here." Mr Sweet was the first to spot the green army truck heading along the pathway, coming up from the direction of the beach. "Just stay calm and do whatever they tell you."

Feck. It was for real! I watched as the army truck sped towards me, coming to a sudden halt about 20 or so yards away. Seconds later, a group of uniformed soldiers, four in all, jumped out, while one soldier remained on the truck, staring across at me. His look, like a mourner at a funeral, I didn't like at all.

The sudden realisation that this was really happening to me had by now hit home and was having an overwhelming effect. I was confused about the whole situation I found myself in and whatever little confidence I possessed had quickly sunk beneath the wave of panic rising through me. I had an instant urge to chuck the mortar high into the air and run like hell. But deep down I knew that whatever I decided to do would almost certainly go wrong. I was doomed. I could feel my knees trembling and knew, as brave as I felt I was, they would ultimately buckle beneath me the minute I attempted to make a move. I was resigned to let fate deal the cards to me. But if this mortar bomb was the real deal and I was blown to kingdom come, then that gormless fat eejit Barnes was not getting away with it. At the end of the day, he was to blame for all the goings on.

"Sir!"

"Are you okay, Rhattigan?"

"It was Barnes's fault, sir! He said it was a toy one."

He had not used those precise words, but he did say it was harmless, which amounted to the same thing in my book. Hopefully, if I ended up six feet under, he'd get his comeuppance, with at least a few months' loss of privileges and six of the very best – if not more.

I watched as two soldiers made their way over to Mr Sweet and struck up a conversation with him, though I wasn't privy to what they were saying. The other two soldiers standing at the back of the truck now headed across in my direction, before stopping some 10 yards away from me. Strangely, they seemed to be wearing what I could only describe as… oversized padded oven gloves?

"What do you have there for us mate?" asked one of the soldiers, a grin spread across his face. But I was not going to answer his stupid question and instead, threw him a scowl. I couldn't understand why he was smiling, considering the predicament I was in, but if he couldn't see what I was holding in my hands, then we were all up shit creek.

"What's your name, fella?"

"Tommy." I was still scowling.

"I'm Sergeant Smethurst, but you can call me Roger if you like. And this is Corporal Anderson. You can call him whatever you like."

"It's not a real one," I found myself making the statement rather than asking the question, while looking into the Sergeant's eyes for any giveaway signs. But they were telling me nothing.

"We'll soon have it sorted," was his answer. "Okay Tommy, here's what's going to happen. We're going to lower a large water tank from the back of the truck. Once it's in place, I want you to slowly make your way over to it. I'll give you further instructions when we get there. Understood?"

"Can't you just take it off me now?"

"We'll do that once we are over there," he said. Then he and the corporal walked back to the rear of the truck, leaving me alone, holding the mortar close to my chest.

I could do nothing else but watch as the large container held by chains hooked to a hydraulic arm slowly moved off the back of the truck and settled on solid ground. The Sergeant then called to me, telling me to carefully and very slowly make my way across to him, and I set off in his direction. It seemed to take an eternity before I came alongside the waist-high water tank, though in reality it must have been seconds.

"Okay. Now for the easy bit." The Sergeant dipped his gloved hands into the water. "Okay, Tommy. I want you to place that thing into the water and into my open hands. But don't let go of it until I say so. And when I do, I want you to hurry straight over to your teacher, understood? Good fella."

Doing what the Sergeant had instructed, I placed the mortar bomb into the water and into his open gloved palms, not daring to let go of it until he said so. When he did, I quickly ran over to Mr Sweet, who was shaking his head disapprovingly, but nothing more than that.

The following morning at assembly, Mr Lilly, not mentioning me by name, gave us all a stern warning about the dangers of picking objects up off the beach. He went on to give us advice on what we should do if we came across such objects in the future. And there was no more said about it. My life had been on the line and the whole incident had been played right down.

Face to Face with Evil

I was once asked by Mr Lilly, "What are you hoping to achieve with your life when you are older?" I suppose it was about the hardest question he or anyone else could have asked me. Because I simply hadn't the faintest idea. I had no aspirations about where I wanted my life to be at that moment in time, let alone in some far-off distant future. I suffered from vertigo, I was also claustrophobic and, so I had been told on many occasions, I was crazy. So I supposed fireman, pilot, astronaut, miner, psychiatrist, or anything else to do with heights, confined spaces, or the medical profession were all non-starters, not leaving many options open to me.

The idea of being a spy sounded good. I thought the cloak and dagger aspect of it would be very exciting and I reckoned I'd be good at catching other spies and traitors, shooting them if I had to. Lilly would certainly be the first on my hit list.

The reason for his question to me wasn't because he was interested in setting me on the road towards any ambitions I may have had. Far from it. He'd put the question to me in front of the morning assembly, in his feeble attempt to belittle me for peeing out of the van window on our way back from seeing "Born Free" at the cinema in Southport.

I'd been dying for a pee and I had asked Lilly if I could go to the toilet before we'd set off in the van. He'd refused, telling me I should have gone before I left the cinema. But I had already asked him halfway through the film and he'd said then that I should have gone before the film had started and I'd have to wait until the end. And then, at the end of the film, we were bustled out of the cinema and straight to the van.

It was always the same with him. "You should have anticipated this, you should have anticipated that." Jaysus, if I'd spent my whole life trying to anticipate what was going to happen next, I'd never have moved from a single spot. How was I supposed to have anticipated that the traffic lights were going to turn red and that he was going to stop the van just as I'd slid open the small window and started peeing out of it? How was I supposed to have anticipated the auld dragon pulling up alongside the van on her scooter a split second later, in the exact spot I was relieving myself?

Looking back, I'd always felt I had a sixth sense and the gift of being able to read people's emotions by looking into their eyes. This, I am sure, had kept me from potential harm as a vulnerable seven-year old roaming the streets of Manchester. So it had come as a complete and unnerving shock for me to look up at the television screen one day and suddenly see the images of the man and woman I'd once encountered on the streets of Hulme, and discover they'd been found guilty of murdering three children!

At the time I'd been playing cards with Collins and Barnes in the recreation room, while Donkey sat watching us. He couldn't play cards to save his life, no matter how much we had tried to teach him. But he was happy enough just to sit and deal the cards out to us, though he even mucked that up at times. But when it came to playing snap, he certainly had the edge, always catching us off guard and causing us to jump with fright when he spotted a matching card, slamming his hand down and almost breaking the table as he screamed "Snap!"

Glancing up at the TV, I recall my heart almost jumping into my mouth as I instantly recognised the man and woman on the screen as the couple who had taken me home in 1963 for a slice of bread and jam. They were being identified as Myra Hindley and Ian Brady. I especially remembered the woman, Myra Hindley, and how she had enticed me with her kind eyes to follow her home. How will I ever forget that moment when I had looked up into her eyes and saw the kindness drain out of them?

Looking back, the two of them had not seemed out of the ordinary and certainly no different from any of the other people we usually came across when begging on the streets of Manchester. There were those who would tell us to "piss off home to yer mam and get her to feed yah", and others who found it necessary to punch, kick or spit at us. But there were also those compassionate people who would give us a few pennies, or take us to a nearby café, ordering up a meal and paying for it on their way out as they'd left us to get on with it. And there were others who would invite us into their homes for a bite to eat, and we'd willingly tag along, chatting away to them, without any fear or thoughts for our own safety. To us, this was nothing compared to the everyday dangers we were already facing in our young lives.

I just knew something wasn't right when I'd sat at the table in the blonde woman's house and my eyes had briefly fixed on hers as she'd plonked down the plate with the thick slice of bread and jam on it, almost snapping at me to hurry up and get it down me. "So we can get you home," she'd said. But I had already noticed the sparkle she'd had in those eyes, when she'd first spoken to me in the park and invited me back to her house, was no longer there.

I was hungry. I remember my stomach letting out a rumble and my mouth watering at the sight of it. And yet, my first thought was to notice that there wasn't any margarine on the bread! How absurd and selfish that seemed.

Usually, when people had rustled up a snack for us to eat, they'd sit down and talk with us, interested in knowing at least something about what was going on in our lives. But Hindley and Brady didn't do that. I remember her swigging from a glass tumbler full of sherry. I knew it was sherry because I knew the smell of it very well and hated it. My parents, both being alcoholics, lived off the disgusting stuff. And I think it was around this point that I had suddenly decided I didn't like her much.

I am still haunted by seeing the television expose of those two evil child killers, Myra Hindley and Ian Brady, and of realising how close I had come to being another of their victims. I am still haunted by the guilt I felt at the time, the coldness, the panic, the fear deep down inside me, while inner voices were screaming at me to get out. I didn't understand all those goings-on in my head, I knew only that I shouldn't have been there and I had to escape.

Why didn't I tell them I wanted to leave? Why didn't I make a run for the door instead of leaving through the window? What was I so frightened of? Not for one second did I imagine they were deliberately going to harm me. They were just ordinary people, she was like any other ordinary young woman. A sister, a mother! And yet I'd had this instinct that made me fear the worst in them.

"Fucking wait!" I'd heard Ian Brady say those words as I had made my escape. "Fucking wait!" I know I will never forget those words. Nor can I ever forget that heart-stopping moment when the sash window I was attempting to force open had momentarily stuck, before I'd managed to open it all the way and scramble out, as Hindley grabbed at my ankle.

Now here they were on the TV! It was the first time I had seen their faces since that day back in 1963. I was now able to put a name to those faces and, for the first time, know them for the evil murderers they were. And I will be forever scarred by that knowledge. It is very difficult to comprehend that, in those moments when I'd been following the seemingly kind woman to her home, I had been walking to my potential death. By luck or some innate sense of self-preservation, I was still alive, nothing had happened to me. But my thoughts are, and always will be, for the children murdered by those two evil bastards.

"I went back to their house for a jam butty, sir," I heard myself tell Mr Sweet, who was on duty at the time.

"And they sent you off home with a lucky bag, did they?"

"No sir, I climbed out the window and ran away."

"Well, run away now, Rhattigan," sighed Sweet.

Not Caring or Sharing

My twelfth birthday had been and gone. It was the usual affair, everyone singing Happy Birthday and not meaning one word of it, the same homemade Victoria sponge with the one candle on it. When I say the same Victoria sponge cake, I don't mean it was the exact same Victoria sponge used for everyone's birthday, though it might as well have been, judging by the state of some of them. And, of course, they couldn't divide one small Victoria sponge cake into 48 pieces, unless it was shared out in crumbs, so we had to pick no more than five friends to share it with. The frustrating thing about this was that we couldn't pick fewer than five friends, in the hope of getting a bigger slice.

"Pick me, Tommy!" "I'm your mate, Ratty!" "I'll be your friend!" "It wasn't me who stole yer footie cards!" "I'll kick your head in if yah don't pick me!" This lot would have sold their grandmothers to the devil, if they'd not done so already.

I would never forget the first birthday I'd had at St Vincent's. I'd never celebrated a birthday before as such, and so couldn't believe all that lovely Victoria sponge cake was mine. And it wasn't! I'd only discovered this after blowing out the candle, when I picked the whole lot up in my hands, ready to greedily devour it.

"What are yea doin' with that?" bawled Sister Ignatius.

"I'm eatin' it Sister." What did she think I was going to do with it?

"Not all ta yerself yer not." She'd ordered me to put it back on the plate. "Yea can pick five friends to share it with."

"I don't have one friend, let alone five."

"Then choose anyone."

"I don't want ta choose anyone."

"Then I'll choose for yea."

"I'll choose, I'll choose," I pleaded, eyeing up the cake, as her shovel-size hand hovered over the top of it.

"Er – ah…"

"Hurry it up," she bawled. "We haven't the whole day."

"Him!" I blurted out, pointing in the direction of the table across from me, but not to anyone in particular.

"Barlow?"

"No. The boy next ta him."

"Murphy?"

"I'm not sure."

"Murphy. Bring yer plate over here an' get yerself a slice of this cake."

Got it! I wasn't sharing it with any false friends! And with her attention diverted away from me and the cake, I'd managed to grab the whole lot up off the plate as she was giving Murphy the surprise news.

"What in heaven's name?" screamed Sister Ignatius, when I attempted to stuff the whole cake into my gob. Her big, gobstopper eyes were almost popping out of their sockets and I had visions of them knocking her glasses off her nose. "Yah greedy, inconsiderate pig yah!"

She made a grab for the cake, which was all over my face, before she suddenly upped with her fist and boxed me one straight in the mouth, knocking me senseless and causing me to almost die choking as I'd swallowed the mouthful of cake already in my mouth (about half of it) and it had stuck in my throat.

I remember feeling giddy with the sense of panic rushing through me as I became lightheaded, and the dining room began spinning. By this point Sister Margaret had joined in and was banging her fists on my back. I wasn't sure whether she was attempting to save my worthless life, or if she'd just decided to join in the assault and battery on my person. But whatever her intentions, it did the trick and I was able to cough up the cake blocking my throat.

Having been frogmarched off to the office by the witch herself, I was taken aback when she said she wasn't going to cane me, because it was my birthday. And like an eejit, I'd thanked her.

"There's no need ta be tanking me," she said. "Yea can get back here tomorrow mornin' and be havin' yer punishment then."

Lesson learned, from then on I always shared my birthday cake with Donkey, Collins, Barnes, Butler and McGinley, just as they all chose me. But even so, I did teasingly point at other lads, seeing the excitement on their faces suddenly turn to scowls when I then called out Barnes, Collins and the others in turn.

The good thing about having reached the age of 12 was that I finally got to wear long trousers. This set me apart from the younger boys, with Miss Peggy having to triple check my inside leg measurement for my new kecks. I don't know why she had to check it so many times (probably forgetful), but she'd seemed happy enough to do so, with her big watery blue eyes smiling at me.

I was chuffed to have been picked to play on the right wing in the upcoming game of football on Saturday. Playing against a team from a posh public school in Crosby, who called themselves the "Taylors Boys".

It had been more than two years since we'd been allowed to play against an outside football team. Mr Lilly said this match, arranged by the Catholic Diocese, was a very important game for St Vincent's, giving us the opportunity of showing humility and civility towards our Fellow Man. I took this to mean the organisers were telling us we were to roll over and play dead. But that was very unlikely.

We were all looking forward to the game, especially since we'd been told the posh school had only ever played rugby, cricket and hockey. So not only were we excited about the idea of playing against a team that didn't know much about football – this was our opportunity to win back some pride. The last match saw us getting thrashed 16-0 by another local school, with 14 of those goals being penalties and the other two scored by our own cowardly fullback.

That had been the first and only football match we'd ever played against an outside team, following the mass brawl at the final whistle. We had gathered around the referee (their referee) and told him he was a cheating bastard, along with every other vile name we could muster at the time. In the tussle that followed, he'd dropped his whistle and had bent over to retrieve it – which, under the circumstances, was entirely the wrong move on his part. And though he'd probably dropped his whistle on many occasions and retrieved it without mishap, I'm sure he wouldn't have expected the toe end of Johnny Hills' football boot to have caught him straight up the backside!

The incident had only lasted for a minute or two, with the opposition team doing all the pushing and shoving and then backing off immediately like big girl's blouses when we started throwing punches and the odd bite. As was always the case when we were involved in things that went wrong, we were the ones to blame. Father Patrick from the Catholic diocese had called us mental retards in his letter to the school. But even if he did have a point, that still didn't give the referee the right to cheat.

That said, it was well worth the condemnation from the old priest, just to watch the hunched referee walk slowly and purposefully off the pitch, as if walking over burning coals, with a painful expression written across his face.

Mr Sweet had woken me up again the previous night, as he did every time he was on sleepover duty. Besides there being the night watchman, there was always a member of staff sleeping over at the school, in case of emergencies. He would usually nudge me awake, never saying anything to me, before leaving the dormitory. I slipped out from my bed and followed him along the side corridor to the staff bedroom, only a short walk away. I hated being suddenly woken from my deep sleeps: usually it took me a while to come to my senses. But luckily, I was so used to being woken in this way, I was automatically able to find my way to the staff bedroom without putting too much of an effort into fully waking up. Once inside the room, I would undo my pyjamas and drop them around my ankles for him to decide what he wanted to do to me.

Sometimes he would sit me down on the bed and make me suck him before making me kneel up on the bed and pushing himself inside me. He'd stopped playing with me a long while back as he used to do in those first few months when I'd accepted his attention and would show my eagerness to please him. But not any more. I was aware that he was now just using me for his own pleasure. There was an expectation from him that I would do whatever I had always done, without him having to coerce me, or do anything for me in return. He expected me to do whatever he wanted, at his command.

I was maturing and knew how my body worked. So, whenever I wanted to, I could pleasure myself senseless without the need for his attention, even if it was at the risk of going blind! But I still did what he asked of me because I didn't know how to say no. I didn't want him. I didn't enjoy what he was doing. But if I refused, I knew, as he also knew only too well, how easily he could make my life a misery all over again.

This was his last night on duty for the next few weeks, and when I'd entered the bedroom, his pyjama bottoms were already off and he was ready for me. "Kneel up on the bed," he whispered. I climbed up on the bed, as I had done many times, onto my hands and knees. I felt him on the outside of me, expecting the usual gentle push, but he rammed himself into me with force, causing me to fall forwards, face down with him on top of me. I was unable to breathe properly with all his weight bearing down on me and I was panicking, trying to push my hands behind me and up on him in my futile attempt to ease the pressure on me, too afraid to call out to him to stop. Seconds later, he got off me, telling me to go back to my bed.

Fridays were fish days, as all practising Catholics should know. Not that Daddy ever gave us any fish on a Friday, or any other day for that matter. The nearest we ever came to eating fish was buying battered potato scallops, which were fried in the same oil as the fish. We bought this ourselves from the fish and chip shop from the money we'd earned from begging.

"Abstaining from eating meat every Friday and sticking to fish instead is a small sacrifice for the sacrifices given by Jesus when he was crucified on the cross," said Father Tierney. Well, I wouldn't have minded furthering my sacrifice and having fish for dinner every day of the week, excluding Saturdays, which was sausage and mash day. And Sunday's roast. The rest I could live without if I could have fish instead.

Reflecting on the previous night, I think Mr Sweet might have been in a bad mood about something or other. He'd already smacked a few lads around their heads that morning, just for being too loud, which caused them to be even louder with all their whingeing. I'd given up trying to make sense of anything that happened in that dump. And I'd also given up on my attempts to rob the petty-cash tin from the office. I'd broken three fingernails trying to force another brick out of the feckin' wall, only to come up against the iron girder. Seven months of my life down the drain, with 10 and a half bricks and a thick lump of iron to show for it. Whoever built this place had certainly wanted to keep the loonies in.

I was not usually one for giving up easily, but I was giving up on that. By the time I got through into the office, I'd probably have worn my fingers to the bone, grown a five-foot grey beard, and died of old age. It wasn't as if I was desperate for the money. I didn't need it, considering that I could get most of the things I needed without having to pay for it. I suppose it was just the idea of being able to do it (which I obviously couldn't) and to put something aside in case of everyday emergencies, just as me auld Granny used to do, putting any of her spare pennies into the small tin she'd kept up on her shelf in her kitchen. She'd told me at the time, "It's for a rainy day", which had baffled me. She hardly ever went out of the house on a nice dry day, let alone when it was teeming down with rain! And even then it was only if she was heading for the pub.

Friday was also library day. There were only around 20 or so boys aged 10 and over who had joined the local library. I didn't understand why there weren't more of us, considering we could go there every Friday unsupervised. Some of the boys weren't even interested in reading books, but joined anyway, just for the opportunity to get away from St Vincent's for a short while. We were allowed out for one hour maximum, which gave us plenty of time to make the 15-to-20-minute journey there and back on foot, and to search out a couple of good books to read.

We were sent out in small groups of four at various times of the day. I usually made the journey on my own, simply because I wasn't (and didn't particularly want to be) friends with anyone. By this point I had distanced myself from my gang of misfits. I couldn't imagine myself ever being true friends with anyone there, if there was even such a thing as true friends. To my mind, friendships were all about keeping secrets, trusting one another and being honest with one another. Not this lot. They couldn't even be honest with themselves, let alone with others. Anyway. I felt I was better without them.

Betrayal

It was 9.30am in the morning and I was off to the library. On the way, I passed the cottage where I would often get a glimpse of the old woman peering out of an upstairs window. Her bright, flower-filled garden had a huge rusting ship's anchor resting in the centre of the lawn. Sometimes, I'd see her pottering around the garden with another old biddy. I wasn't sure if they were ever aware I was passing because they never looked my way, even when I would pause to read the poem written on the large piece of grey slate standing by the front door of the cottage. And though I had already learnt it off by heart, I would always stop to read it again, every time I passed.

> The kiss of the sun for pardon,
> The song of the birds for mirth,
> One is nearer God's heart in a garden
> Than anywhere else on Earth.

It did make me wonder why churches didn't have such beautiful flowered gardens, instead of their dismal grey cemeteries.

Miss Little, one of the two women librarians, was always very friendly towards me, even though she was aware I was from the approved school. She was younger than the other librarian, though not as tall. I thought she might be pregnant, as she had a large, swollen tummy, though I didn't dare ask her, just in case she wasn't. Every time I visited, she always seemed to have a pleasant smile and she'd tell me about new books that had recently arrived, even suggesting a book to me that she thought might be of interest.

By stark contrast, Miss Flower, the other librarian, had such a miserable-looking face. A skinny, lanky woman, she must have been at least twice as tall as Miss Little. I'd always thought miserable people were only miserable because God had given them one kind of affliction or other to be miserable about. But, other than her being as tall as a beanpole, I couldn't see anything else seriously afflicted about her. There was something about her which, for some obscure reason, reminded me of Harpo Marx. She had tight blonde curls (which could have been a wig) and staring eyes, and she never struck up a conversation – at least not with any of the boys from St Vincent's, unless it was to throw a few sharp words our way. And she could think again if she thought for one minute I hadn't noticed, when I was on my way out of the library, her shifty eyes checking out the contours of my trousers, on the off-chance I'd a book stuffed up my jumper or down my kecks. (I never had.) I'd given her something to look at the previous week, when I'd stuffed a sock with paper and shoved it down the front of my trousers on the way in, deliberately parading in front of her. Miss Little thought it was funny. She didn't say as much, but I could tell by her wide grin. Miss Flower just choked on her coffee.

I believe her dislike of the St Vincent's lot had come about some months back, when Alistair Jones jokingly asked both librarians a question. "Miss Little," he asked, "are you called Little 'cos you are small?" To which she chuckled and said, "Probably". Then turning to the old dragon, he'd asked her, was she called Flower because she "was a flower?"

"Oh, and what sort of flower do you suppose I am?" asked the unsmiling old bat.

"Cauliflower!" came the punchline, which didn't go down well with her, though there was a loud guffaw from everyone else. She'd barred Jones from the library for three months, but he never did go back.

Walking along the public pathway running between a group of houses leading to the common, I could have sworn I'd seen two boys dressed in grey trousers and grey jumpers through the gap in the high garden fence on my right. I could see that the lads from my group were all together and walking across the common in the direction of the library, which was just across the main road. So, I knew it wasn't any of them. Unable to resist a nose, I pulled the twisted fence panel slightly towards me, allowing a bigger gap for me to peer through.

It was 13-year-old Michael Farr, and that little squirt James Thompson, who was 10. Farr had his hands cupped together, giving Thompson a leg-up to a side window. The police had been to the school three times over the past few months, making enquiries about a spate of burglaries in the local area. And as these two eejits had only been at St Vincent's for a short while, I wondered if they were the culprits.

Giving them no more thought, I made my way to the library, to find another lady, Miss Watmore, working in place of Miss Little. She told me Miss Little had given birth to a baby girl, and would probably not be back for some while, though she didn't say how long that while was going to be. I was disappointed, sad even, to think I wouldn't be seeing her again for ages, but Miss Watmore seemed to be alright and not like Miss Flower, who was eyeing me up and down. Not wanting to prolong her unwelcome gaze, I handed the sour woman my returned books and hurried off in search of another two, choosing *Great Expectations* and *Oliver Twist* by Charles Dickens as my new ones.

I still had half an hour to get back to the school, so I decided to take a different route, the one I would usually take when I had extra time on my hands.

Compared with Hulme, the streets of Formby seemed a whole world apart. There were no alleyways, or dirty streets, or row upon row of terraced houses, or gas lamps. I never saw neighbours standing on their doorsteps, gossiping about anything and nothing. There were no bombed houses, or crofts, or kids playing noisily outside. Everywhere was clean, even the air I was breathing was so different from Manchester's coal-polluted atmosphere. Formby was bright and colourful, with beautiful houses, all with gardens, front and back. And all those la-di-da people living there, amid the different smells of flowers and cut grass. And yet how I still missed Hulme and all the things about it that Formby didn't have.

I'd only just plucked the apple off the long branch hanging right over the garden wall, within my arm's reach, when I heard the car pull up behind me. A quick look over my shoulder told me it was a police car. St Vincent's was only around the corner and my first reaction was to make a run for it. It would be easy to jump over the school wall and make good my escape, using the trees and shrubs as cover. But on second thoughts, I hadn't done anything wrong and so stood my ground.

"Did you just steal that apple from that tree?" asked the copper as he walked right up to me, armed with his notebook and pencil. The other copper, a young woman, remained behind the wheel of the panda car, staring out at me suspiciously through the windscreen.

"What tree?"

"Don't get smart with me, sonny."

"You're not my daddy."

"Right, name?"

"Malone." Jaysus, why did I say that?

"Are you aware that taking an apple from someone else's tree without their permission is theft?"

"That's a branch, not a tree. And anyway, it's not on the property, so how's that stealin'?"

"Listen, clever clogs, the apple tree belongs to the owner of the property. And you are committing a serious offence by stealing the owner's apples."

"It was only the one apple. And anyway, I found it on the ground and was putting it back."

"Oh really?" smirked the copper, looking happy that he'd got his man. "I was putting it back on the tree," he muttered, as he wrote in his little black book.

I must admit, it did sound ridiculous when hearing the copper repeating it back. But I hadn't meant it the way it came out. And if I'd been a judge, I would have found myself guilty straight away. It seemed the Formby coppers were also a world apart from those coppers in Manchester, who'd have probably plucked off a few apples higher up the branch for me. Surely he wasn't being serious?

"Even if you found it on the pavement, it still doesn't make it yours."

He was being serious, he was bonkers. "There!" I threw the apple over the wall into the owner's garden. "I've put it back. Can I go now?"

"First name."

"Paddy."

"Paddy Malone. Are you Irish by any chance?"

Jaysus, he was clever. But I wasn't answering that question, afraid I'd probably dig a deeper hole for myself.

"And where does Malone live?"

How would I know? I'd just made the name up.

I was saved by the copper in the police car, who was now making hand gestures for Sherlock to hurry back.

"Your lucky day, Malone."

Plucking another apple off the tree as the police car sped off, I arrived back at the school with a good five minutes or so to spare. As I turned the corner of the school block, I was sure I'd just seen 10-year-old Peter Loss hurry in to the boot-room. And as curiosity always got the better of me, I quickly made my way across the yard to see what he was up to. By all rights, he should have been in class.

Opening the door, I saw he wasn't in the boot-room, so I moved quietly to the door leading through into the changing rooms at the back of the stage, where Mr Sweet took me from time to time. The door was usually locked from the other side, so, when I gently turned the handle, I was surprised when it opened inwards and even more so when I heard a few muffled sounds, which caused me to freeze instinctively. I knew where they were coming from and I knew what was happening in there. I could feel my heart pounding in my ears, as I slowly bent down and looked through the keyhole of the old gym equipment storeroom. I couldn't see anything because the key was in the lock, but I heard Peter Loss whimper and Mr Sweet tell him, "Shh, I'm not going to hurt you."

My worst nightmare! The feeling of betrayal made my legs turn to jelly and almost buckle underneath me. I couldn't believe, I didn't want to believe this was happening. I was stunned. Shocked. Numbed. I held back the tears I felt welling up. I had never felt so much intense and all-consuming hatred, leaving my thoughts in turmoil.

I don't recall taking the bootlaces from the football boots. I don't recall tying them together or climbing the tree. I don't recall tying the bootlace around my neck or tying the other end to the branch. I don't recall jumping. But I do recall the moment my right knee hit me under the chin, splitting it wide open. I do recall lying in the tall grass, hiding myself from the world. No one knew I was there. No one had witnessed what I had just done. And life still went on. The birds were still singing. The pilot in the glider high above me had no notion that I was there. No one cared.

I so hated the world, I hated myself, I hated everyone and everything about this life I was living. It was pointless. It meant nothing to me and gave me nothing. I so wished I were dead. And yet, I was so glad I was still alive!

Father Tierney said, "God gave us life. And then left it to us to make our own choices. Therefore, each one of us will have to stand alone and bear the consequences of our own choices." So, I only had myself to blame for everything that had gone on in my life. After all, it had been my choice, it was what I had wanted. And I would have to bear the consequences of that and of the fact that I so hated the bastard! From that day forwards, I was going to pray night and day for Sweet to die.

Fighting Back

In the earlier part of the afternoon I'd been playing a game of war with some of the other boys, when I'd spotted Thompson and Farr making their way into the grotto. I thought Farr may have had something hidden up under his jumper, but I was unable to see properly once his back was to me. They were not part of our game, but even so, I wanted to find out what the pair of them were up to. Continuing to crawl through the tall grass bordering the whole outside of the playground, I made my way to the edge of the grotto and watched them disappear into the old shed, closing the door behind them. They were back out within a couple of minutes, which led me to assume they'd been hiding something – they'd been far too quick to have been smoking cigarettes or getting up to things with each other.

I'd afforded myself a quiet smile as the pair of them walked past me, without realising I was only a matter of a few feet away, skulking in the grass. And once I felt they were at a safe enough distance, I headed for the shed.

"What were they hiding?" I wondered aloud, as I scanned every inch of the shed. I soon spotted the disturbance marks on the wooden floor where the large rusting grass roller had been dragged out of the way before being put back haphazardly. Dragging it a foot or so away from the old garden tools standing behind it, I peered down over the top, just noticing the edge of the brown handbag poking out from behind a couple of rusting shovels. Taking a peek inside, I was shocked to find a pile of £5 notes, along with a mixture of coins, jewellery, and a collection of army medals staring up at me. So that's what they'd been up to when I'd seen them through the gap in the fence on my way to the library. "They must have burgled that house," I thought.

I had bad memories of how my daddy had made me climb down coal holes into the cellars of other people's houses in Hulme, using me to open the front doors so he could rob whatever took his fancy. Then, I'd had no choice other than to do his bidding. But now at least I was able to do something about these two feckers.

Forgetting I was a Nazi paratrooper in the middle of our war game, I pushed the old roller back into position, before leaving the shed and crawling out from the grotto, making my way back through the long grass until I was further down by the school block, where Mr McGuinness was standing.

"Mr McGuinness."

"Yes?"

"If I tell you something that's really bad, will you not say it was me that told you?"

"It depends on how bad it is." His crinkled, weather-beaten face creased into a smile. I really liked Mr McGuinness and often wondered why the teachers couldn't have been more like him. Though much older than they were, he seemed able to tolerate us much better, without resorting to violence or having to scream at us.

I hesitated, unsure whether I was doing the right thing, fearful of anyone finding out I'd snitched.

Mr McGuinness noticed my hesitancy. "If it doesn't involve you in any way, then I won't mention your name to anyone."

"I've just seen Thompson and Farr hiding a lady's handbag in the old shed up in the grotto. It's behind some old shovels, behind the big roller."

"Off and play," he said, not looking in the least surprised or interested. And I wondered if he thought I was making it up.

Later that day, Mr Marron surprised us all with the news that we would be playing a friendly football match against each other, before the big game the following day. The team playing the Taylors Boys would be playing against another home team, which he would choose. I don't know why they called it a friendly match. We took our football seriously.

At least it was dry for this game, unlike the match we'd played a couple of weeks back, when it had belted down with rain. It was no wonder it had ended in a goalless draw: the ground was so waterlogged the ball was only able to travel about three yards, if you could even manage a kick at all. Slipping and sliding was bad enough, but heading the ball was out of the question.

Little Paddy Gavin, our goalie, had stopped a potential goal with his head. I could have sworn his neck had disappeared between his shoulder blades as his head and the ball made contact, with the ball seeming to momentarily stay on the top of his little head for a second or two, before dropping to the soggy ground in front of his feet, where he'd retrieved it safely enough. But we'd then watched in amazement as he'd staggered off the pitch, still holding onto the ball and ignoring the calls from Marron for him to come back. Two of the lads were sent to fetch him and they brought him back onto the pitch. But it was obvious to us all, his brains had been knocked senseless by the weight of the ball. So Marron ordered the two lads, much to their annoyance, to take him off to Matron, who'd put him in sick bay for a few hours of rest.

Getting my football boots from the boot-room, I made my way to the assembly hall, excited by the game ahead. The smell of White Horse liniment hit my nostrils as some of the boys, already in their kits, rubbed it all over their calves and thighs. Not that many of them would be doing much running around on the pitch to get aching muscles.

I was about to take off my jumper when I noticed, from the corner of my eye, Mr Sweet heading over in my direction. I could feel my stomach turning, because I knew what he was going to say to me. But not only did I not want to miss the football match, I didn't want him to touch me ever again. My thoughts, along with my heart, were racing. I was unsure how I was going to handle the situation, but I could feel an overwhelming surge of anger towards him rising inside me. Suddenly I heard Father Tierney's voice: "God gave us the choice, and we must bear the consequences of our choices." Thank you, Father Tierney! The choice had always been mine. Today, I was going to make the choice and would accept the consequences, rather than making a choice driven by the need to be loved.

"I want you to stay back and help me with something," Mr Sweet said in a low voice.

"I don't want you ta love me any more." I said it! My anger had taken over any fear that I had of him, or anyone else for that matter. And there was no turning back. "I'm not doing anything for you. So feck off and leave me alone." I swore at a teacher!

I felt the bang to my head as it hit the wall, and both Mr Sweet and Mr Marron, who was nearby, suddenly attacked me. But I had already made my choice and I was fighting back. I caught Mr Sweet with a kick to the side of his leg, Mr Marron had hold of my hair and was shaking my head from side to side. This only made me angrier. They could beat me all they wanted, I was no longer aware of any pain. I was not giving in to this pair of vicious, bullying bastards. I would rather die fighting.

Mr Marron managed to get his arms around me from behind, holding me in a bear hug. But not before I knocked Sweet's glasses off his fat reddening face. Between the pair of them, I was half carried, half dragged out of the hall, still struggling and trying to kick my legs free from Mr Sweet's tight grip. I could hear Donkey hee-hawing and other voices shouting at the two teachers to leave me alone, which lifted my spirits.

The pair of them managed to get me halfway through the door of the tiny kit store, but they couldn't get me all the way inside because my hands were free and holding tightly on the door frame. Well, they were until Mr Sweet gave my balls a hard squeeze and I was forced to let go. Throwing me onto the floor of the kit-room, they swiftly left, locking me inside as I kicked the door and continued to use every swear word I could muster.

I didn't know how long I had been in the kit-room. It seemed time had a knack of always passing slowly when I was waiting in silence. I had eventually calmed down, having had the time to reflect on what had happened. And although my anger had subsided, the sense of betrayal still lingered inside me. I wondered what was going to happen to me now, having done what I'd just done. But to be honest, I didn't care. I was sensing an imminent turning point in my life.

Breaking Out

Nearly three years had passed since I had first arrived at St Vincent's and Sister Ignatius had given me her welcoming bone-crushing handshake. Father Tierney told us we should use the time the Almighty gave us on this earth to do good for our fellow man, though there was never a mention in his boring sermons about doing good for ourselves. And just as it was plainly obvious the grown-ups were not listening to what the old priest was telling them, the Almighty never listened to my prayers, otherwise half of that lot in there would have been under the ground by this point.

For me, time was meaningless, invisible. I had no hopes or plans for tomorrow, or for next week, or for the coming months and years to follow. The reality of my life and the lives of the boys I was living among was that we had no futures. We lived only for the days we found ourselves in. Yesterday was already done and dusted, and tomorrow didn't exist.

I looked forward to the end of each day, sometimes willing them to pass quickly, so that I could go off to my bed and creep back into the silence of my dreams, where I felt safest. But reality always found a way of kicking us in the teeth, dictating that tomorrow came around to push our dreams to one side, and leaving us no say in our own destiny.

Eventually let out of the kit-room, I was frogmarched down to the school block, with Mr Marron leading the way and Mr Sweet following behind us. I'd decided to stay calm and keep my composure, not wanting to be beaten by those two again. But when Mr Keenan snapped at me to bend over his desk, I stubbornly refused to do so, telling him I had done nothing wrong. But he wasn't interested at all. Not giving me the opportunity to explain my behaviour or get one word in edgeways, Marron and Sweet suddenly grabbed me and between the pair of them, managed to get me over Keenan's desk. And there, with each of them holding one of my hands across the opposite side of the desk to prevent me from standing upright, Mr Keenan forced down my trousers and pants and beat my backside viciously with the cane, drawing my blood.

I never did get to play in the match against the Taylors Boys, which had ended in a nil-nil draw, leaving my dream of scoring the winning goal in tatters. But it was great to have witnessed history repeating itself, when both team captains had gone in for a tackle on the ball and our captain, Paddy O'Neil, having taken offence to a poke in his eye, began battering the other captain's head against the ground, leaving a dent in the pitch. The ensuing brawl, which was more violent than the previous one, saw blood spilled on both sides, but (I'm proud to say) St Vincent's came out on top – again! And I am sure the toffs came away that day having learnt a valuable lesson: when putting your dukes up like the boxer Gentleman Jim, it is always wise to bear in mind that your opponent might not be as gentlemanly. And so leaving your bollocks unprotected wasn't a good idea.

The school did receive another letter from Father Patrick on behalf of the Catholic diocese, with him complaining about having put his own head on the block, only for us to chop it off. The letter had gone on to repeat all the previous personal insults, as well as informing us of the life ban on us ever playing against any other outside schools. Their loss!

As I had anticipated, Mr Sweet started his campaign of bullying me again, and though the physical attacks were few and far between, some of the cruel things he would say to me were just as bad as the physical stuff. His behaviour towards me wasn't obvious to anyone else, as he had made sure no one could see what he was doing or saying. On one occasion, he'd deliberately stood on my hand, breaking my thumb, as I crawled out from one of the grass dens we used to build after the football pitch and grass areas around the playground had been mown. In the past, the teachers had not minded us doing this, having no idea of some of the things going on inside them. But Mr Sweet suddenly decided to put an end to the dens.

"Out! Now!" he'd bellowed at a group of us inside the huge grass den, which we'd only just put the finishing touches to. And, as I had crawled out and looked up at him, he'd suddenly stood on my right hand and twisted his foot, grinding his heel and my hand into the ground and breaking the knuckle of my thumb. I could see the evil in his eyes as I screamed out with the excruciating pain. But he just looked down at me, a wry grin spread across his face.

I ran off to Mr Lilly's office and told him what had happened. He wasn't all that interested and called Matron to have a look at my thumb. Like her husband, she didn't believe a word of what I had told her, even suggesting it was an obvious accident, "if, in fact, it had even been Mr Sweet's foot", she argued, as she'd bandaged my hand up, made me a sling and sent me on my way.

Thompson and Farr were eventually caught by Mr Alston and Mr Marron. They set a trap for the lads after Mr McGuinness passed on the information I'd given him about seeing the brown handbag hidden in the old shed. We'd all watched from the windows, with some of the boys cheering loudly, as the pair of them, crying and pleading their innocence, were marched out in handcuffs and driven out of the school in the police car, never to be seen by us again.

As I knew all too well, all good things have a habit of ending badly. In the process of searching the shed, on the suspicion that Thompson and Farr may have hidden other things there, a hoard of contraband was found. Cigarettes, a pipe, lighter, matches, eight miniature bottles of spirits, money and condoms, amongst other things. The discovery resulted in the shed being demolished and the old gardening equipment given to the scrap merchants. What happened to the contraband was anyone's guess.

Now vulnerable to unwanted attention from some of the older boys, it had become increasingly difficult, if not impossible, for me to keep my head down and avoid all of them. I eventually came around to accepting the fact that it was pointless to keep saying no and risking a beating, while still getting bummed for my trouble. So, I let the inevitable happen and just got on with it.

But there came a point when I decided I could no longer accept what was happening to me. I not only hated, loathed, and despised most of my peers and the adults around me, I had come to hate, loathe and despise myself. I'd been getting these sudden urges to cut my wrists or throw myself out of an upstairs window. I was losing control of all my feelings and emotions, unable to stop the urge to hurt myself. Something was eating away at me from the inside out and I didn't know how to make it go away.

I came up with the idea of running away from St Vincent's, and confided in Pete Collins. He begged me to take him along too, almost crying real tears, and I could do nothing else but agree, swearing him to secrecy. The plan? There wasn't one, save to slip off under cover of darkness, when everyone was sound asleep in their beds.

The night we'd decided we were going, Collins and I crept, fully dressed, from our beds and out of our dormitory, only to see Donkey and Barnes, fully dressed and tiptoeing up along the corridor in our direction.

"I told you not to say anything," I berated Collins under my breath.

"I didn't tell them anything, I swear."

"He didn't tell us anything," whispered Donkey. Barnes backed him up, swearing on his granny's life, which convinced me Collins was telling the truth.

"I'm sorry," I said.

"That's alright," said Collins with a sheepish grin.

"It was Butler that told us!" blurted Donkey. "He told us, Pete told him."

Shaking my head in dismay, I quickly moved off, not bothering to see whether the others were following or not. Creeping down the middle stairway to the ground floor, with the others in pursuit, I made my way to the back door leading out in to the playground. The door was always locked, but the key hung on a hook next to it. Opening the door, I slipped the key back onto the hook and we were out.

It was a strange, exhilarating feeling to be outside, feeling free and wanting to be there. I could feel the heavy cloak of despair suddenly fall away from me, as the four of us quietly strolled across the playground, like ordinary kids with all the time in the world to get wherever it was we were going. Not that I had any clue as to where we were going.

"Look!" Donkey stopped suddenly in his tracks and pointed in the direction of the grotto.

"What is it, Donkey?" I asked.

"The ghost!"

"What ghost?" said Barnes, cowering behind us.

"The nun!" We had all heard about the ghost of Sister Agnes, who allegedly haunted the toilet block.

"I can see her!" I'd spotted the faint outline of her head and shoulders above the tops of the flowers. "She's praying." I was excited to see her for the second time since coming to St Vincent's. The first time was a few months after my arrival. She'd seemed so real to me when I'd walked into the beautiful grotto and had knelt alongside her, by the statue of Our Lady, and silently prayed with her. Having not seen her again (until now), I was never sure if she'd been another figment of my weird imagination, which had conjured many strange apparitions in the past.

"Who's praying?" asked Barnes.

"The ghost," said Donkey.

"What feckin' ghost?"

"Can't you see her?"

"All I can see is you two idiots taking the piss."

"Shite! The night watchman's peering out the window!" I spotted the light out of the corner of my eye as the curtain moved. "Keep still. He won't be able to see us from there." I was confident about that, considering he was half blind and wore thick-lensed glasses.

We could see the old fella's face pressed up against the window as he peered out through the glass pane for a minute or two, before he let the curtain fall back into place.

"Come on." I made to head off.

"I'm not going near any ghosts," said Barnes, refusing to budge from the spot.

"She won't hurt you," said Donkey.

"I know she won't, 'cos I'm not fuckin' going in there."

"Well I am, because it's the best way to go," I declared. "You can go another way if you like. Or you can go back. But this is the way I'm going. Anyway, look, she's gone."

"Are you sure?" Barnes, still cowering behind me and Donkey, peered out over our shoulders. "She could be hiding from us."

"If it'll make you feel better, I'll go and take a quick peek." I didn't wait for his reply and made my way into the grotto, seeing no one else but the statue of Our Lady standing in her usual pose, gazing down on the spot where the water used to flow but didn't any more. I stood for a moment looking at the grey figure, before quietly sneaking back past the other two, coming out from the shrubbery behind Barnes. "Boo!" I shouted, frightening the life out of him so that he screamed and farted simultaneously.

"The night watchman's looking out the window again," I lied, and ran towards the boundary wall, scrambling over it and dropping to the other side, with the others in hot pursuit.

Freedom

We spent the rest of that first night sleeping on the sand dunes of Formby beach. Waking early the following morning, cold and tired, we headed in the direction of Blackpool. I don't know why. It was just the first place I'd thought of when I'd decided to run away. I'd been to Blackpool once before, when my brother Martin and I were in Lynwood Children's Home and we were all taken there for a one-week holiday.

My memories of Bellevue amusement park in Manchester will probably stay with me forever. But so too will the memory of those mesmerising illuminations of Blackpool, which ran the full length of the promenade and surrounding streets. The amusement park, the noise, the vast crowds, the rain, the hysterical laughing man! All part of a memory of a happier time. And I just wanted it all over again.

From the high sand dunes near Formby it was easy to spot Blackpool's tall tower far off in the distance and having it in my sight went a long way to lifting my spirits. And even though it was still a long way off, we were not in that much of a hurry to get there. This was an adventure – our adventure! And it was all that more exciting because we had no one to bawl us out.

I wouldn't have a clue as to how far we walked that day along a seemingly endless desert of sand. The people had now gone from the beach, the light was fading, and the incoming tide had forced us off the beach and back onto the sand dunes. The others looked tired and a little sullen, and I was wishing they hadn't come with me. I didn't share their dreams and aspirations and I wouldn't have minded if they'd decided to give themselves up. I had nothing to give them.

We eventually came across a large metal road sign telling us we were nearing Southport. Then the heavens opened and it teemed down with the rain, gently at first and then much heavier. I usually loved being out in the rain, but not at that moment in time. I was not feeling that exhilarating sense of freedom I would often get standing out in it (the heavier and stormier the better) and always having to be the last one to get inside, much to the annoyance of those telling me to get in out of the rain.

Walking along one of the avenues, we came across a small tin workman's shed standing on a stretch of road that was being re-surfaced. By now the light was beginning to fade fast. Barnes forced open the door with his bare hands to reveal a pile of workers' tools and some large containers of liquid tar, which ponged. In front of them was a short, tar-stained yellow plastic bench, probably used by the workers to sit on when they were having their lunch. We managed to squeeze into the shed and onto the bench before closing the door, which was only a matter of a few inches from our faces. And there, in the relative safety of the cramped dark shed, we fell asleep, listening to the sound of the rain beating its loud rhythm on the roof.

In the early hours of the morning, I was woken by Barnes. The others were standing outside the shed, in the grey, dismal light. They looked dishevelled, cold and hungry and I did feel sorry for the pair of them. Donkey was very quiet. In fact, I hadn't heard him say much since he'd cussed out loudly after banging his elbow on St Vincent's boundary wall when scrambling over it during our escape. Looking at him now, I wondered what might be going on in his simple head. He caught me staring over at him and he threw me a big grin.

Running up along someone's front path, I helped myself to the two bottles of milk standing on the doorstep. Barnes shared his with Collins, while Donkey and I shared the other bottle. The milk made me feel even colder, and I could tell from their silence that the others were probably having second thoughts about running away. I was almost expecting them to tell me they wanted to go back to St Vincent's. But they said nothing.

We wandered aimlessly through the empty streets as the minutes and the hours ticked by. I suggested we should knock on people's front doors and beg for something to eat. "I did it all the time in Hulme and we always got food." This seemed to lift their spirits.

"What sort of food?" asked Donkey.

"Any sort of food," I told him.

"I don't like cabbage."

"Who the fuck eats cabbage for breakfast?" growled Barnes, sourly.

"Rabbits?" replied Donkey after a long pause.

"I'll do the knocking and the asking," I said quickly, defusing the argument I was sure would kick off between Barnes and Donkey.

Not long after we'd started our door knocking, a police van pulled up behind us, and two coppers got out, heading in our direction.

"Run!" I shouted, turning on my heels and charging off along the street. A quick look over my shoulder told me I had a copper on my tail, while Barnes, Donkey and Collins stood talking with the other copper as if it was a Sunday afternoon outing! They'd given up. What did I do now?

I had this dreadful fear running through me that the copper chasing me wasn't going to catch me. And the thought of being on my own, now that I knew I was going to be on my own, was so overpowering, I felt as is if I was drowning in my own fear. I was petrified. I didn't want to be alone. What was going to happen to me? Where was I going? I was bombarding myself with questions to which I had no answers.

It seemed the only thing I had in my life at that moment was the ability to run and to hide. Nothing else. I'd even lost the ability to beg for food, so it seemed, because no one had offered us a scrap of it. Not even a cabbage! With the realisation that there was nothing I could think of doing that was going to make me feel any better or worse about myself, I decided to slow down to give the copper a chance to catch me. But even then, he seemed too out of breath and wasn't getting any closer to me. I couldn't believe I was going to do this, but I was forced to deliberately trip over my own foot, hurting my elbows, just so the unfit, lazy sod could catch me.

It turned out we'd been reported by a woman for begging at her door. I felt sure it must have been the old bag with the huge red and blue veined hooter. When she'd opened her front door, she'd taken one look at us before slamming it back in our faces, almost catching her conk in it. And that was the response we'd had from all those people who'd opened their doors to us: a quick once-over and the door in our faces.

It was difficult to understand how people, well fed and comfortable in their warm houses, could look into the eyes of hungry children and suddenly go blind. But that is what seemed to have happened. For them, it had been all too easy to not see us.

Back at St Vincent's, we were not asked to explain our reasons behind running away, nor were we asked if we were hungry or feeling ill. Instead, we were told we were ungrateful, untrustworthy, despicable children with not an ounce of achievement or a brain cell between the four of us. That last part of the comment seemed to cheer up Donkey and he hee-hawed a laugh, which earned him a clout around the face. We knew we were not going to escape without punishment. But I was shocked by the viciousness of the beating dished out to us, because it was Mr Alston on the other end of the cane.

Of all the staff at St Vincent's, Mr Alston was the only one I'd had the slightest respect for. Unlike the others, he had never beaten me before this. I had always thought him to be much more tolerant and understanding towards us than all the others put together. But I was wrong. My respect for him vanished the instant he struck the first blow across my bare backside. While the other three cried, I just stood there glaring defiantly up at him and I was sure he could see the hatred in my eyes.

We were marched down to the communal shower area and made to strip off while Mr Alston and Mr Sweet stood watching us under the cold shower. To feel so small, isolated and insignificant wasn't anything new to me. I was used to it, if the other three weren't. It was painful, of course it was. I felt bitter and sad to be treated in such a way, but I was helpless. There was nothing I could do but accept it as the norm.

After we had showered and dressed in our clean change of clothing, the three of us joined the others as if nothing had happened.

The Season to be Jolly

Only two months to go until another Christmas was upon us. There was the usual buzz of excitement in the air, with most of the boys looking forward to going home for their two-week break. Except for me. I wasn't excited about going home because I wasn't going home. But I was excited about the prospect of having the whole place to myself again. The only downside was that it was over all too quickly. It didn't bother me in the least being alone. And though it was a little bit spooky during the night times, once my head was under the covers I was usually okay. I wasn't that afraid of ghosts, I'd never been hurt by them and I only hid my head because I didn't want to see any ugly ones that would probably frighten me to death.

The first Christmas I'd spent on my own wasn't anything out of the ordinary. On Christmas morning, Sister Ignatius handed me a large orange and an apple, telling me I should be thankful for small mercies, which I was. I hadn't been expecting anything at all, let alone something from that mean-spirited witch.

To be honest, it wouldn't have surprised me if she had ordered me out on the streets to beg for the poor Sisters of Mercy, with the life of poverty they'd have us believe they lived.

This would, at least, have filled up the rather boring days for me. However, I'm not sure I would have given her any of my takings – if I'd actually received anything from that town's tight-fisted community.

That had been the only direct contact I'd had with Sister Ignatius and the rest of the nuns during that whole Christmas period, which for me was an extra bonus. Perhaps they'd been too busy, purging themselves and praying for absolution from the sins they'd committed throughout the past year, before a new year began.

Miss Peggy and her friend, who she'd introduced to me as Eileen, were the only two people I'd had any official contact with during that first Christmas. There were people around the place, such as the cleaners, gardeners, and handyman, who had always acknowledged me with the odd hello. But other than that, Miss Peggy was on hand to give me my clean changes of clothing and torture me with her cooking. I'd pretend to her the food was lovely, because I didn't want to upset her.

Even though Sister Ignatius hadn't been visible, I'd had this strange feeling the auld dragon was keeping a beady eye on me, peering around every corner with her piercing gobstopper eyes. My suspicions were justified when I'd caught sight of her ghostly image out of the corner of my eye, her nose pressed right up against one of the stairwell windows as she stared out at me. I pretended not to notice her as I climbed up onto the large tractor tyre, making it roll a few yards before losing my balance and having to jump off it.

This was a pastime that would keep most of us amused, with us taking it in turns to hop up on the tyre and see how far we could make it roll by walking it along, before falling off it. It was hard to keep your balance and stay on the tyre as it rolled along, but it was great once you had the knack of it. There were only a few boys, besides me, who were able to walk the tyre the full length of the playground, which was some achievement.

Climbing back up onto the tyre, I made it roll for about 10 yards before losing my balance again. And I bet the witch had put a curse on me, willing me to fall off, so I gazed across and up at the window, letting her know I knew she was there. She'd done likewise, staring back at me, and for a moment we stood with our eyes fixed upon each other, before I blinked, and she suddenly vanished from view. With little else to do throughout the days, I continued practising for hours on end, until eventually the tyre became my legs. And by the time the other lot got back from seeing their mammies and daddies, I'd been able to walk around on the tyre for hours without once losing my balance, which had really annoyed everyone waiting for their turn.

This year, we were putting on a Christmas show for the local community. Mr Lilly was doing a magic act, whilst Mr Keenan had got together a group of the best singers in the school to do a Black and White Minstrels show. He was also doing the props for it. In fact, Mr Keenan was writing, producing and choreographing the whole thing. I'd asked him if I could lend a hand, but he said he didn't need anybody's help, least of all mine. "It seems everything you do is doomed to failure," he explained.

"We'll soon see about that," was my first thought, as I started to plan out ways to get even with the creep.

I hated his smug face, which always reminded me of a miserable-looking bulldog, only with long, bushy eyebrows, which he would often preen and twist with his fingertips, bringing them to a point. He knew nothing about me. And whatever he thought he knew was down to what the snitchers in St Vincent's had told him.

"Can I do a solo?"

"So low we can't hear you!" He laughed at his own feeble joke. "No one is doing a solo," he snapped. "I might consider letting you and Walters do a duet. But," (there was always a but) "I don't want the pair of you attempting to out-sing each other, otherwise I'll send both of you off the stage. And if you don't like it, I can always get someone else to do it."

"Can we sing 'The Carnival Is Over' by The Seekers? It's my favourite song. Please," I pleaded.

"Absolutely not," he snapped. "I'm picking all of the songs and you'll know soon enough what they will be."

I have no favourite season, but I'd always thought that Christmas was the most miraculous time of the year. It has always amazed me how, when Christmas comes around, the atmosphere takes on a different meaning, with everyone wishing goodwill to everyone else when they don't mean it. And then there are the year-round, tight-arsed miserable buggers who suddenly become happy. It's as if, at a certain time in the calendar, an automatic switch inside their brains suddenly flicks on and they suddenly realise 'tis the season to be jolly.

Unsurprisingly, we didn't get much in the way of presents at St Vincent's. Not that I ever expected anything from Santa Claus. What kind of a saint was he supposed to be? He couldn't even be bothered to fly over our house in Stamford Street, unless it was only to stick his two fingers up at us and yell down, "You're getting nothing, yah little bastards!" And if the previous year's gifts at St Vincent's were anything to go by, I wasn't going to get too excited about this year's offerings.

It's the thought that counts, so we were told, when we moaned about the crappy presents Santa had brought us. This only proved to us that no thought had gone into them. It wasn't as if we could even swap the rubbish. We all got the same things: an orange, a pen and a diary. A diary! What the feck did I want with a diary? I was 12 years old. I had no dates to remember, no appointments to keep, no friend's names and addresses or telephone numbers to write in it. I decided if I got another one this Christmas, which was more than likely, I'd leave it lying around, like I did with last year's, for someone else to pick up if they felt the need for an extra diary.

I was about to discover that this Christmas was going to be different from previous ones at St Vincent's. It was the dreaded maths class and I was trying to learn my times tables, which were written up on the blackboard. I hated maths. In fact, I hated most subjects, barring English and music. I found maths boring and a complete waste of time. Adding numbers, dividing numbers, multiplying numbers, then taking them away – and for what? To know we were getting the right change back from the shopkeeper? Well, I wouldn't be buying anything from a shopkeeper, so maths wasn't much use to me.

Mr Lilly walked into the classroom. All 16 of us immediately jumped to our feet and stood ramrod to attention, just as we had been drilled, with our arms straight and our hands tucked tightly into our sides, with thumbs pointing downwards, like a squadron of boy soldiers. What a terrible prospect – the idea of us fighting a war…

Mr Lilly threw the briefest of glances in our direction. I was sure I'd caught his eye, before he turned his back on us and had a brief conversation with Mr Marron, who kept glancing over in my direction. This caused me to wonder what I might I have done to deserve his attention. When Lilly left the classroom, we all breathed a heavy sigh of relief and I went back to my sums.

"Rhattigan!"

"Sir?"

"Headmaster's office."

"I haven't done anything, sir."

"That's nothing new," Marron retorted, prompting a few sniggers from the other morons. "Pronto!"

It was odd seeing 15 pairs of bespectacled eyes gawking accusingly at me. Odder still was the fact that every boy in St Vincent's wore a pair of the round, wire-framed glasses the optician recommended. The lenses of my glasses were no stronger than the window panes I looked through every day. And it was impossible to reflect a death-ray of light through them, so that I could burn ants or flies to death. The lads wearing thick bifocals could incinerate all sorts of things in seconds.

What a sight they were to behold. Big eyes, little eyes, squinty eyes, frog eyes, cross-eyes! I wondered why the headmaster wanted to see me. I was feeling guilty already.

Could It Be Magic?

Making my way up along the corridor in the direction of the headmaster's office, I came across Brian Walters and Paddy O'Neil sitting outside the dentist's room. They didn't seem very happy, and no wonder. We all had previous experiences of our visiting dentist, affectionately known as "The Butcher". There wasn't a lad in St Vincent's place who didn't have a mouthful of lead fillings.

As I went to pass the pair of them, Walters stuck out a leg in a feeble attempt to trip me up.

"Missed, gobshite." I hopped over his outstretched leg.

"Your mum's the biggest whore in Ireland," he informed me.

"Who told yah? Yer dad?" I laughed in his face and he jumped to his feet, just as Mr Alston walked into view. I walked off, with the threat of "later" ringing in my ears.

"Where are you off to?" asked Mr Alston.

"Headmaster's office, sir."

"What is it this time?"

"Nothin'."

"That's unusual."

There yah feckin' go. I was guilty if I did something wrong and I was guilty if I did nothing wrong. There was no point in even thinking about defending myself, because it would only make me look guiltier.

"You're still very welcome to come and write letters to your brother, you know," he smiled.

"I don't want to write to him any more," I lied, dropping my gaze and hoping he would get the picture and realise I didn't want to talk to him.

"Well, you'd best be off before you get yourself into more trouble," he sighed.

I knocked on Mr Lilly's office door. There was no answer. I knocked again, only louder. But there was still no answer. I was sure the fat German-speaking slob was deliberately keeping me waiting, just for the fun of it. I had a sudden urge to pick up the nearby fire extinguisher and smash it against the office door. That would make him answer.

"Yes." Lilly's voice called out, just in time to save his office door. For the devil of it, I knocked on the door once more. "Yes!" said the voice, more insistently this time. So, I knocked again.

A couple of seconds later, the door swung violently inwards. "Are you deaf, boy?" snapped the red-faced headmaster, as he glared at me.

"I didn't hear, sir."

"Get in. And close the door behind you," he snapped again, moving back inside his office and plonking his fat backside down into his red leather chair, which squeaked under his weight.

Closing the office door, I made my way over to his desk and stood to attention. He said nothing. It was as if I was completely invisible to him. I watched as he picked up a tea biscuit from the small plate and chomped away at it, getting a few tiny crumbs stuck on his Hitler-style moustache. He then picked up his cup and glugged the remaining coffee in it down his saggy neck.

"I've some good news for you, Rhattigan," he said, his dark eyes beaming. "You won't be staying here over the Christmas period." The shock was sudden and I could feel all the butterflies in the pit of my stomach fly off at once.

I said nothing and just stared back at him, as he silently studied me. I think he wanted me to beg the question, why? But I wasn't going to do that. Why couldn't he just come out with what he had to say, instead of building it up in dribs and drabs, for me to try and second guess him? If I wasn't staying in this dump, then what dump will I be staying in? I wasn't going to ask, and so I waited for him to let his secret out.

"You are going home to your parents for Christmas."

"I'm not!"

"You are."

"No, I'm not. I don't want to."

"You don't have any choice in the matter."

"Why?"

"Because the powers that be believe it's time to integrate you back where you belong, if that is at all possible," he said, looking down his nose at me. "I'm sure your parents will have their work cut out."

"I don't have parents."

"Well, according to the Social Services reports, you do."

Social Services? Who the feck were these faceless people who made all the decisions on my life without ever bothering to ask me how I felt about it? Who were they, these invisible people, who had decided I needed their care and protection and yet had never been to see me, or give me this so-called care and protection?

Yes. They were there alright to give us their shitty, hand-me-down clothing and the odd tatty old piece of furniture. They were there, banging on our front door, wanting to know why we hadn't been to school. They were there, tearing my family and our lives apart, on the premise of them knowing what was best for us, the children. But where had they been for me since I had been incarcerated inside the walls of this Catholic school, where I was ignored, beaten, abused and used by the very people charged to care and protect me?

"I hate the Social Services, I hate the Catholic Church, I hate the Nugent Care Society and I hate my parents. And I don't want to go home to them." Unusually, Mr Lilly didn't even bat an eyelid at my outburst.

"That may be the case. But you've no choice in the matter."

"I can kill myself."

"That would certainly settle matters." His smug, smiling eyes laughed at me from behind his gold-rimmed spectacles. "I see your brother Martin is happy about the arrangements."

"Is he going, too?"

"As far as I am aware."

Why didn't he just say all this in the one go and save me arguing the toss with him? If Martin was going, that changed everything.

"I take it you've decided to live a little longer then? Right, we're done here. If you are still breathing on 20th December, you are off to your family in Chatham for the holidays."

"Is that in Manchester?"

"It's in Kent, better known as the Garden of England. Oh, I almost forgot. I'm looking for a magician's assistant for this year's Christmas show."

"How do yah mean, sir?"

"I hear you are interested in magic?"

"I love magic."

"That's settled, then?"

"Will I be able to do a magic trick?"

"Well, perhaps I might consider showing you one or two easy ones you could do. But I don't want you showing every Tom, Dick and Harry how they are done. Magic is a secret and has to remain a secret."

"I'm good at keeping secrets, sir."

"Well, now you are here." He suddenly pulled a packet of Players cigarettes from his jacket pocket and took one of them out. Then, moving the coffee cup and plate to one side, he wiped the sleeve of his jacket across the desk, making sure the surface was clean, before laying the fag down on the desk top. "Watch the cigarette carefully," he said. And I stared down at the fag as he twiddled his fingers just above it, as if summoning up his magical powers, while adding some garbled utterings that could have been German for all I knew. Putting his index finger an inch in front of the cigarette, he moved it across the table towards me, and the fag followed his finger.

"Can I see it again? Please, sir." I was pretending to be amazed by the trick, clever as it was, but I was sure I saw the tiniest piece of a biscuit crumb (which must have fallen from

278

his moustache) suddenly vanish off the table top just as the cigarette moved.

"Once more and that's it," he said, going through the same routine to summon up the magic to his podgy fingers. "Keep your eyes on the cigarette."

"I'm watching, I'm watching." Was I feck! I was keeping my beady eyes on his lips.

I was right. "You blew it!" I was all excited, having sussed him out. "I saw you, sir."

"Get out of my office." Lilly's face, like magic, had suddenly turned red.

"But sir, I was clever, wasn't I?"

"Out!" His face had turned scarlet.

"Can I still be your assistant?"

"Get out!" He threw the packet of cigarettes at me, missing the side of my head by a whisker and I did a quick disappearing act.

A Bang on the Head

I had a swollen eye and a bit of a sore head after being whacked in the face a couple of days previously. I didn't remember much about what had happened, it was that quick. I'd hurried into the outside toilet block but was unable to have a pee because Allen Jarvis was standing at the latrine, peering over at me. His face was already messed up, with two black eyes and a bruised hooter, the handiwork of Allan McGowan (one of the Geordie lads), who had beaten Jarvis up after he had given McGowan the come-on in the bathhouse.

I could tell Jarvis wasn't having a lag because the drain was down my end and there was no pee heading in my direction. So, taking a quick peek, I'd caught him peering at my privates. Worse still, he could see I could see him, and yet he stood there flashing his dick at me, with a grotesque grin spread across his face. Lost for words, for once, I just laughed at him and hurried out of the toilet block.

The next thing I remember is the pain, as my brain exploded into millions of shooting stars, and the sudden darkness. It reminded me of the time, back in Manchester, when I'd decided to walk along the top of a high wall and lost my balance, falling off and landing head-first on the pavement. Left with a lump the size of a duck egg protruding from my forehead, I remember having a constant headache along with this strange, ripple-effect mist, hanging in front of my eyes for days on end. I'd been fortunate my brother Martin was with me at the time, so he was able to guide me around the streets, keeping me safe. I'd vomited a few times, which Daddy had ignored, while Mammy blamed it on something I must have eaten, "with the shite yah pick up off the streets every day".

I so missed Martin. I still recall the agony I'd felt the moment I'd realised we were to be separated from each other. I had cried so much and I could feel the physical pain of a broken heart, which was so bad I thought I was going to die. The night times were always the worst. I would lie in my bed, unable to sleep, constantly thinking about those happier times when we were so free and together, roaming the streets of Manchester without a fear in the world because we had each other for protection. Not that we had too many worries about needing protecting from the streets we'd once roamed. They were relatively safe and good to us. Knowing Manchester like the back of our hands, we were always confident. Perhaps at times too confident for our own good.

I remember when we were once searching through a bombed bakery shop a few streets away from where we lived. I was out in the backyard, twisting a piece of lead piping away from the wall, when I noticed a sudden movement from the corner of my eye. It was only slight, but it had been enough to tell me that the roof was about to cave in at any second. And then it did.

"The roof!" I screamed at the top of my voice, as I ran backwards away from the building, just managing to get out of the way in the nick of time, as the whole roof collapsed in on itself, sending plumes of dust skywards. "Martin! Martin!" I'd dashed over the debris through the blinding cloud of dust in my desperation to find my brother. Most of the back part of the roof and ceiling had fallen in and down into the ground floor of the shop, where the floorboards had been ripped out.

"Martin!" I'd frantically called his name time and time again as I scrambled, half blind, over the grey slates, my caked eyes streaming with tears and a mouth full of grit.

"Give us a hand, kid."

"Martin!" He was alive. The joy I'd felt that day when he'd called out to me is beyond description. How my heart had skipped as I looked down to see his dirty face peering up out of the coalhole, his big smile spread from ear to ear.

"I'd seen it before yah shouted ta me." He'd spoken so calmly, as if it were no big deal. And I suppose at the time it wasn't such a big deal, especially to him. "There's some coal down here!" he declared.

Back then, we had no fears or thoughts for our own safety. But now, no longer having each other to watch out for, I constantly worried about him. I was always afraid something bad was going to happen to him and I wouldn't be there to protect him. It was so frustrating, but what could I do except continue praying for his safety and keep wishing we could be together again.

I wanted to know who had whacked me in the head and why. Norman Butler told me Johnny Johnson had told him that his friend Paul O'Connell told him he'd seen the two Welsh cousins, Hugh and Peter Williams, rushing around the corner of the toilet block seconds after I'd came staggering around, holding my face. Not having had any run-ins or any contact with the two Welsh cousins in the past, I was finding it difficult to believe they had anything to do with it. Unless someone had put them up to it? Walters? Possibly. But then again, he always wanted to be involved in his own dirty deeds, provided he had his back covered by his goons.

There was only one person I knew I'd recently upset: Mr Lilly. Could he possibly have bribed someone to hit me? I'd heard little Gary Percival bragging to some of his friends about the fact he'd been chosen by Mr Lilly to be his assistant for the Christmas show. The pair of tosspots! I was already thinking of ways to ruin their little act.

If there is one important lesson to be learnt in life, it would have to be, See Nowt, Hear Nowt, Say Nowt. And certainly, never let on to anyone that you know their secrets. Just as importantly, never let your friends know your secrets. That way, if things go tits-up, you only have yourself to blame. As well as putting together a plan of action to spoil Mr Lilly's act, I thought I might also have come up with a way to get information from the two taffy cousins.

In the later part of the afternoon, Mr Alston took 12 of us for choir practice. He had been hoping for at least 20 volunteers but couldn't muster up any interest, no matter how much he'd threatened. He'd eventually had to throw out three of the choir – Donkey being one of them – after telling them they couldn't sing a full note in the right key if their lives depended on it. It was true of course, they were awful. Especially Donkey. Jaysus, it was bad enough him being a beat behind the rest of us, singing the last word to every line a split second after we'd already finished it, but he would also elongate the last feckin' lyric.

It was funny at first, but it didn't take too long for it to become a distraction to the rest of the choir. Donkey was upset to be told he was no longer needed, and I had felt sorry for him. As it turned out, he was soon cheered up when Mr Alston offered him an alternative role in the show, telling Donkey he could stand on stage alongside him, and turn the sheet music while Mr Alston played the piano.

Not long to the show and our timing was still a little out, though the difference in our performances without the tone-deaf loonies was miraculous. But nothing is ever perfect in life – there is always a downside. Mine was the fact that Brian Walters was one of the chosen 12. Worse still, I'd been picked to duet the Christmas carols "In the Bleak Midwinter" and "Silent Night" with him.

"That's good." Alston looked up from the piano as the pair of us practised. "Keep the harmonies like that. Don't try to out-sing each other and it'll be great."

Out-sing each other! It was Walters trying to out-sing me, as usual. And I wasn't going to let the tosspot get away with it. I'd cursed him in the hope that his voice would break, which would put an end to those comparisons between him and a singing angel. There was no way that fecker was ever going to heaven!

The sight of him gawking at me while I was singing and shaking his head at me with a big smirk all over his face really got up my nose. Cowardly feck! He was too afraid to say anything to my face because he didn't have any of his mates to back him up. I felt so angry and had a sudden urge to rush at him and push him off the stage. With a bit of luck and a shilling on the side, it wouldn't be his voice breaking but his scrawny neck…

On second thoughts, rushing at him would only mean me out of the show and him being the star and getting all the plaudits (not to mention sympathy if he ended up in a wheelchair), which he would have loved and milked for all it was worth. No. I would bide my time. So help me. I would get him.

"Right boys! Let's have you all singing 'Distant Drums'!"

"We've no drums, sir."

"You will just have to make some drum sounds for now. Drums and tambourines will all be here tomorrow. Ready? After three."

"I hear the sound (dum, dum, dum, dum, dum, dum), Of distant drums (dum, dum, dum, dum, dum, dum), Far away (dum, dum, dum, dum, dum, dum), So Far Away."

"Da-da-da-da-da-da-daah!" I improvised.

"What's that racket all about, Rhattigan?"

"It's a bugle, sir."

"Bugle? It's a bloody racket. Just stick to the drums. Okay, that's all for today. Final rehearsal tomorrow."

A Bellyful of Bangers

At tea-time, I stood at the back of the queue as it slowly snaked its way up along the side corridor and through to the serving area. Two sausages, a large spoonful of home-grown peas, a dollop of watery mashed potatoes (without the eyes) and two thin slices of bread was our ration. Matron came around the tables pushing the tea trolley in front of her. She filled our plastic half-pint mugs from the large metal tea urn on the trolley, which she always left at the other end of the dining room, for any of us to help ourselves if we wanted a refill.

I had no idea why I was doing it, but I was staring at Peter Loss's plate, wishing for his peas to scatter everywhere. He was getting on my nerves, talking with his mouth full and spraying bits of food everywhere. To my amazement, as he cut through his sausage, his knife suddenly slipped, causing most of his peas to fly off his plate. Jaysus! I was filled with a mixture of excitement and trepidation. If I had the power to do that, just think what else I could do!

My eyes followed Mr Lilly's short, stubby legs, as they slow-marched up and down the middle of the polished dining room floor. I was concentrating all my thoughts, willing his legs to fall off, leaving him to support his stumpy body on his arms. But he marched past me without a second glance, before doing a regimental about turn and walking back the way he'd just come.

"Who's taken me feckin' sausages?" I looked up from my plate to see the gormless Dave Given, sitting directly across from me, almost choking on a mouthful of food as he attempted to quickly swallow it down his scrawny neck.

The other lads sitting around the table thought it was hilarious. The guffaws from Carl Winner, sitting opposite Given, reminded me of a snorting pig. He had tears of laughter streaming from his eyes, so I let him have a handful of my hot, watery potatoes, straight in the eye. But he just wiped off the mess with his hand and ate it.

"Sir!" I raised my hand in the air.

"Yes." Mr Lilly stopped slow-marching.

I was about to tell him my sausages had suddenly vanished off my plate, when I felt something sticking into my ribs. 12-year old Gordon Turner (one of the other Geordie lads) had his fork pressed into my side. He said nothing to me – he didn't have to. The madness in his eyes had already said what I needed to know. And knowing he was a mad bastard, I changed tack.

"I need ta go to the toilet, sir."

"Why didn't you go before you came into the dining room?"

"I didn't need to go then."

"Well, you'll have to wait."

"It's popping out sir." I deliberately made my face go red to emphasise the point. "I don't think I can hold it back, sir."

"You've two minutes. Get out."

I didn't need a second invitation. I was out of the dining room, doing a good impersonation of Groucho Marx as I squeezed the cheeks of my backside together and held a hand behind me at the ready, as if I was expecting something to drop out at any minute.

Hurrying down the slope and past the toilets, I stopped at the entrance to the serving area and took a quick peek inside. I could see Matron through the glass partitioning dividing the serving area and the dining room. She was busy at one table chatting to the boys, pretending she was interested in how they were getting along, when it was common knowledge to all of us she only wanted to give them a flash of her cleavage as she leant forward. Anyway, you couldn't even see all the way down her blouse.

Deciding to make my move, I scurried across the floor on all fours towards the hotplate. A quick peer over the top of it and I homed in on the nine sausages. Yummy! I greedily grabbed all of them in my hands. They were boiling hot, but I was prepared to put up with the pain rather than drop them. Pulling up the bottom of my jumper into a fold, I dropped the sausages into it before scurrying back the way I had come. Making my way up to the toilet block, I sat happily on the bog and scoffed down the lot, before heading back into the dining room.

"Those of you for seconds, raise your hands," said Mr Lilly.

That'll be a miracle! I sucked the last remnants of sausage from my teeth as I watched Matron head off into the serving area. She reappeared seconds later with a bemused look on her face, making her way to Mr Lilly, she stood on tiptoe to speak into his ear.

I may not have had the power to make Mr Lilly's legs fall from underneath him, but I did feel good, sitting there, smiling on the inside, with my hand raised high in the air, along with 47 other hands. I was the only one, besides the two of them and God, who knew what she was probably whispering in his ear. And with all hands raised high in the air, he was unable to single out a possible culprit.

"You can all put your hands back down," snapped Lilly, while his shifty eyes gazed out at us. But I kept up my hand, as I saw the chance to carry out my plan on the two taffy boys.

"What is it now, Rhattigan?"

"Can I get some more tea please, sir?"

"Get on."

"Thank you, sir." I slid a small portion of my sloppy mashed potatoes off my plate and hid it in the palm of my hand, before taking my plastic mug down to the urn and filling it with hot tea.

On my way back, just as I reached the table where the Welsh cousins were sitting, I dropped the potato slop on the floor and pretended to slip on it, throwing my tea over Peter Williams' lap. Jaysus, talk about quick! In the blink of an eye, he was up out of his chair, pulling his trousers and underpants down around his ankles, giving everyone a good laugh.

"Sorry sir, I didn't mean it, sir. I tripped on that sir." I pointed down to the potato skid.

"Blithering idiot."

"I didn't see it, sir."

"Get back to your seat."

"Can I get some more tea, sir?"

Mr Lilly said nothing. Instead, he raised his eyebrows and glared at me. Taking that as a no, I quickly moved off, back to my chair.

"Come with me," said Matron and Williams shuffled off after her, with his hand cupping his private parts.

"Pull those pants up, you buffoon!" bellowed Lilly.

That evening, I managed to collar Hugh Williams in the small recreation room. To my surprise, and without me having to utter a single threat, or give him any clue as to my suspicions about him and his cousin, he spilled the beans.

Admitting it had been him, he was quick to point out it had, apparently, all been a terrible case of mistaken identity. A lad called Chris Holland had told them to give Jarvis a beating, with threats of dire consequences if they didn't. I couldn't understand how they could have mistaken me for that beanpole Jarvis. Williams went on to explain that it was his cousin who had thrown the punch, not him.

"I was watching out in case anyone came around the corner, honest. We didn't know it was you 'til it was too late."

"I thought Holland and Jarvis were bum-chums?"

"They were, 'til Holland caught Jarvis with Martin Flanagan. We're really sorry."

"Yeah, I believe you." I was happy to accept Williams' apology.

"Are you going to get your own back on us for that?" he said, pointing to my swollen eye.

"Nah, yer alright." It was Holland I blamed for starting the whole thing, and I was already forming a devious plan to give him his comeuppance.

Later that evening, I collared Jarvis in the small playroom. He was getting thrashed by Michael Flynn in a game of chess.

Flynn, without question, was one of the better chess players in the school, even if he did come across as an eejit. I remember the first time I'd challenged him to a game, with us putting up 10 football cards each as winnings. At the time, I had genuinely thought I was good enough to beat him, especially having thrashed all the other idiots who'd challenged me previously. Finn had only just managed to beat me, in a tough, tense game that had taken us just over an hour to play.

"You're really good," he'd smiled at me. "I thought you were going to beat me."

I'd offered him double or quits and he'd jumped at the opportunity, the patronising hustler. I lost 20 football cards in two or three minutes, which was about as long it had taken him to put me in checkmate. I should have realised the other goons I'd played against were completely hopeless, leading me in to a false sense of invincibility. It wasn't fair, I told myself.

After telling Jarvis his ex-bum-chum Holland had set him up for a bashing, I was taken by surprise when he suddenly burst into tears like a little girl.

"For feck's sake, Jarvis! He couldn't have been much of a mate."

"He was more than just a mate to me."

Jaysus, the face on the fella. It was bad enough he had two black eyes and a bigger conk than usual, but now he was sobbing and making those strange guttural noises from his throat. It was taking me all my willpower not to laugh.

"Come on Jarvis," I encouraged, pretending to care about the big fairy. "It's not as if it's the end of the world. There's plenty of fish in the sea. If yah want ta go fishing that is."

I'd heard my uncle Frankie Gavin saying this to his sister, my Aunty Mary, when she'd kicked her husband Jimmy the Gurk out of the house, because (according to Aunty Mary) he was "like a dog on heat, sniffing around the floozies like flies around a lump of shite. Only, a dog would be a lot fussier!"

I continued to talk Jarvis around. "Anyway, he can't be much of a mate if he can do that to yah. Can he?" I sat on the edge of the old armchair, throwing a comforting arm around his shoulders, and to my amazement the tears suddenly stopped, like a tap being turned off.

Wasting no time, I asked him if he could get me a box of pins from the clothing store, where he worked every Saturday, helping Miss Peggy.

"What are you going to do with them?"

"If the bird sang, the cat would eat it!" I tapped a finger to my nose, though I was sure he wouldn't have a clue what I meant.

I'd made the saying up, having listened to Uncle Paddy telling the family one of his many stories when they were all in the house, singing and dancing and laughing as they'd celebrated Grandad's passing. I remembered how the back room had suddenly gone silent, when my uncle had staggered to his feet and took to the floor.

"One cold and frosty winter's day," he began, "a young sparrow is flying high over the Irish countryside, mindin' his own business, when his feathers begin to freeze up. Feck this, says the sparrow. I must find meself a place ta land and keep meself warm. Otherwise I'm a dead duck. Spotting the wide-open doors of a barn, he aims himself towards them, miraculously surviving a bumpy landing on the cold stone floor inside the barn.

"Unfortunately, the barn is completely empty and the bird, almost half frozen ta det, resigns itself ta die. That's when the cow walked in ta the barn and stood over the sparrow, before dropping its load all over it. Gad the stench! It was terrible. But at least the warm shite began ta warm the bird. And, happy in the knowledge he was going ta survive, it began whistling a merry tune. Along came the farm cat. And on hearing the whistling cowpat, he parted it with his paw, saw the whistling bird and ate it!

"Now, there's tree morals ta this story. One: if someone puts yah in the shit, it doesn't mean ta say he's yer enemy. Two: if someone gets yah out of the shit, it doesn't mean ta say he's yer friend. And lastly. if yah ever find yerself in the shit, sometimes it's better ta keep yer gob shut."

The Best-Laid Plans...

It was very early Sunday morning. Barring the sounds of heavy breathing, I could hear nothing else. Assuming everyone was asleep, I slipped my feet over the edge of the bed, before quietly tipping back my bedside locker and retrieving the small box of pins that Jarvis had stolen for me from the clothing store. Moving barefoot out of the dormitory, I cautiously made my way down the side stairs to the dimly lit corridor on the ground floor, hurrying past the kitchen and the headmaster's office in the direction of the small chapel.

In the semi-darkness, I could hear the large grandfather clock ticking away, its loudness exaggerated by the silence, as it duetted with the sound of my own heart beating loudly in my ears – as it always did when I was up to no good and scared of getting caught.

Opening the chapel door, I sneaked inside, leaving it just slightly ajar, so I could listen for any sounds that might tell me someone was on the prowl. The chapel was only a small affair, with an altar and eight pews at the front, then a short step up to the back area with a further eight pews, used whenever we had an overspill of worshippers. It was light inside the chapel, with the moonlight shining in through the high windows running the length of the longest wall.

I could make out the statue of Jesus, with his hands held outwards showing the bloody wounds on the palms of his hands, where the crucifixion nails had gone through them. Yet despite his obvious pain, he could still afford a gentle smile. I genuflected to him, blessing myself with the sign of the cross, before making my way past him to the other end of the first pew, where the Virgin Mary stood on her own plinth smiling down at me. Getting down on my knees, I looked up guiltily at the Holy Mother and recited the Hail Mary in a whisper, "… pray for us sinners, now and at the hour of our death, amen". It gave me comfort to know that, while I was in there up to no good, she was praying for my forgiveness.

The front pew was the only one decked out with individual, thin seat cushions, put there for the benefit of the adults and the two altar boys, Holland and that lanky, walking skeleton, Nigel Bones Cuthbert, who was always allowed to have second helpings, yet never seemed to put on any weight.

"Tommy." I heard the faint, ghostly whisper, just as I turned over the end cushion, where Holland always sat.

Jaysus! I saw Donkey's ugly mug leering at me from the doorway.

"What are yah doing down here?" I whispered.

"I couldn't sleep, so I followed you. Have you come to play the organ?"

"Play the organ? Oh yeah, I tiptoed all the way down here, just ta wake the feckin' dead." Donkey's stupidity never failed to amaze me.

"Can I have a go?" he asked, oblivious to my sarcasm.

"No yah can't. Give us a hand, will yah?"

I watched as Donkey scrambled over the pews and joined me down on his knees. God, he was a sight for sore eyes. The dim light flowing in through the high windows threw shadows across his startling, ever-changing features. And if I hadn't known him and how soft he really was, I'd have been frightened to death meeting him in the dark.

"Here." I tipped the small box of pins out on to the cushion. "Help me stick these in, like this." I sank a pin into the fabric to demonstrate. "And push them right down to the heads."

"Holland sits there," Donkey informed me.

"Not for long he won't."

"But they'll stick in his bum."

"That's the idea."

"Ouch!" Donkey shot up suddenly.

"Keep the gob down!"

"A needle stuck in my finger."

"Just think how many will be stuck in Holland's arse tomorrow. Sssh, don't laugh!" I was forced to stick a hand over Donkey's hairy gob to stop him from heehawing. "Ye'll get us murdered." I was glad to see the last pin, about 30 in all, go in. And we blessed ourselves before slipping out of the chapel and back to our beds.

I didn't like any days in St Vincent's, let alone Sundays, even if it was a day of rest and we didn't have to scrub and polish the floors. But this was a Sunday I wouldn't have wanted to miss for anything.

After breakfast of dried scrambled eggs on toast, we lined up before being marched out of the dining room to the chapel. I could already feel the butterflies in my stomach, as I pushed my way to the third pew from the altar, where I knew I should be able to get a pretty good view of Holland doing the high jump.

And there he was, leading the way into chapel, dressed in his red and white altar boy's cassock and his fake saintly face, surrounded by the white smoke billowing from the incense burner he was swinging to and fro. He was followed by Cuthbert, whose head was lost somewhere in the cloud of smoke, though we could hear him coughing. Father Tierney followed next, with Mr Lilly and Matron following him. And then, following behind them were two nuns I'd not seen before.

What was going on? Holland and Cuthbert walked past their usual seats and were standing instead beneath the statue of the Virgin Mary, with their backs up against the wall. Mr Lilly was now showing the two nuns to their seats – Cuthbert and Holland's feckin' seats! I was conscious of Donkey looking at me from the other end of our pew and when I glanced over, he threw a grotesque grin in my direction before I quickly looked away.

"*In nomine Patris et Filii et Spiritus Sancti, Amen.*" Father Tierney blessed the congregation with a lazy wave of his hand. "You may be seated."

"Feck!" I was anticipating the loud scream ringing out and around the chapel. The poor nun. She was going to be leaping in the air like a wild banshee. Not that she probably didn't deserve it. I wondered how high she would jump? And I had already put my best dumbfounded expression on my face, ready to let everyone see I was as shocked as they were.

It was a miracle. Both nuns had plonked themselves down on the pew and there wasn't a peep out of them. The one sitting on the pin cushion did a little shimmy to settle her hefty backside in, but not a whimper out of her. She either had the Almighty protecting her from harm's way, or she was wearing a metal pair of undies.

Holland was looking in my direction. He had a smirk on his face, and I wondered, was he trying to tell me something? The smirking goon then gave me a knowing nod, as if he had read my thoughts. It seemed to me he knew about the trap beforehand, otherwise that nun should have been jumping as high as a kite. But how could he have known? Then the smirking goon shifted his gaze in the direction of Donkey, who grinned back at him.

"Yah feckin' eejit!" I snapped under my breath at the missing link. "Tosser," I added, shaking my head in despair as the gormless goon gave me the thumbs up.

"What did yah just call me?" Paddy O'Neil, sitting to the right of me, suddenly threw an elbow out, catching me a hard blow to the funny bone and causing the fingers on my right hand to go into spasm. I'd often wondered why it was called the funny bone. It wasn't as if I was rolling around on the floor in fits of hysterical laughter as the pain shot straight down my arm, causing my fingers to take a funny turn and momentarily freeze into a claw – perhaps that was the funny bit?

"I was talking ta that eejit." I nodded in Donkey's direction. "Not yea."

I flexed my paralysed fingers into a ball, which O'Neil took the wrong way.

"It's a fight yer feckin' looking for, is it?"

"It's me fingers. Look at them, they've gone all funny after yah accidently knocked in ta me."

"Sister Agnes will now take the first reading," said Father Tierney, turning to the correct page in the large book of Missals. The middle-aged nun (who should have been in agony) made her way to the altar and stood behind the lectern, while the old priest made his way across to the little altar chair, just to the left of Our Lady.

"The Jews. According to John 10:3-42," began Sister Agnes. "The Jews fetched stones to stone him, so Jesus said to them –"

"Ye bastards!" came the sudden cry from Father Tierney, leaping high into the air as if his arse had just been set on fire. "Yer all heathens!"

We watched him rush out of the chapel with the pin cushion still attached to his backside and him angrily muttering all sorts of extremities to himself. Donkey exploded into fits of hee-haws, which started some of the other lads laughing.

Mr Lilly and Matron hurried along after the two old nuns, who were chasing after the old priest. On his way out, the headmaster stopped to have a few quiet words in Mr Marron's ear.

"Right you lot. Quietly make your way down to the assembly hall, one pew at a time – I said quietly!" barked Mr Marron. "Holland, you and Cuthbert clear all the hymn books away and get changed before making your way down."

No number of threats from Mr Lilly was ever going to get anyone to own up to putting the pins in to the cushion. And I suspect he knew this himself. Yet there he was in the assembly hall, spewing his usual rhetoric, his eyes bulging with rage as he held up the cushion.

"I know who the imbecile is. But I want to give him the opportunity to own up before I name him."

What he meant was, he hadn't a clue who it was. Yes, we may have been imbeciles with nothing going on in our tiny, wasted lives, but we were not falling for his lies. So, it was no surprise that our answer to him was a cold stone wall of silence.

"Because of the selfish act from one despicable, spiteful individual, you will all suffer the consequences. Is that what you want – is it?" His shifty eyes moved along the sea of indifferent faces staring back at him. He was searching out guilt, which easily put us all in the frame. "This," he declared, holding up one of the pins in his hand, "is one of 40 pins that I pulled from this." He held aloft the cushion in his other hand as he performed a slow death-march along the front row of boys, letting each one of them get a good look at the offending objects. "This is a callous, cowardly act on a defenceless man of the cloth. And as painful as it is, infection could be a more serious consequence."

Talk about exaggeration. I was sure we'd only stuck 30 pins into that cushion, and I was a little peeved that I wasn't able to correct the headmaster on that point. Instead, we had to listen to him go on. "No home leave. No pocket money. No swimming. No camping. Library. Beach. Cinema." He called them out one by one, which was a complete waste of time, considering most of us were placed in the approved school because we were doing nothing constructive in our everyday lives. And so, the loss of privileges wasn't going to make much difference.

He kept us standing to attention for another hour, before telling us he was extending the opportunity for the culprit to come along to his office for a chat. In other words, he had given up, like he always did, knowing he had better things to do. I noticed he never mentioned anything about cancelling school or Mass. Or the Christmas show – seeing that his awful magic tricks were the star attraction.

The Show Must Go On

There must have been over a hundred people sitting in the assembly hall, waiting for the show to begin. The Mayor had turned up, along with lots of other dignitaries, though Father Tierney, who would usually open the show with a blessing, was noticeably absent. We'd not seen the auld priest for weeks and it was likely we wouldn't be seeing him again, as we had a new priest, Father Gilmore, who was there to see the show.

The previous day I'd had a showdown with Brian Walters. Well, it was hardly a showdown. Paddy O'Neil was over by the swings, talking with Walters and a couple of his chums, when he'd looked across and called me over. I'd no problems as such with Paddy, though I did wonder why he was mixing with creeps like Walters.

"Alright Tommy?" Paddy gave me a big smile and immediately I sensed he was up to something. I'd readied myself to make a quick run for it if anything kicked off.

"I'm alright, Paddy," said I.

"I hear yous two don't get on?"

"The truth is Paddy, I don't like him an' he doesn't like me. An' he can't fight his own battles unless he's got his bum-chums with him." I glared at Walters before scowling at his three grinning mates.

"I don't need an army to beat you up, Wall Talker," snapped Walters. "He talks to walls. Did you know that Paddy?"

"No, I didn't. Why d'ya talk ta walls, Tommy?"

"So I don't have to talk with tosspots like them lot."

"Get him!" ordered Walters to his gang.

"Touch him an' I'll murder the lot of yah," warned Paddy.

I was taken aback by his outburst because I didn't think Paddy (who could look after himself) would be interested in me, let alone back me up for a fight. But he was. And he did. Turning to Walters, he gave him an ultimatum: "Yea can either fight him, or yea can fight me. What's it ta be, yah little maggot yah."

Two years! That's how long I had waited to get a fair fight with this evil, bullying bastard. And now I'd been given the chance, I was determined to take it.

It's strange how the brain can think things out in seconds. And as I stood facing Walters, I'd already decided I wasn't going to stand toe-to-toe with him and fight a boxing match. Especially having already faced him in the past, with the gloves on, when he'd given me an idea of what the Milky Way looked like, before kicking me in the mouth.

"Come on then, Wall Talker," goaded Walters, as the pair of us circled each other. "You can't even punch your way out of a paper bag, you girl's blouse."

"You can have the first punch," I invited, expecting the snide to take up the invitation and come straight for me. But instead, he suddenly bent over and grabbed a small handful of the dried grit around the swings, throwing it at my face before taking a lunge at me.

But I had been waiting for the sneak to do something like that, and I'd turned sideways on to him, closing my eyes and throwing out the hardest right-handed punch I'd ever mustered in all my life. I felt my fist make contact and watched as the cowardly squirt fell on to his hands and knees.

"Kick his feckin' head in!" Paddy shouted.

"I don't kick like a coward," I said. "Get up ya tosser yah." I'd given a little confident shimmy of the legs as I stood back from Walters, not believing my luck, that I had knocked the fecker down with the one punch. "Up!" I shouted. "So I can knock them teeth down yer neck." I held up my right fist, ready to give him another one in the gob if he dared to get up. But he wouldn't. Lifting himself into a sitting position, he stayed on the ground, spitting blood out from his cut lip, looking gormless and dazed. His so-called mates had already walked off, leaving him to it.

Now, we were standing next to each other on the stage, along with the rest of the choir, waiting for the curtains to open and the show to begin. He hadn't spoken a word to me, nor I to him. Perhaps he hadn't recognised me. We had, after all, got blacked-up faces, as the show had a Black and White Minstrel theme. But I had easily recognised his ugly mug.

It was difficult to contain our excitement as we waited, with bated breath, for Mr Keenan to finish his boring, long-winded Christmas speech. Even his attempt at humour only raised the odd laugh.

"Without further ado," he announced, "ladies and gentlemen, boys and girls (there were no girls in the audience), will you please give a warm welcome to the Black and White (we were all black) Minstrels!" The curtains opened and Mr Alston struck the first chords on the piano.

"Mammy, Mammy."

"Mammeee!" Jaysus, Donkey had decided to join in the singing.

"The sun shines East, the sun shines West."

"Weeest!" echoed Donkey.

"Get off!" Mr Alston suddenly pushed Donkey's hand away from the piano. But Donkey kept stabbing a finger down on any key he could get at. As they fought over the piano, we were singing out of tune. "Get away, you freak," said the deputy headmaster, before slapping Donkey hard across the face. This was obviously the worst thing he could have done, because Donkey started crying like a donkey, as we continued with the chorus.

"I'd walk a million miles —"

"Haw-hee-haw!"

"For one of your smiles —"

"Hee-haw! Hee-haw!"

"My Mammy!"

To be honest, I expected the audience to have wished they were a million miles away from the awful sound, but for some strange reason, they were loudly laughing and applauding — probably out of sympathy.

We managed to get through the rest of our part of the show without too many problems. Mr Alston handed the spare tambourine to Donkey, letting him join us on stage. I wasn't sure if he did this out of the goodness of his heart, or whether he'd just decided nothing could get any worse. But it did cheer up Donkey no end, and he played that tambourine like I'd never seen anyone play a tambourine before.

I was also taken by surprise when Walters and I did our duet of "Silent Night" and he harmonised all the parts softly, instead of attempting to take all the limelight, which for once was all mine.

Next, Mr Keenan introduced the Great Wizard and his assistant, Ramondo. Mr Lilly and Gary The Ponce Percival were dressed in long black capes and looked more like a pair of gormless vampires than magicians. And that should have been me!

We stood in the wings, supposed to wait until Mr Lilly finished the closing act of the show. But, as I had a plan of action to get off the ground, I slipped off, unnoticed, to the back of the stage. Making my way through the small door leading underneath the stage, I crawled over to the secret trapdoor. Above me, I could hear the footsteps of Lilly and Percival The Ponce. The applause was a sure sign that the first couple of tricks had gone down well. But then Mr Lilly set up his little magic table close to the trapdoor. And I knew, because I'd had a sneak preview of them rehearsing, that little Ramondo would be standing on the trapdoor for three of those tricks. Well, that was their plan. But if my plan went the way I wanted, he'd be involved in just the one, unrehearsed, great trick.

Back went the two trapdoor catches. Job done! Before you could say *Hey Presto!* I had returned to join the others in the wings.

"And now, my assistant Ramondo is going to show you all a special trick."

Oh, the joy of watching Percival rush around to the other side of the little table where the black top hat sat waiting for him to pull out the stuffed rabbit, followed by the false flowers and all those rainbow-coloured ribbons. Only before he could do that, he disappeared into thin air, along with the hat. The audience gave a hearty clap. Mr Alston began to play "Roll Out the Barrel" on the piano to disguise the loud groans coming up from the open trapdoor. Why that song? I hadn't a clue, but the audience were happily singing along to it.

Mr Keenan took two of the older choir boys to help get Percival out from under the stage. A moment or two later, his head popped up through the open trapdoor and he gave Mr Lilly the good news. "I think he may have broken his leg." I rushed straight out to the front of the stage, volunteering myself to be the substitute assistant. I had banked on there being virtually nil chance of the Great Wizard telling me to clear off – and I was right.

"Just do as I say and everything will be fine, understand?" growled Mr Lilly under his breath. I obeyed every instruction to the letter and, with the magic show going well, I could see he was pleased with my performance, though he told me to stop bowing at the end of every trick – probably because he wanted all the plaudits.

"And now for the grand finale." Mr Lilly gestured with a hand to the tall box that had stood on the stage throughout the show. "When I tell you," he whispered, looking like a ventriloquist with a false smile on his face and hardly moving his lips, "I want you to stand inside the box. And when I have closed the curtain, I want you to open the black curtain behind you and stand at the back of the box, until I give you further instructions. Am I clear?"

"Yesh shir," I said, without moving my lips.

"My assistant will now stand inside the box."

Following his instructions to a tee, though I couldn't see the point of it, I stood inside the box and smiled out at the audience. When the front curtain was pulled closed, I opened the black curtain behind me and stood behind the box, waiting for further instructions. I had done exactly what Mr Lilly told me, yet he clearly wasn't happy afterwards, angrily telling me I'd made him a laughing stock of the Magic Circle!

"But sir," I protested, "you said nothing about closing the black curtain again once I was at the back of the box."

Home Sweet Home

The woman from the Social Services was standing in the main hall of St Vincent's, waiting to take me to the Garden of England, where my family now lived. I had with me a small brown case, which contained the new clothing the school had bought specially for me to take home, in order to give a good impression. The woman introduced herself as Mrs Newton, before telling me Martin was waiting outside in the car.

"Can I go to him?"

"Yes, of course!"

Needing no second invitation, I ran outside and I saw my brother's face in the back of the car, looking in my direction. His smile filled the whole side window before he jumped out and ran across the driveway to me.

"Tommy!"

"Martin!"

How tightly we held on to each other. I didn't want to let go of him, or he of me, and I'd shut my eyes, praying this wasn't a dream, before opening them wide again, to see and feel he was still there and holding on to me. It seemed unreal. I'd never dared dream that I would ever hold, or be held, by someone who I truly loved. And although I was desperate to cry, I just could not find a tear to shed.

On the long drive to meet our family I felt anxious because I hadn't seen any of them for so many years. I had never forgotten their faces as they had stood watching me and Martin taking off from the driveway of Nazareth House Children's Home on that January day in 1964. My biggest fear was that they might not recognise us, which Martin and I discussed in the back of the car. And despite the very long drive from Liverpool to Kent, the time flew as we talked non-stop, all the way to our destination.

The woman told us that if this short stay over the Christmas period went well, we would probably be able to come home permanently. Having had no wish to see my parents, I wasn't sure about this, especially as my memories of them were still raw. I was only going because it gave me the opportunity to be with Martin once again. As for my other siblings, it was difficult for me to feel emotionally attached to them after all the time apart, but I was looking forward to seeing how they'd turned out.

Turning left at Chatham train station, the car drove along Hills Terrace and past St Michael's church, before pulling up outside a row of terraced houses. Three houses down, the end one had a big sign hanging outside, telling us it was the Rose in June pub. It couldn't have been a better location for my parents.

"Here we are," said Mrs Newton, looking at her watch.

"What's the time?" asked Martin.

"It's eight-thirty."

"Mr Lilly said our house was in the Garden of England?" My comment made the Social Services woman laugh.

If that laughter was because of what we were seeing

through the car windows, then I could see the joke. Though I wasn't laughing. Garden of England my arse! It was a dump. A tip! There wasn't even a weed in sight, let alone a blade of grass or a flower. Though admittedly, it was still a vast improvement on Stamford Street.

Perhaps it was me. Perhaps I'd been so used to living in St Vincent's, I'd forgotten what it was like living in a hovel!

Mammy opened the front door of number five. She hadn't changed since the last time we'd seen her, except for the colour of her hair, which was now blonde instead of dark brown.

"This is Martin and Tommy." Mrs Newton introduced us to our own Mammy! And Mammy shook our hands. "Oh, I nearly forgot," said Mrs Newton, opening her handbag and taking out a large brown envelope, which she handed over to Mammy. "This is for the boys' keep."

"Ta missus," said Mammy. Only then did she stand aside and allow us to walk into the house and through into the back room, with her following us. "Yea can leave them auld bags on the chair there an' go an' play with yer brothers. Der out the back way – somewhere." She left us and went back to the open front door where Mrs Newton was standing.

I followed Martin out the back way. It was dark so we couldn't see much, but we could see the high chicken run, which took up the whole of the garden. We couldn't see the chickens, but we could hear the racket they were making. The path out the back way led out on to a street, dimly lit up by an electric streetlamp. Across the way, we could see a group of kids playing in the playground of St Michael's Primary School, which was closed for the Christmas holidays.

"Tommy! Martin!" Our younger brother Nabby was the first to spot us. Squeezing through the gap in the metal fencing, he was followed closely by Michael and Gosson, who were tiny babies the last time we'd seen them. We didn't throw our arms around each other, like Martin and I had done. But that didn't mean to say we loved them any the less. Martin and I had a special bond, which was the only difference.

"Have yah seen Uncle Oliver and Raphael and the old man yet?" asked Nabby.

"There's only Mammy in the house," said Martin.

"She'll be in the Rose in June by now," said Nabby. "The whole family are over there. The old woman was just waitin' in the house for you to turn up."

We suddenly heard breaking glass, followed by loud, angry voices.

"Quick!" Nabby ran off in the direction of the side road, which led back around into Hills Terrace.

Following our three brothers, we rushed around the corner, just as a chair came through the pub's side window. At the front of the pub, we were met by a riot of 30 or more people, all fighting outside on the road. Our Uncles Oliver, Paddy, Raphael, Christy and Frankie, plus some aunties and a few cousins – and daddy – were all there. Fighting.

Mammy had a young fella in a headlock. She was reaching down for one of her high heels, but was having a problem getting hold of it because the young fella was struggling to get out of her choke-hold and was knocking her off balance. Rushing over to her, I slipped her shoe from her foot and handed it to her. She paused briefly, gazing into my eyes, before thanking me. Then she started beating the fella over the head with her shoe.

I looked across to Martin and, as our eyes met, we both knew what the other one was thinking.

"We're home!"

Acknowledgements

Two of the toughest things I've ever had to deal with in my life were acknowledging my past – and then willingly walking back into it.

For years I have suffered in silence with my mental health. My voice was muted by the ghosts of my past, which were leering, snarling, laughing, tormenting me. I was dragged down into an abyss of suffocating darkness – while the voices spewed their garbage of obscenities and accusations, daring me to do away with myself, launching a tirade of abuse at me: 'Filthy animal! You asked for it! You're disgusting! You're the guilty one! You got what you deserved! Shame on you! Come here, you little bastard! Fool! Fool! You'll never escape your ugly tortured destiny!'

And I wake to find I have pissed myself again.

Having taken a massive overdose of drugs at the age of 15, which should have put paid to my suffering, the psychiatrists attempted to help me cope with the traumas blighting my everyday life by throwing more drugs at me, while teaching me coping strategies, such as recognising the issues and talking them through. Or avoiding 'trigger' situations at all costs. My preferred strategy! But as for redressing the pain I had been caused, how could I do this when I still felt guilty at the hands of my abuser?

For me, 'avoidance' is the ultimate denial. The unconscious incarceration of the past, locked away in a cold dark corner of my mind, receiving no recognition as to its existence – for fear of it destroying me. And yet, sacrificing my past was in fact destroying me.

It is difficult to live a 'normal' life when you've had no control over the start of it, before being cast out into the wide world, which you have no understanding or experience of. Nor the world of you. Your only expectation is of being lonelier than ever. And so, left to take back control, the only way for me to do so was to lose control.

I was exasperated by a never-ending spiral of self-harm. Alcohol abuse. Drug abuse. Self-hatred. Guilt. Shame and suicidal ideation. The love of my beautiful wife and my close family could slow all of this down, but never halt it. It was only a matter of time before the ghosts would have me for themselves and my pain would ultimately end for good.

And then, out of the blue, a letter arrived for me from the Merseyside Police. Brief and to the point, it was about to turn my world upside down.

Dear Mr Rhattigan,

While looking through our records we have noted you were resident at St Vincent's Approved School, Formby, Liverpool, between early 1965 and late 1968. We are making inquiries into various allegations we have been made aware of. As you were resident during the period of our investigation, if there is any information that you have which might assist us, you can contact us at the above address.

Yours Sincerely

Chief Constable of Merseyside Police

Or words to that affect.

I'd been given the one opportunity to exorcise my demons, and I knew there wasn't going to be another chance! But even if I wanted to – how could I tell? How could I betray myself, my secrets and the secrets of the demons that bind us together?

Distressing and desperate as those moments had been for me, I sat for days on end, going over the letter time and time again, wondering what I should do. With encouragement from my wife and children, whose love, understanding and belief in me was so overwhelming and empowering, I was convinced to go for it.

It took a couple of weeks to build up the courage for *me* to lift the receiver and telephone the Merseyside Police, but I did it!

I was nervous, of course. I was so scared of not knowing where this was going to lead me. For all those years, I had kept my past imprisoned, and now I was letting it free! And at the precise moment I placed the receiver back down, I felt the heavy burden fall from my shoulders and an overwhelming feeling surging inside me. I knew my new life was about to begin.

With that in mind, I would like to acknowledge and offer my profound and sincere gratitude to Graham Thomas, and all those police officers serving with the Merseyside Police Force, who persevered with their investigations under extreme circumstances, having to listen and then write up so many harrowing statements while maintaining their own forced composure, their professionalism, while wrapping a coat of dignity around me and those many other survivors, telling their stories to them for the first time. 'Thank you' seems such a pitiful response, when you consider the enormity of what you have achieved! Some say, 'You went trawling.' I say, 'I cannot find the words to thank you enough for catching me in your net and handing me back my life!'

I'd also like to offer my special 'thanks' to my former Psychiatric Nurse, Christofer Fay (my mate for life), manager of the East Kent Mental Health Service, who helped me trust him to lead me through the darkness towards the light. How could I have ever found my way without you, Chris? I don't know. I want to acknowledge the fact that you were the initial inspiration for me to write this and my first book, *1963: A slice of Bread and Jam*, 'once the healing process had kicked in.' It took a long time, as we both expected it to! But I can now look back on my past and see so many wonderful memories beyond the mist. Thank you.

If you need support and more information on some of the
issues covered in this book, please contact:

http://thesurvivorstrust.org
Free, confidential helpline: 08088 010 818
(Mon-Thurs 10am-4pm & 6pm-8pm/Fri 10am-4pm)

Safeline.org.uk

Samaritans.org
116 123 (UK)

Also by Mirror Books

1963 - A Slice of Bread and Jam
Tommy Rhattigan

Tommy lives at the heart of a large Irish family in derelict Hulme in Manchester, ruled by an abusive, alcoholic father and a negligent mother. Alongside his siblings he begs (or steals) a few pennies to bring home to avoid a beating, while looking for a little adventure of his own along the way.

His foul-mouthed and chaotic family may be deeply flawed, but amongst the violence, grinding poverty and distinct lack of hygiene and morality lies a strong sense of loyalty and, above all, survival.

During this single year – before his family implodes and his world changes for ever – Tommy almost falls foul of the welfare officers, nuns, police – and Myra Hindley and Ian Brady.

An adventurous, fun, dark and moving true story of the only life young Tommy knew.

Also by Mirror Books

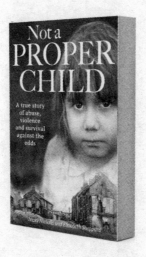

Not A Proper Child
Nicky Nicholls and Elizabeth Sheppard

Left as a newborn in a box outside Stoke City Football ground, Nicky's grandparents took her into their home, but instead of finding refuge - she was subjected to sexual abuse. In 1951, at the age of six, her estranged mother 'rescued' her. But Nicky's hopes of a safe and loving home were soon dashed, and her world became darker still...

As a result of her broken young life, Nicky spent years as a homeless alcoholic, ending up in prison, where she encountered Moors Murderer Myra Hindley and glimpsed pure evil.

Nicky's compelling life story captures her rare spirit of survival against the odds, and charts her rise from the horror of a deeply damaging childhood to a positive, creative and independent life.